P9-DMI-977

Broke, USA

ALSO BY GARY RIVLIN

Drive-By

Fire on the Prairie

The Godfather of Silicon Valley

The Plot to Get Bill Gates

From Pawnshops to Poverty, Inc.—

Broke, USA

How the Working Poor Became Big Business

Gary Rivlin

HARPER
BUSINESS

An Imprint of HarperCollins*Publishers*
www.harpercollins.com

FIRST EDITION

Designed by Jennifer Ann Daddio / Bookmark Design & Media Inc.

Library of Congress Cataloging-in-Publication Data

Rivlin, Gary.
    Broke, USA : from pawnshops to Poverty, Inc. : how the working poor became big
business / by Gary Rivlin.—1st ed.
        p.   cm.
    Summary: "A unique and riveting exploration of one of America's largest and
fastest-growing industries—the business of poverty"—Provided by publisher.
    ISBN 978-0-06-173321-5 (hardback)
    1. Working poor—United States. 2. Poverty—United States. 3. United States—
Economic conditions—21st century. I. Title.
HD8072.5.R58   2010
339.4'60973—dc22
                                                            2010002874

10 11 12 13 14   OV/RRD   10 9 8 7 6 5 4 3 2 1

To

DAISY

and

OLIVER

And in honor of two extraordinary people
who passed away during the writing of this book,

SANDRA ROTHBART COHEN

and

DANIEL SHEAFE WALKER

"Annual income twenty pounds, annual expenditure nineteen nineteen and six, result happiness.

"Annual income twenty pounds, annual expenditure twenty pounds ought and six, result misery."

—Wilkins Micawber, in *David Copperfield,* by Charles Dickens

Contents

Prologue

Tommy's Angel

DAYTON, OHIO, DECEMBER 2008

Seventy-three-year-old William T. Myers lives in a forlorn trailer park on the industrial outskirts of Dayton, Ohio. Pine View Estates, a tightly packed community of about 250 mobile homes, sits along a heavily trafficked commercial thoroughfare battered by a nonstop, noisy parade of dump trucks, cement mixers, and other heavy equipment. Despite its name, Pine View Estates has no pine trees—nor are there any views except those of the trailer park's closest neighbors: a metal salvage yard and a large asphalt plant. When giving directions to his home, Myers, who goes by the name Tommy, jokes about the railroad tracks a visitor must cross to reach the modest gray and white aluminum-sided trailer that he, his wife, a dog, and a cat have called home over the past few years. "I suppose you can say I live on the wrong side of them tracks," Myers said in a high, reedy voice. He punctuated his crack with a crazed, Walter Brennan–like cackle.

I met Tommy Myers and his wife, Marcia, in 2008, shortly before Christmas. I was still in my car when a small, wiry white man built like a bantamweight fighter bounded out of his trailer and made a beeline for my door. "Ain't no way you want to park there," he advised in a squeaky voice tinged with the Appalachian twang one hears a lot in southwestern Ohio. His next-door neighbor, he explained, stands at least six foot five inches tall and belongs to the Outlaws motorcycle club. Apparently I was taking the space the man considered his personal parking spot. "It might be best to just move your car," he said. I did.

Inside, a spindly, sparsely decorated Charlie Brown Christmas tree sat by the entranceway. There was a living room large enough to fit a couch, a couple of chairs, and a tiny dining room table.

"It's not too bad," Myers said.

"Easier to clean than the house," Marcia said.

"We make do." A large wooden crucifix was nailed to one of the living room walls. A lot had happened in Myers's life over the past ten years but the cross reflected a recent change. A neighbor had invited the couple to a screening of *The Passion of the Christ* and soon Marcia and Tommy were attending church for the first time since either was a teenager. "She made me start going to church with her," Myers said. "It's been a blessing ever since."

Tommy Myers has a pleated face and a broad, toothless smile. He had five kids from his first marriage, to a girl he had gotten pregnant shortly before graduating from high school in Dayton, and a sixth if you include the baby Marcia had given birth to less than two months before the couple met. He has worked as a delivery driver for most of his life. For years he drove a truck for Pepsi, then for a beer distributor. More recently he made deliveries for a restaurant supply company. Marcia, whom Myers sometimes calls "Momma," is a cafeteria worker at a local high school. "My wife's tougher than a crocodile and alligator combined," he said, causing Marcia to roll her eyes. She has a nice smile, a round face, and a curly mop of thick strawberry blonde hair that was somewhat wilted after a long day over the cafeteria's steam tables. "She knows it's best sometimes just to ignore me," Myers said with a shrug, flashing his gums and emitting another whoop. Marcia, who was dressed in flannel sweatpants and a blue "Life Is Good" T-shirt (a freebie from the school), drifted in and out of the room as we spoke. She hates to even think about the topic that had brought me to their trailer on the outskirts of Dayton that day.

The pair met in West Palm Beach, Florida, when Myers was thirty-five and Marcia was nineteen. Tommy had grown up in Dayton, but after his divorce he arranged a transfer through Pepsi. There he worked with Marcia's brother and played with him in a softball league, which is how Myers and Marcia came to meet shortly after she had given birth to a baby boy. Life was good in Florida, Myers said, but he missed Dayton, and eventually they moved north.

Home in Florida had been a trailer, but once in Dayton the couple decided to buy a home they found in a white working-class neighborhood. The house cost only $60,000, but for Myers, who was about to turn sixty, and Marcia, in her forties, it felt like a small palace. There was an upstairs and a downstairs and a finished basement with a washer-dryer. The place had three bedrooms, or four if you included the utility room that seemed a wild extravagance after so many years fitting their lives into a cramped double-wide. They had a decent-sized backyard, where Marcia liked to tend to her plants. The monthly payment was $526 including property taxes and insurance. They painted their new home white and, because Marcia loved her home team, trimmed it in Miami Dolphins teal.

Myers started thinking about retirement. He would turn sixty-five in 2000 and it would be nice to slow down. But then Marcia got sick and he thought about all the calls he had been getting from a man he's now inclined to refer to, sarcastically, as his guardian angel. He was a salesman for the consumer finance giant Household Finance Corporation, phoning one name on a long list of prospects. By 2001, when the Myerses borrowed $95,000 from Household, this venerable U.S. corporation would rank as the country's top subprime lender.

Household Finance was established in 1878 by a Minneapolis jeweler named Frank J. Mackey, who sensed the money to be made through loans to people of modest means. Through the late nineteenth century and into the twentieth, banks were conservative institutions that loaned money to affluent citizens at a slightly higher interest rate than they paid those same citizens for their deposits. In the name of reducing risk, they categorically excluded potential customers who had jobs but did not look, act like, or even speak the language of their prosperous, mostly property-owning clientele. So Mackey started loaning money to those heretofore excluded people out of the back of his jewelry store at an interest rate high enough to protect against the increased risk but low enough to remain affordable.

Business was good for both Mackey and his credit-starved customers. The working people who borrowed money from Mackey—the working poor, if we were talking about them today—proved themselves to be a diligent and largely dependable lot. Mackey created a system by which people made regular partial payments on what they owed him. That enabled families living paycheck to paycheck to purchase big-ticket items such as furniture and iceboxes and handle emergencies too great for their weekly paychecks to accommodate. Mackey might have seen himself as doing nothing more ambitious than providing credit to people at the bottom of the economic ladder but essentially he invented the unsecured installment loan. He moved his company to Chicago and, in the 1920s, HFC went public.

It was an enormously profitable business that for decades could be sustained simply by opening offices in new locales, but in the 1960s the company grew restless. Flush with cash, HFC acquired an airline, a car-rental company, and a supermarket chain, among other properties. None proved anywhere near as lucrative as the personal loan business, however, and in the second half of the 1970s management decided that it would follow in the footsteps of giants such as Citibank and American Express and transform itself into a one-stop financial supermarket. It sold off most of its recent purchases, bought an insurance company, and moved into branch banking and even private wealth management. When this new strategy produced the same disappointing results as the previous one, the company decided to look for a new chief executive outside its senior ranks.

Their savior was a Brooklyn-born dockworker's son named William Aldinger, who had been working as a top executive at Wells Fargo. Aldinger sold off the insurance company. He gave walking papers to those who had been hired to beef up its private banking business and fired the company's art curator. The people generating the real profits, he understood, weren't those in shiny shoes and sober dark suits looking to woo the business of the very wealthy. It was all those salespeople in their off-the-rack JCPenney specials manning the company's mini-empire of strip mall storefronts. Under Aldinger, the company's consumer finance division would no longer need to compete for the brass's attention.

The turnaround reigns as one of the financial world's classic feel-good tales, and it fell on a *Wall Street Journal* reporter named Jeff Bailey to tell Household's story in 1996, two years after Aldinger's arrival. During that time, Household's share price had more than doubled. "At Household, formerly a sprawling and ill-focused conglomerate," Bailey wrote, "a single-minded devotion to consumer loans is leading a significant turnaround." Aldinger had refocused Household on what Bailey dubbed "lunchpail lending." Loaning money to the little guy, whether via a credit card, a used car loan, a home equity line, or a furniture store, was proving far more profitable than nearly any alternative banking activity—and Wall Street was beginning to notice.

On one level, Aldinger, a man with humble beginnings, was returning Household Finance to its original roots. Yet it seemed the new Household and the company Frank Mackey had started more than a century earlier shared nothing aside from the same core customer base. Before Aldinger, Household had competed for consumers by offering lower interest rates. Under Aldinger, the company raised its rates but also intensified its marketing efforts. The gambit worked. Loan volume went up, not down, and profits soared. The company would deluge working-class neighborhoods with mailers—and then follow up these come-ons with repeated phone calls. "Nobody applies for a loan," a Household executive told Bailey. "It's all push."

To make its point, the company invited Bailey to play a fly on the wall at a branch the company operated on the suburban fringes of Chicago. There, in an office next to a Jenny Craig weight-loss center, he sat watching as local branch manager Bob Blazek and his staff trolled an internal database in search of customers deep in credit card debt who also owned a home. "I love to see five to ten" credit cards, Blazek explained. "We target them first." When Blazek reached a couple who owed $28,000 on eight cards, he treated them like prime prospects rather than dangerous credit risks. He sold them a high-rate home equity loan sized to pay off their credit cards and upped their credit by another $20,000, "just in case the spending bug bites again." Later, Blazek confessed to Bailey that had a second customer, a retiree, gone to a conventional bank instead of talking with him, he almost certainly could have gotten much more favorable terms than the 15.25 percent annual interest rate he would be paying to Household.

The company made little effort to collect from borrowers who were falling behind on payments. Those customers, executives explained to Bailey, were instead treated as top prospects for a new loan—at a higher rate, of course, and with a new set of up-front fees tacked on. Many salespeople chose to leave the company, and Household fired another three hundred during Aldinger's first two years for failing to meet company quotas. The company, Bailey found, experienced a 60 to 70 percent annual turnover rate among its salespeople. Those who could stand the pressure, though, were paid far more than they were likely to earn elsewhere. Branch managers were paid a salary of $40,000 a year plus performance-based bonuses that let top managers such as Blazek make as much as $100,000 a year.

In 1998, a few years before Tommy Myers would become a Household customer, Aldinger made his boldest move yet. Household bought its best-known competitor, Beneficial Finance. So where once HFC could claim roughly 1,000 storefronts in working-class neighborhoods across the country, the company now operated nearly 2,000. The deal increased Household's debt, placing even more pressure on the sales staff to make loans. The Beneficial employees, who had been working on a straight salary, saw their wages slashed and replaced by the possibility of the rich commissions and sales bonuses they might earn peddling Household's high-priced products.

Not everyone was as impressed as Wall Street by the creative means that businesses like HFC were devising to earn fat profits off those with thin wallets. "They're sucker pricing," one critic, Kathleen Keest, a deputy in the Iowa attorney general's office, told Bailey. Keest's quote high up in the *Journal*'s story—and the presence of the phrase "sucker pricing" in the article's headline—showed that even the paper sometimes called Wall Street's daily bible was queasy about the changing nature of lunchpail lending.

Unfortunately, Tommy Myers didn't read the *Wall Street Journal*.

The calls started shortly after the Myerses moved into their home in 1995. "Every month we were getting another letter from Household," Myers said. After a time, the phone started ringing as well. "Hello, Mr. Myers, how are you today?" It was the same man who was signing the letters from Household. "I was never so popular," Myers said, "as when I owned that house."

Myers doesn't consider himself a sucker. The mortgage on his home was a standard A-grade loan obtained through a mainstream lender. He's never resorted to borrowing money from a pawnshop and he never wasted a 2 or 3 or 4 percent share of his paycheck relying on a check casher. He can't imagine himself ever going to one of those rent-to-own stores that long ago figured out how to sell $500 television sets for $1,200. I asked if he'd ever gone to one of the thousands of shops around the country offering "rapid refunds" to people so desperate for quick cash that they'll give over a portion of their tax refund to save waiting a couple of weeks and Myers looked at me as if I'd insulted him. "Never, never, never," he said. "I would never pay a third of my money for that."

His reaction to a question about payday loans was even stronger. Stores offering a cash advance against a person's next paycheck were sprouting up all around Dayton starting in 1997 yet he had never been tempted to stop at one. The rates they charged, he said, $15 on every $100 borrowed, were too high. "I may just have me a kindergarten education," Myers said, "but they ain't never getting me with one of them things."

At first the salesman from Household was as easy to ignore as the rest of these peddlers of high-priced credit. He'd employ any number of gambits, Myers recalled, to convince him to start using his home as a kind of ATM machine. You're building up equity in your home, he would counsel; make that equity work for you. Fix up your home. Consolidate your bills. Take that pretty wife of yours on a trip, he'd cajole. Myers would always politely decline.

But then in 2001 Marcia started to have trouble breathing. Walking up a flight of stairs left her feeling as if she had just run a marathon. She couldn't go to work and then the news got worse when the doctors discovered a congenital heart problem and told her she needed surgery. The long recovery meant the pair would be without her paycheck for the better part of a year.

Myers puzzled over what to do about their new, more perilous financial situation. They were suddenly carrying more than $10,000 in credit card debt. They were paying a relatively low 7 percent on their mortgage but getting hit by interest rates as high as 10 percent on their three credit cards. "My thinking there was 'Let's refinance the house, put everything in one bill, it'd be easier to handle,'" he said. Now it was Myers who was calling Household.

It turns out that the salesman who had been calling was also a Household broker who could write loans. "He tells me, 'How about me taking your house, your credit card bills, everything, and we'll combine it into a single loan at 7.2 percent?'" He would end up owing more in principal and pay a slightly higher interest rate than they were paying on the mortgage but one that was significantly less than the interest on their credit card debt. That sounded great to Myers, who told the man to draw up the papers. "We want to get this all taken care of and get you back on your feet," Myers remembers him saying.

The nearest Household Finance office was just off the interstate in a first-ring Dayton suburb called Huber Heights. There on a Friday evening in the fall of 2001, out by the big air force base, in a shopping center populated by an Applebee's and an Uno pizza parlor, they met with the salesman who had been calling them. He greeted the couple with a toothy Dentyne smile—and right away Marcia was mistrustful. "She flat tells him," Myers said of his crocodile wife, "'Anytime I talk to somebody and all I see is teeth and eyeballs, I don't trust 'em.'"

"I can tell a phony grin from a mile away," Marcia said. "And this man was too smiley for me." The phone rang and things went from bad to worse. It was a friend of the broker calling, apparently to work out the details of a trip to a nearby amusement park the next day. "This is a big deal to us," Myers said, "but we're sitting there for like twenty minutes—"

Marcia: "*At least* twenty minutes."

"—at least twenty minutes while he's talking about this trip and all the rides he's looking forward to."

The man was all business once he was off the phone. It was Myers's impression that he was in a rush to get home. Myers would kick himself in the coming months for acting so accommodating despite the stakes, but Saturday was a workday and there was Marcia to worry about. She didn't feel anything close to 100 percent. Marcia had spoken up one final time. "I don't want to do this whole thing," she said, but then she abdicated to her husband. You're the one who understands this stuff, she said. You're the one who handles the money. "I don't understand interest and that whole mess," she remembers saying. "So if you think this is the right idea, then go for it." Myers felt confident he was making the right decision. He thought he knew the questions he needed to ask. This particular broker might feel wrong to him but the deal felt right.

Anyone who has been to a real estate closing knows that disorienting feeling that comes while staring at a thick stack of impenetrably complex documents, each reading as if written by the Committee for the Full Employment of Lawyers. Myers fixated on a single detail: the new interest rate. "I asked him point-blank, 'So what I'm signing here, this means I'm paying 7.2 percent,'" he said. "And he looked me straight in the eye and said, 'Just trust me. You make your payment every other week, that brings your interest rate down to 7.2.' I didn't think too much about it. I just thought, 7.2, good, that's right."

The rest of their meeting was a blur. They signed and initialed until their hands cramped up. The Myerses had thought it was just the three of them in Household's offices that night when a man appeared out of the gloaming when the time came to have the papers notarized. They were there less than an hour, including the time the broker was on the phone with a friend.

"You make your payment every two weeks . . ." Those words gnawed at Myers's subconscious all weekend but it wasn't until Monday that he pulled out the papers and asked one of his daughters, who knew something about mortgages, to take a look. "She says to me, 'Dad, you got took.'"

Under Ohio law a borrower has three days to change his or her mind about a home loan. Myers didn't contact Household until the next morning, four days after they had signed the papers, and the man he met with on Friday night refused his request to rescind the deal. "Partially it's my fault for not saying I want to come back when we're not all in this big rush," Myers said. It was when he received the bill for his first mortgage payment that he began to appreciate the magnitude of his mistake. He knew his monthly payment would be higher than the $526 he had been paying but he was figuring on a bump of maybe $50. Instead it had nearly tripled to $1,400 per month.

The main culprit was the interest rate. The annual percentage rate, or APR, on the loan Household sold the Myerses was 13.9 percent, not 7.2 percent. In time, it would be revealed that Household agents around the country were routinely claiming that customers would be paying lower interest rates than they were actually being charged. Each used the same sleight of hand: Because its customers were required to make biweekly payments, they were making the equivalent of thirteen monthly payments during the year rather than twelve. Financial planners recommend making thirteen payments each year because by doing so borrowers pay off a standard thirty-year fixed-rate mortgage in just over twenty-one years. The mortgage holder is paying the same interest rate on the money, of course, whether he or she is paying the standard twelve months a year or thirteen, but over the life of the loan they'll pay significantly less interest because those extra payments are whittling away at the principal on the front end. Yet even this rhetorical trick practiced by Household agents doesn't get a borrower from an interest rate of 13.9 percent to 7.2 percent.

People with tarnished credit, naturally, can expect to pay a higher interest rate than those with good credit. They present a greater risk of default and lenders need to charge a higher rate to cover any additional losses. But Tommy and Marcia Myers had excellent credit. The generally accepted definition of a "subprime" borrower is a person with a credit score of below 620 on a scale between 300 and 850, though some institutions use a cutoff of 640 or higher. But the Myerses weren't even close to the margins. Myers contends that the couple had a FICO score (FICO is named for the Fair Isaac Corporation, which created the credit rating system) in the mid-700s. If so, that meant that had Myers gone to a traditional bank rather than Household, he would have secured the loan he had been seeking.

A credible lender might charge its subprime customer an interest rate one or two percentage points more than what its customers with good credit receive. But in his interview with the *Journal*'s Jeff Bailey, Household's William Aldinger dismissed this idea of competing on price. They would compete instead using aggressive marketing and sales techniques. The Myerses thought they were borrowing $80,000 at an interest rate of 7.2 percent. That would have meant a monthly house payment of $543. Instead they were charged an APR roughly seven percentage points higher than the rate a prime borrower could have secured in the fall of 2001. That translated to a monthly payment of $942.

But the interest rate proved only one factor in the near tripling of the monthly payment. The Myerses ended up borrowing $95,000, not $80,000, because of a pair of extra charges Tommy learned about only after the fact. Everyone carps about closing costs, the fees that lenders invariably tack onto a mortgage: escrow fees, loan origination fees, attorney's charges, and the like. Commonly those add a percentage point or two to the cost of a loan. Fannie Mae, the quasi-government mortgage finance company that sets the standards for the industry, won't approve a loan if the fees and points exceed 5 percent of the total cost of the loan. In the case of the Myerses, though, Household hit the couple with slightly over 8 percent in points and fees. That bumped the amount the couple needed to borrow by $7,700.

Myers admits he didn't even notice that number on that Friday night they were in Household's offices signing papers. "My mind was on two things," he said. One was that 7.2 percent interest rate; the other was his wife's health. "She was fixing to have her operation and I wanted to get these obligations out of the way so I could pay attention to her," he said.

The other nasty surprise was an insurance policy he had unknowingly purchased. Myers acknowledges that the broker had brought up the issue of insurance during the closing, but he figured it was part of the deal, like a warranty automatically included as part of the purchase. He certainly didn't mention its cost, Myers said.

"He tells us, 'I had a couple of people, had the loans for two or three months when they got injured; we paid the loans off and everything.' He's telling me how this is this great thing, part of the loan we're getting. Well, I got to reading the fine print: $7,600 for insurance." Without quite realizing it, Myers had fallen into another costly and controversial financial trap, the so-called "single-premium credit insurance policy." For years single-premium policies were a staple of subprime loans. Those selling the policies argued that they protected borrowers in case of death or an accident, but banks and other lenders rarely even bothered to pitch the same product to those in the market for a conventional loan. That's because a middle-class borrower is more likely to buy a standard life insurance or disability policy to protect against disaster.

People typically make monthly or annual payments when buying an insurance policy. Single-premium policies, however, are paid off in one lump sum at the start of the contract. If that contract is financed, as it invariably is, that means interest accrues on the entire cost of the policy. That's what happened to the Myerses. The policy, as written, expired after five years, but Tommy and Marcia would be paying off its costs over the entire life of the mortgage. At 13.9 percent interest, that meant the actual cost of the policy would work out to around $32,000, not $7,557.

Myers received the final shock a few weeks after signing the deal when the couple received a second bill from Household. At roughly $325 per month, this one was much smaller than the first bill but it enraged Myers more than any other aspect of the loan. While working their way through a stack of papers at the closing, they had unknowingly signed the paperwork for *two* loans: the original home refinance and also a home equity loan. This was becoming a common tactic inside Household: Agents would lend money through a home equity loan at the same time they were writing a refinance, even though that often meant (as in the case of the Myerses) that customers were left owing more than the actual value of their homes. Household charged the Myerses an interest rate of 19.9 percent on this second loan.

"We knew nothing about a second bill coming in," Myers said. "A home equity loan? First we hear a thing about it is when this bill here comes in the mail." (Myers would claim that later when he had a chance to examine all the loan documents, he noticed initials that looked nothing like his or Marcia's.) He rushed to the Household office the first time he had a free moment to confront his broker. "You must think I'm awfully fucking dumb," he began. He laid out his case in one big emotional gush but he casts the man as smug rather than defensive. "You can't sue me, there's nothing you can do, you signed the papers," he remembers being told.

"I said to him, 'You snookered me on that 7.2 percent interest. But you ain't snookering me on this line of credit at 19.9 percent.'" Myers was resigned to paying the monthly amount on the new mortgage; he felt he had no one to blame but himself for agreeing to a lousy deal. But he wouldn't pay a dime on the home equity loan. "He tells me, 'You have to pay.' And so I says, 'We'll see about that.'"

Myers phoned his state senator, where an aide informed him that a lender can charge basically whatever he wants so long as the terms are spelled out in the contract. He heard pretty much the same from an aide inside the governor's office, who told him that even if everything he said was true, it wasn't against the law. Myers phoned the White House. He tried reaching the secretary of the U.S. Department of Housing and Urban Development (HUD) and the U.S. attorney general. He ranted at random Beltway bureaucrats who seemed indifferent to what had happened to him. But mainly he pestered the people at Household.

Myers could have paid his bill by mail, but then he would have denied himself the pleasure of stopping by the Household office before work every other week. "I enjoyed seeing 'im," Myers said of his broker. "I enjoyed sticking it to him for the screwing they took me for." He'd park right out front and wait for them to open and invariably be the first person in the door. "I'd basically raise hell every time I'd go in there," he said. "I'd razz him for being a crook; I'd talk about what a job they did on me. I didn't care who was in there. I'd just give him what for.

"I'll be honest with you," Myers said. "I'm very, very stubborn. I try and be fair about things. But don't tick me off. Just don't tick me off."

Among those Myers called to complain about Household was a local advocacy group called the Miami Valley Fair Housing Center (Dayton is located on the Great Miami River). Myers is white and the Fair Housing Center was a group known for fighting the racial discrimination that denied homes to qualified black buyers in the Miami Valley, but he figured someone there would know something about abusive lending practices.

Actually, the mission of the Fair Housing Center was already starting to change by the time of Myers's call. Just as strong currents of change were beginning to flow through a newly deregulated financial world, the strategies of housing activists were shifting with them. It was no longer a matter of lenders refusing to make loans in certain neighborhoods; rather, it was now something like its opposite: Lenders were now targeting those same neighborhoods and aggressively peddling mortgages and home equity loans on terms that left borrowers worse off than if they had been denied a loan in the first place. This new scourge had first shown itself in the city's black precincts but quickly spread to its white working-class neighborhoods and to the crumbling first-ring suburbs. Myers didn't realize it at the time but his hometown had become a hotbed in the fight against predatory lending, and Fair Housing's executive director, Jim McCarthy, was one of the people pushing hardest for a confrontation with these lenders. The county had recently given McCarthy and his allies $600,000 to fund a public awareness campaign to warn people about these abusive loans and to create a group they were calling the Predatory Lending Solutions Project to help people untangle themselves from situations like the one that had ensnared Tommy and Marcia Myers.

Fair Housing opened more than 650 case files in 2001 and nearly 900 more the next year. McCarthy invited me to go through the center's files, where I found the names of more than seventy-five people who had contacted their organization about a Household loan. Not every person who showed up in their offices was a victim, McCarthy said, but many shared tales not all that different from the one that Tommy Myers told. He remembered Myers—remembers liking him and feeling great sympathy for what had happened to him—but called up his file to refresh his memory. He filled me in on details that Myers had left out, such as the stiff prepayment penalty Household had written into his loan terms—another staple of abusive mortgages. Just as it had cost Myers dearly for the privilege of taking out a Household loan, it would cost him plenty to get out of the loan inside of five years. Myers also didn't mention that Household had paid a subsidiary of itself to do the appraisal on his home and then stuck it on his tab. Technically that's not illegal but it's certainly not the accepted practice, either. Phone logs for the organization showed that Myers had initially contacted the Fair Housing Center to ask whether it was true that there were no predatory lending laws in Ohio. He was told that there weren't.

McCarthy could sympathize. Since the late 1990s, he and his allies had been trying to alert people in the state capital, Columbus, about the destructive practices of seemingly legitimate subprime lenders like Household Finance. "We were met by this very arrogant 'Who are you, you're just a bunch of community organizers, we know and you don't' attitude," McCarthy said. For the time being at least, there would be no help from the state or, for that matter, the federal government.

In the meantime, Fair Housing beat the hustings in search of local lawyers willing to take on the cases of those believing themselves to be victims of predatory loans. Among the few who answered the call was Matthew Brownfield, an attorney who lived in Cincinnati, one hour to the south. Brownfield filed a class-action suit against Household in November 2001, listing the Myerses among a small group of named plaintiffs. The basis of the lawsuit was the charge that the company had violated federal mortgage disclosure laws and therefore the loans should be rescinded. The suit claimed more than one thousand potential plaintiffs. Gary Klein, who as a staffer for the National Consumer Law Center in Boston had helped write the materials that lawyers across the country use when litigating these types of cases, helped Brownfield. That gave Myers a tickle: A big-time lawyer from Boston was helping him go after Household.

Brownfield encouraged the Myerses to remain in the house. Household—perhaps because the Myerses had sought legal protection—had yet to take action against them over their failure to pay on the home equity loan. Don't worry about the main loan, either, he advised the couple. Pay a set amount each month into an escrow account I'll help you set up. That way you can demonstrate good faith to a judge.

Myers, however, was thinking about the aggravation this whole mess was causing Marcia, who was still recovering from open-heart surgery. So at the end of 2001, six years after they had bought their first home but not five months after they walked into that Household Finance office in Huber Heights, the Myerses walked away from their house and mortgage and moved into a trailer park in a suburb south of Dayton. The place wasn't too bad, they said. Space was tight but they had access to a community swimming pool. There were trees, the grounds were well maintained, the neighbors were nice. All in all, it didn't seem too terrible a place to recover while waiting for the courts to rule on their claim.

The Myerses wouldn't need to wait terribly long; the company's aggressive new lending policies were sparking lawsuits all across the country. Household Finance was facing legal action for its alleged deceptive practices in Illinois, California, Oregon, New York, and Minnesota. The community organization ACORN had filed a national class-action suit against the company, charging it with widespread consumer fraud, and AARP joined a similar class-action suit filed against the company in New York.

The company was also attracting the attention of regulators around the United States, starting with Christine Gregoire, then the attorney general of Washington state. One case that spurred Gregoire into action was that of a seventy-year-old Bellingham man who had been talked into buying a credit insurance policy limited to those sixty-five or younger. There was also the family of five in Auburn, paying $900 more a month than they had been paying before they turned to a Household salesman for a refinance. A group of attorneys general began meeting with company officials in the summer of 2002 and a joint settlement was announced that fall. Household agreed to $484 million in fines— the largest consumer fraud settlement in U.S. history—and assented to a series of reforms, including a 5 percent cap on up-front fees and utilizing "secret shoppers" whom the company would hire to police its own salespeople. William Aldinger even claimed he was sorry after a fashion. In a written statement, he apologized to the company's customers for "not always living up to their expectations" but did not admit to any specific wrongdoing.

The $484 million settlement sounded enormous—until one did the arithmetic. The money was to be divided among the roughly 300,000 people in forty-four states who had refinanced with Household between 1999 and the fall of 2002. Even forgetting about legal fees and the money set aside for compliance, that worked out to an average of $1,600 per person. Household, by contrast, had logged sixteen straight record quarters in a row. In 2001 alone, the year the Myerses signed their deal, Household reported $1.8 billion in profits. The company had made big promises but its executives told analysts that they didn't expect its consent agreement to cost them more than ten cents a share over the coming year. Household's share price spiked by one-third in the forty-eight hours after news of the settlement spread. Investors seemed relieved that the penalty hadn't been larger or the reforms more sweeping.

The national settlement presented the Myerses with a difficult decision. The state attorney general had announced that Ohio residents who did business with Household could receive up to $5,200 per family. But agreeing to a settlement meant the Myerses would have to drop out of their lawsuit. They opted out of the negotiated deal so they could continue to press their specific case in court.

In the end, it hardly made a difference what they chose. The confidentiality agreement Myers and Marcia signed with Household means they can't reveal the size of their cash settlement, but suffice it to say that in retrospect the monetary difference between the two deals was minimal. They received a better payout than the state would have given them but not so much more that it had been worth all their anguish. The bottom line is that it was a mere pittance compared to what Household had cost them. "It wasn't worth all the fuss, I'll tell you that much," Myers said. "I told my lawyers, 'The only ones making any money on this are you people.'"

One month after settling with the attorneys general, William Aldinger stood before the cameras for one more blockbuster announcement: Household was being acquired by HSBC, the London-based financial giant, for $16.4 billion. Later, long after the financial crisis of 2008 had done so much damage, Floyd Norris, the *New York Times* columnist, would dub this acquisition, consummated in 2003, "the deal that fueled subprime." This sector, the CEO of New Century Financial, a large subprime lender, said at the time of the acquisition, gets "beat up on a regular basis. So it's refreshing when a highly-qualified suitor sees value." Under the deal, Aldinger was paid an immediate bonus of $20.3

million and given a new contract that guaranteed him at least $5.5 million a year over the next three years.

Myers was not nearly so fortunate. Even factoring in his wife's medical costs and the loss of her income for almost a year, Myers figures that he would have saved enough to retire in 2002 or 2003 at the latest if he had not been lured into a deal with Household. Instead, shortly before resolving their legal case, the Myerses filed for bankruptcy. "You know, you hear all these people saying they're ashamed to have filed bankruptcy," Myers said. "That's not me. They screwed me, and the way I figure it, one screw job is good for another screw job."

Myers was still working when I visited him at the end of 2008, a week shy of his seventy-fourth birthday. He was too old to be delivering boxes to restaurants so his boss put him to work in the warehouse, packing boxes of tomatoes and the like. His workweek starts on Saturday night at midnight. He works until 8 or 9 A.M. on Sunday morning and then returns to the plant Sunday night to work the same hours. He picks up a third shift during the week. "Ain't too bad," he said with an amiable smile.

Harder to swallow has been their slide down the housing hierarchy. The trailer park in the south suburbs, the one with trees and a swimming pool, raised its rates to $400 a month, which proved too steep a price for a part-time produce boxer and a cafeteria worker. That meant the Myerses had to move—again. They looked for a place that cost $200 a month or less, which is how they ended up at Pine View.

Marcia misses her old flower beds. The small patch of dirt available to her now is nothing like the garden she had in those few years they owned a home. But she tells herself she had lived in trailers before and they would do just fine in one now.

It helped that they had recently visited the old place. The couple was shocked by what they saw. They had read about foreclosures in the paper but it was nothing like seeing it up close. The old place was still white with the teal trim but it was as if the house had been physically moved out of the stable working-class neighborhood that they knew and dropped into a deteriorating ghetto. There were vacant houses everywhere, with plywood over windows and garbage strewn about. Several payday lenders had opened storefronts in the area, as had a check casher and a rent-to-own place. "We didn't feel so bad after that visit," Myers said.

Yet he can't help but feel lousy sometimes, he said. It's not the lost house, or the fact that he's still working hard into his mid-seventies. It's the feeling that he let Marcia down and also himself.

"After I first found out about the shafting I took, I felt dumb," he said. "I felt really, really dumb for a good long while there." He confessed as much to one of his attorneys. "He says back to me, 'Hey, there are people with a lot more mental capabilities than you that got took. We got police chiefs in these lawsuits, we got schoolteachers.' He listed off a bunch of people with better educations than me.

"It made me feel better. At least it was everyone who was took."

One

Check Cashers of
the World Unite

LAS VEGAS, 2008

The stomping piano chords and tambourine slaps blaring over the loudspeaker are at once familiar. They are the opening notes to the early Motown hit "Money (That's What I Want)." The nation's check cashers and payday lenders have a dangerously low sense of irony, I mused. We are a respectable business, their leaders have been saying since the founding of the National Check Cashers Association in the late 1980s. Sure, we cater to a hard-pressed, down-market clientele but we are not the money-grubbers the popular culture makes us out to be. We provide a useful service critical to the working of the U.S. economy. Our products are heavily regulated and fairly priced. Yet here they were kicking off their twentieth annual gathering in October 2008 with a musical production based on a song whose lyrics repeat, more than thirty times, that what the singer wants, more than love and more than happiness, is lots of money.

The convention was being held in Las Vegas. The women dancing across the stage were young and buxom and dressed in skimpy sequined outfits. The men were buff and tan and similarly underdressed. We could have been sitting in any show room on the Strip except that the lyrics had been rewritten for the occasion. Instead of an unconscious self-parody the skit was actually aimed at a handy target in those dark and unsettling days in the fall of 2008: the country's bankers. If not for the behavior of the banks, their industry would not be nearly so robust. The banks abandoned lower-income neighborhoods starting thirty years ago, creating the vacuum that the country's check cashers filled. The steep fees the banks charge on a bounced check or overdue credit card bill fuel a lot of the demand for payday advances and other quick cash loans. The big Wall Street banks had stepped in and provided money critical to the expansion plans of many in the room, but never mind: These entrepreneurs selling their financial services to the country's hard-pressed subprime citizenry are nothing if not opportunistic. The nation's narrative, they argued, was theirs. The banks, who were booed lustily throughout the two-day conclave, would serve as the poverty industry's new bogeyman.

"I get my money (when I want), I get my money (when I want)," the troupe sang as they danced and pantomimed various financial transactions. Those playing the part of bankers (picture a tie over an otherwise naked male torso) were emphatically shaking their heads "no" ("At the bank I feel like I'm on trial; I'd rather get fast service and a smile"), but when those in the role of customers knock on the door of their local "financial center," they are greeted by friendly people who are only too glad to cash their checks or to loan them cash until their next paycheck. Apparently salvation is sweet. Suddenly a dozen or so very good-looking young people were dancing through a blizzard of fake twenty-dollar bills while singing, "I got my money (and it works for me)." The extravaganza brought down the house.

There's no single gathering place that routinely brings together more of the many strands of the poverty business than this one, held this year in a cavernous hall in the bowels of the Mandalay Bay convention center. Those who pioneered the payday advance industry in the mid-1990s started showing up at meetings of the National Check Cashers Association because they didn't know where else to go and, over time, other parts of this subculture of low-income finance—the pawnbrokers, Western Union and MoneyGram, the country's largest collection agencies—followed. Eventually the check cashers hired an outside consulting firm to give them a new name, and since 2000 their organization has been called the Financial Service Centers of America, a rebranding at once more respectable and opaque. When expressed as an acronym, FiSCA, the name sounds quasi-official, like Fanny Mae, Freddie Mac, or some other agency playing a mysterious but vital role in the U.S. economy.

Business remained good in the poverty industry, despite hard economic times and also because of them. People struggling to get by, after all, are often good news for those catering to the working poor and others at the bottom of the economic pyramid. Everywhere I looked there were people flying their corporate colors. Competing battalions were dressed in look-alike pants and pullover shirts bearing company logos, each representing another big chain booking hundreds of millions of dollars in revenues each year, if not billions.

Yet despite flush times, the weekend felt like one extended, oversized group therapy session for an industry suffering from esteem deficit disorder. The CEO of one of the industry's biggest chains, ACE Cash Express, even brought a video created for the occasion aimed at bucking everyone's spirits. A montage of warm black-and-white photographs flashed on a screen hovering above the stage as an ethereal cover of the song "Over the Rainbow" played and a narrator intoned, "They need to pay their rent. They need to feed their family. They need someone who understands them." Joseph Coleman, the group's chairman, had offered similar self-affirmations in his welcoming remarks. Virtually every person in the room made his or her living catering to customers with tarnished credit. So Coleman opened by assuring them that they were not to blame for the financial hurricane that was leaving the global economy in tatters. Feel proud of what you do, he told an audience of more than one thousand people. "While consumer advocates were organizing against us for charging fifteen dollars on a two-week loan," Coleman said, and while well-meaning community activists and pinhead bureaucrats were wringing their hands over those choosing to pay a fee to a check casher rather than establishing a checking account, "the big boys were selling toxic six-figure mortgages that threatened to bring down the worldwide financial system."

"No one matches the service we give our customers," Coleman, who runs a small chain of check-cashing stores in the Bronx, New York, reassured his cohorts. "No bank matches our hours. Our products fit our customers' lifestyle." Look at any member of the easy-credit landscape, whether the used car dealer offering financing to those who could not otherwise secure a loan or those who saw the fat profits that could be made pitching faster IRS refunds to the working poor. We're ubiquitous in the very neighborhoods where businesses tend to be scarce, Coleman said. We're willing to serve these people who otherwise would do without. And yet—here a picture of Rodney Dangerfield appeared on the giant overhead screen—"we don't get no respect." With that the room erupted in appreciative applause.

The business of making money off the poor dates back to the first time a person of means held a ring, a brooch, or a pocket watch in hock in exchange for a cash loan plus interest. The Chinese supposedly served as the globe's first pawnbrokers and in fifteenth-century Italy the Franciscans ran nonprofit pawnshops called *monte di pietà*— translated, the "mount of pity." In his *Inferno,* Dante reserved the lowest ledge in his seventh and final circle of hell, below even the murderers, for moneylenders guilty of usury, and of course Jesus famously knocked over the tables of those moneychangers conducting business in the temple. More recently, a person could get Cadillac-rich by running an inner-city policy wheel or reign as a minor land baron on a small patch of dirt running a tenant farm in the rural South. There no doubt were ghetto grocers and poverty pimps long before the coinage of either of those terms and it was the writer James Baldwin who famously noted that it was very expensive being poor. But the poverty industry—making money off the impoverished and the working poor as big business—can be said to have started in 1983 when an oversized Texan named Jack Daugherty sought to strike it hundreds-of-millions-of-dollars rich as a pawnbroker.

By that point Daugherty had burned through $300,000 in savings. He had lost money pursuing his fortune in the oil trade and frittered away more of it on a Dallas area nightclub. Left with nothing except the small pawnshop he had opened in a suburb of Texas while he was still in his early twenties, Daugherty told himself that men had started with less. He dubbed his new business Cash America and set out to buy up as many pawnshops as he could.

He tried arranging financing through Merrill Lynch, Goldman Sachs, and the other big investment banks but none would even agree to meet with him. Rich acquaintances shunned him as well. The pawn trade meant dealing with people with grime under their nails and mud on their boots, and, depending on the state, it meant charging shockingly high interest rates that ranged between 60 percent and 300 percent annually. "If you said 'pawnshops' at one of the local country clubs," Daugherty said, "they wouldn't even talk to you." But he was not a man easily deterred. He grew the business more slowly, one store at a time. He focused on mom-and-pop pawnshops run by aging couples whose children wanted the cash more than the headaches of running the family business.

Daugherty was up to thirty-five stores when he convinced an investment bank to take his company public. In 1987, Cash America began trading shares on the American Stock Exchange. The AMEX lacked the cache of the Big Board or Nasdaq but Daugherty was able to raise $15 million and fund his first buying spree. By the end of 1988, Cash America, based in a suburb of Dallas, operated 100 pawnshops. By 1995, it was up to 350, including 33 in Great Britain and 10 in Sweden. The company changed its name to Cash America International and was invited to join the New York Stock Exchange. By 2009, Cash America was operating 500 pawnshops in the United States and another 100 in Mexico. By that time Daugherty was doing business with many of the same brand-name lenders—Bank of America, Wells Fargo, and

JPMorgan Chase, to name just a few—that had ignored him when he was just starting out.

Competition was inevitable and it's no wonder, given the numbers Cash America was reporting. In the early days, Daugherty's people were borrowing money at 9 percent and loaning it out at an average annual interest rate of 210 percent. Its profits grew by more than 20 percent a year, ranking Cash America among the country's hottest growth companies. Several more pawn companies went public in the late 1980s and at the start of the 1990s. To the prosperous, the pawnshop might have seemed an archaic, throwback business that hit its zenith in around 1955 but those with poor credit or no credit knew better. The number of pawnshops in the United States doubled during the 1990s. Though the pawn business can seem penny ante—in 2009 the average pawn loan stood at just $90—Cash America now tops more than $1 billion in revenues and churns out in excess of $100 million in profits a year.

Other businesses that belonged to what might be called the fringe financial sector followed more or less the same trajectory as the pawnbrokers. The rent-to-own furniture and appliance business was born in the late 1960s when the owner of Mr. T's Rental in Wichita, Kansas, a man named Ernie Talley, told a family that they had rented a washer-dryer for long enough to have paid for it in full. The enterprise he created went public in 1995 and today is called Rent-A-Center, a company that delivers profit margins more than twice that of Best Buy, which sells, rather than rents, its electronics and appliances. Rent-A-Center, based in Plano, Texas, another Dallas suburb, reported that its 3,000 stores booked just under $3 billion in revenues in 2008 and $220 million in pretax profits. If anything, its closest competitor, Aaron's, based in Atlanta, had an even better 2008 as its stock price soared 38 percent in perhaps the market's worst year since the 1930s.

Wall Street money started washing through the check-cashing industry in the early 1990s when ACE Cash Express went public. Though ACE's senior management, in league with the private equity firm JLL Partners, paid $455 million to take the company private in 2006, today at least a half dozen publicly traded companies are in the check-cashing business, including Dollar Financial, a diversified, $500 million, 1,200-store mini-conglomerate based in Berwyn, Pennsylvania, that sells its customers everything from check-cashing and bill-paying services to payday loans, reloadable debit cards, and tax preparation services.

Yet when compared to the cash advance business, all these other enterprises catering to those on the economic fringes can seem pint-sized. Payday lending was a late entry in the Poverty, Inc. phenomenon—the first payday lender didn't go public until 2004—but it is at once more pervasive than any of its scruffy, low-rent cousins and far more controversial. There were so many payday outlets scattered across thirty-eight states at the industry's peak a couple of years back—24,000—that their numbers topped even the combined number of the country's McDonald's and Burger Kings. An estimated 14 million households in the United States (of 110 million) visited a payday lender in 2008, collectively borrowing more than $40 billion in installments of $200 or $500 or $800. A list of name-brand banks that have helped the industry fund its expansion includes JPMorgan Chase, Bank of America, Wells Fargo, and Wachovia. "Free and equal access to credit for any legitimate business that complies with all laws is a cornerstone of the free enterprise system," a Wells Fargo spokeswoman told Bloomberg News in 2004, representing one of the rare times a large bank was asked about its subprime activities prior to the credit meltdown of 2008.

Payday lenders charged their customers a collective $7 billion in fees in 2008. The country's rent-to-own shops collectively took in about $7 billion in revenues that year. By comparison, movie theaters in North America generated $11 billion in ticket sales in 2008.

The pawnbrokers booked roughly $4 billion in revenues that year and the check cashers $3 billion. Toss in businesses like the auto title lenders (short-term loans in which a car serves as collateral) and all those tax preparers offering instant tax refunds (one chain, Jackson Hewitt, with 6,500 offices scattered across the country, is more pervasive than KFC) and that adds up to $25 billion. By comparison, the nation's funeral business is around a $15 billion a year industry and the country's liquor stores and other retailers sell around $30 billion in beer, wine, and spirits each year. Include the revenues generated by the money-wiring business (Western Union alone did $5 billion in revenues in 2008 and MoneyGram $1.3 billion) plus all those billions the banks and other companies selling debit cards charge in activation fees, withdrawal fees, monthly maintenance fees, and the dollar some charge for every customer service inquiry, and revenues in the poverty industry easily exceed those of the booze business.

There are any number of ways of describing this relatively new financial subculture that has exploded in popularity over the past two decades. I typically used "fringe financing" or the "poverty business" when describing this project, but FiSCA chairman Joe Coleman absolutely beamed when I used the term "alternative financing" to describe his world. Investment bankers tend to stick to even safer rhetorical shores and use the more genteel "specialty financing."

But whatever descriptor one prefers, this sector of the economy encompasses a wider cast than was represented in Las Vegas in the fall of 2008. The Poverty, Inc. economy includes the subprime credit card business—the issuing of cards to those with tarnished credit who are so thankful to have plastic in their pocket that they're willing to pay almost any interest rate (one lender, First Premier Bank, sent a mailer to prospective customers in the fall of 2009 offering an APR of 79.9 percent)—and the used auto financing business. Regulators don't require banks to publicly disclose what portion of their revenues are derived from subprime borrowers versus those with higher credit scores, but the Wall Street financial analysts monitoring the publicly-traded companies issuing subprime credit cards (a list that includes Capital One, American Express, and JPMorgan Chase) estimate that the banks and others in the business are making at least $50 billion a year off subprime credit card borrowers. A sampling of Wall Street analysts estimate the size of the subprime auto financing world at somewhere between $25 billion and $30 billion a year in revenues. And there's also all those subprime mortgage lenders that had peddled products at once so destructive and so popular that they triggered the worst economic downturn since the Great Depression.

In time subprime lenders would target a demographic much broader than those who could reasonably be called the working poor or the lower middle class. CNBC's Rick Santelli would infamously rant on the floor of the Chicago Mercantile Exchange about being forced to bail out neighbors who borrowed to build new bathrooms they could not afford. Even Edmund Andrews, a *New York Times* economics reporter who earned a six-figure salary—he was responsible for covering the Federal Reserve Bank, no less—would write a book about getting caught up in the subprime madness. Rather than rent or find a suitable place in a less expensive neighborhood, Andrews was able to buy a handsome brick home in Silver Spring, Maryland, using what people in the industry called a "liar's loan" because they required so little in documentation that they practically begged an applicant to fib.

Yet long before the subprime loan became an easy way for all those people desiring a $500,000 or $600,000 house on a salary good enough to buy a home for half that price, they targeted people who owned properties worth $100,000 or less. In that regard, the subprime industry serves as more than a unique lens for examining America's prolonged and unhealthy love affair with debt; it also offers a street-level narrative exposing the very roots of the subprime crisis. The poverty industry pioneered the noxious subprime mortgage loan during the 1980s and it was the huge profits generated by companies like Household Finance that inspired the likes of Countrywide Financial and Ameriquest to get into the business and eventually expand their market to include the middle class. In the early days there would be no debate about whether homeowners relying on a subprime loan were greedy or foolish or somehow had themselves to blame. There was something unmistakably predatory about this earliest iteration of the subprime story. Solicitations for easy money came in the mail and over the phone and sometimes with a knock on the door by a home repair huckster working in tandem with a mortgage broker. As it played out in working-class enclaves through the 1990s and into the early 2000s, the subprime mortgage was often a scam, an easy way for many big banks to goose their profits. However, it was nearly always as toxic for a borrower as eventually it would be for the world economy.

There were plenty of would-be heroes offering urgent warnings about the destructiveness of these loans, but they might as well have been wearing tinfoil hats and grousing about radio devices implanted in their teeth; those in power failed to heed their cries. The contagion needed to enter the general population—or at least spread to neighborhoods where editors and reporters and the politicians and their friends live—before the rest of the populace could be warned of its dangers. And then of course it wasn't people's individual tales of woe but the stock market's great fall and the failure of a few investment banks that functioned as a collective smack to the head.

"This whole crisis we're in has been an emergency situation for a long time," said Howard Rothbloom, an Atlanta lawyer who is among those who have been complaining the longest about the perils of the subprime loan. "But it only became a crisis once it was investors who lost all that money."

The country's subprime mortgage lenders and their confederates were generating an estimated $100 billion in annual revenues at the peak of the subprime bubble in the mid-2000s. And no doubt a large portion of that $100 billion a year was still being sold to the working poor. There's a race element to the story as well. How else does one explain all those studies that repeatedly show that a black applicant was several times more likely to be put into a subprime loan than someone white at the same income level and with the same general credit rating? But even if the lower classes account for just half of the subprime mortgage industry's revenues, that would mean the Poverty, Inc. economy was around a $150 billion a year industry at its peak. By comparison, the country's casinos, Indian casinos included, collectively rake in around $60 billion in gambling revenues each year, and U.S. cigarette makers book $40 billion in annual revenues.

"The thing about dealing with the subprime consumer is that it's just a nickel-and-dime business." That's what Jerry Robinson, a former investment banker who had logged nearly twenty years in the subprime business, told me. Robinson's résumé includes stints in rent-to-own, payday, used car finance, and four years with a subprime credit card company. "But the good news," Robinson continued, "is there's a whole lot of nickels and dimes" to be had. All those waitresses and store clerks and home health-care workers might not make much, but in the aggregate they can mean big bucks. Whereas the banker seeks 100 customers with $1 million, people inside the payday industry like to say they covet a million people who only have $100 to their name. Bad credit. No credit. No problem.

The corner pawnbroker can be a lifesaver for the person needing quick cash for a bus ticket home to attend a favorite aunt's funeral. A person without a bank account needs someone like a check casher to survive in today's modern world. I spent a day in Spartanburg, South Carolina, with Billy Webster, who had a net worth exceeding $100 million on the day his company, Advance America, the country's largest payday lending chain, went public in 2004. To him there is something noble about the way he attained his wealth. How else could a person struggling by on $20,000 or $25,000 or $30,000 survive if not for access to the quick cash his company and its competitors offer? "People who use our service like us and appreciate us," Webster said. "It's only the consumer critics who don't like us."

Yet the poverty industry can seem less lofty when one considers the collective financial burden these businesses place on all those that regularly use its services. There are 40 million or so people in the United States living on $30,000 or less a year, according to the Federal Reserve. There are no doubt some people making more than $30,000 a year borrowing against their next paycheck with a payday lender (just as there are people getting by on $20,000 who would never use a check casher or a subprime credit card), but $30,000 seems a useful cutoff if trying to describe the working poor: those who earn too much to qualify for government entitlements but who earn so little there's no hope they'll ever save much money given the rising cost of housing, health care, transportation, and everything else one needs to live life in twenty-first-century America. If each person living on under $30,000 a year donated equally to the poverty industry, that would mean their annual share of that $150 billion is $3,800. For the warehouse worker supporting a family on $25,000 per year, that works out to a 15 percent annual poverty tax.

Publicly traded companies feel great pressure to grow their revenues year over year. So too does any ambitious entrepreneur. It doesn't make a difference that the target market is those who can least afford to lose another $1,000 or $2,000 or $3,000 a year from their take-home checks. The task of teaching the country's payday lenders and check cashers and pawnbrokers tricks for shaking even more from their customers falls to people like Jim Higgins, who arrived in Las Vegas for the twentieth annual check cashers' convention to give a ninety-minute presentation he dubbed "Effective Marketing Strategies to Dominate Your Market."

Higgins, a squat man with silver-framed glasses and aquiline nose who calls to mind Vincent Gardenia, the actor who played Cher's father in *Moonstruck,* gave his talk twice that weekend. The session I attended was standing-room only and Higgins's talk brimmed with practical suggestions. Employ customer loyalty programs, as the airlines have done so effectively. Mine your databases and divide customers into several categories, from those who have only visited you once or twice to those who come in at least a couple of times a month. Devise a targeted mailer for each. Send out "Welcome!" mailers to each new customer and sweeten the hello with a cash incentive to return. For those who are semi-regulars offer a "cash 3, get 1 free" deal. "These are people not used to getting anything free," Higgins said. "These are people not used to getting anything, really." Use these tried-and-true methods, he advised, and you can "turn your store into an effective selling machine."

It's not hard, he reassured them. Pens scribbled furiously as he tossed out specifics such as various ideas for contests and giveaways and other come-ons that have worked for the big boys. Raffle off an iPod or consider a scratch-and-win contest. Do whatever it takes to turn someone into a loyal customer, he counseled them. "Get a customer coming to you regularly," Higgins said, "and they could be worth $2,000 to $4,000 a year."

I had the good fortune to have knocked on the door of the people at FiSCA—and on the doors of any number of swashbuckling entrepreneurs who have figured out how to get very rich off those with very little—at a time when many of the pioneers of this industry felt misunderstood and under public attack. A few harbored resentment toward the press and declined to talk, but most proved eager to meet with me. FiSCA was typical. The check cashers don't normally allow outsiders to attend their events, Stephen Altobelli, who works for an agency that does public relations for FiSCA, had told me. But I was granted an all-access pass that allowed me to roam the halls freely and chat with whoever was willing to talk with me. I had told Altobelli that I would be spending time with critics such as Martin Eakes, whose name had come up any number of times in Las Vegas as the crusader the people in the room most love to hate. I told him, too, that I would be meeting with people, such as Tommy Myers, who consider themselves victims of the poverty industry. He didn't care. "Our people want to get their stories out there," Altobelli said.

That seemed fine by me. Our country was experiencing the worst economic times since the Great Depression and his people resided in an upside-down world in which people with little money in their pockets boded well for their bottom lines. There's something undeniably brilliant about the person who figures out how to make a 150 percent markup on a $500 television by renting it by the week, or a person like Allan Jones who sees the potential to become a triple-digit millionaire several times over by loaning people $200 or $400 at a time. Who are these people who one day wake up and decide that they're going to make their mark and their millions charging potentially confiscatory interest rates to the working poor?

These were jittery times inside the Mandalay conference center. Less than one month earlier the government had allowed Lehman Brothers to fail while helping to arrange a shotgun marriage between Merrill Lynch and Bank of America. The financial industry's future looked tenuous and even if those in this room could expect to see demand for their products go up, so too would defaults rise. If nothing else, the deep credit freeze that had descended on much of the world meant the end, at least temporarily, of the days when a small entrepreneur could dream of the inflated payout from a chain anxious to grow big fast. And then there were the normal competitive pressures of running a business in twenty-first-century America. The big threat in 2008 was Walmart, which was moving aggressively into a couple of the poverty industry's more lucrative areas. Other giant retailers were starting to nibble around the edges of their market as well.

Yet all these seemed minor concerns compared to changes in the political climate. From the podium, in the corridors, in breakout sessions, and in the bars you could hear the fear and also the rage. They were blameless for the current financial meltdown, they told themselves, victims of a crazy housing bubble just like everyone else. But of course that wasn't quite true. They, like the country's subprime mortgage lenders, had taken advantage of the same deep and restless pools of capital looking for a high return. The fall of real wages among working Americans had created an artificial demand for expensive credit and the people gathering in meeting rooms on the grounds of the Mandalay Bay were among those who had moved in to meet the need, amassing fortunes in the process. And even if they didn't buy the idea that they were partially responsible for the nation's financial woes, they recognized that others would blame them. The country's biggest banks and Wall Street's best-known financial houses had belly-flopped into the subprime soup and the members of FiSCA knew they were in danger of being swamped by the wash. "You better hurry on down to Cleveland [Tennessee] if you want to meet with me," Allan Jones, the man who invented the modern-day payday industry, drawled over the phone when we spoke a few weeks before the FiSCA meeting. "I'm not sure I'll have any business to still visit next year." Even as people were commemorating their twentieth meeting, there were already those who were anticipating a much smaller crowd for the twenty-fifth. The obsession in Las Vegas that weekend was Ohio, where, in three weeks, voters would be asked to greatly restrict the fees a payday lender could charge on a loan. Ohio was a top-five payday market and in fact prime territory for any number of Poverty, Inc. businesses.

"Believe me, Ohio was the wake-up call for a lot of us," Joe Coleman said.

All these major corporations, chain franchises, and newly hatched enterprises specifically catering to the working poor—were they financial angels to the country's great hardworking masses, by making homes and cars and emergency cash available to those otherwise shunned by the mainstream financial institutions? Or were these businesses tilling the country's working-class neighborhoods so aggressively that they endangered the very survival of these communities? Were they vultures carelessly adding to the economic woes of a single mother of two working as a chambermaid at the local Holiday Inn? This question, which preoccupied me in my time on the subprime fringes—the morality of making a much higher profit on the working poor than on more prosperous citizens—was also one the country would need to ask once the new administration was out of crisis mode and legislators could turn their attention to various bills addressing the profits being earned by the poverty industry.

"When someone makes a profit in low-income communities, the presumption is that they must be doing something wrong," Joe Coleman had said to me in Las Vegas when I ran into him in the hallway between events. An excitable man, Coleman got so revved up during our talk that he told me that if his life were a movie, he wouldn't be Mr. Potter in *It's a Wonderful Life* but rather the man who protects the working stiff from the rapacious and coldhearted financier. "We're the George Baileys here," he blurted. "We're Jimmy Stewart!"

Two

The Birth of the Predatory Lender

ATLANTA, 1991–1993

I f you think that if only there had been some warnings, the subprime
lenders could have been stopped before they practically destroyed
the world economy, then you should avoid the office of the Atlanta
public interest lawyer Bill Brennan. It would be too upsetting.

Since that day in 1991 when eighty-year-old Annie Lou Collier sat
across from his desk because a bank was threatening to take her home
of thirty-eight years, William J. Brennan, Jr., has been talking about
virtually nothing else but the need for people in power to impose some
basic regulatory standards on the country's lenders. A staff attorney
for the Atlanta Legal Aid Society, Brennan has paid his own way to
Washington, D.C., numerous times to testify before Congress and the
Fed. He has spent more than he wants to admit doing reconnaissance
work at industry-sponsored subprime lending conferences. Over the
years he's put so many flights and hotel stays and subscriptions and
overnight deliveries on credit cards that for a time he put himself and
his spouse, Lynn Simmons, a schoolteacher, in debt. "My wife wasn't
happy with me but we don't need to get into that," he says sheepishly.

His collection of subprime-related material began small: some articles, a few key memos, a legal brief somebody had sent him. But when Brennan reached twenty or so cartons, Simmons put her foot down. She banished every last box from their home, so on top of everything else, Brennan now spends around a hundred and fifty dollars each month on a storage locker.

"Ninety-eight percent of everything good that's happened in the fight against predatory lending is because of Bill," his friend Howard Rothbloom told me. Back in the early 1990s, Rothbloom, then a young bankruptcy lawyer, called Brennan hoping to get up to speed on a new rash of predatory lending he was seeing in Atlanta. "Bill offers to send me a couple of articles he thought I'd find interesting," Rothbloom said—and the next day a FedEx van was delivering a heavy box to his office. "Just quickly . . . ," Brennan will say when leaving a voice mail for his boss, Steve Gottlieb, the executive director of Atlanta Legal Aid. But it's never quick. The Legal Aid voice mail system gives callers five minutes to leave a message but Brennan invariably needs to call again to finish a message and sometimes he needs to call a third time. Gottlieb asked Brennan to stand at his wedding but he has also banned his friend from using the office copier.

Brennan has no tolerance for halfway measures. He became a regular reader of the *New York Times* business section and he bought a subscription to the *Wall Street Journal*. And when he learned that the lenders he was following were reading something called *Inside B&C Lending* (its motto: "Everything you need to know about subprime mortgage lending—making loans with less than 'A' credit"), he decided he would read that as well, though an annual subscription cost $495. He has unusual dedication and focus. Brennan once spotted Steve Gottlieb walking down the street at seven or eight o'clock at night as Gottlieb and his wife were heading to a restaurant for dinner. "Steve! Steve!" Gottlieb heard—and he turned to see Brennan, tall and lanky, dashing toward him with a large packet of materials in his hand. He had stopped his car in the middle of the road and ran from it with the engine still running and a door wide open.

Brennan has a kind, open face and a gentle disposition. He's bald, with a fringe of gray hair, a thin gray mustache, and gold-framed glasses. He has a courtly manner and dresses smartly at the office, preferring ties and blazers and trousers with sharp creases. He smiles a lot, but often it is the pained smile of someone who feels the world's burdens more heavily than the average person does. He stoops slightly when standing, as if apologizing for his height. Jim McCarthy, a housing activist in Dayton, Ohio, was anxious the first time he called Brennan at the end of the 1990s when McCarthy was starting to get involved in the fight against predatory subprime lending. "Here I was, this nasal-voiced kid from Ohio who knew next to nothing," McCarthy said, "and he gave me all the time in the world." Of course, a FedEx box filled with follow-up materials arrived at McCarthy's office the next day.

Bill Brennan wanted to be a Catholic priest, but after entering the seminary he found cloistered life too confining and so transferred to Emory University. His parents, who had grown up poor, pushed their son to attend law school but Brennan felt ambivalent about a legal career even after graduating from Emory Law School in 1967. He took a job teaching at a school for the mentally disabled in a poor black community in Atlanta and threw himself into the politics of the day. He marched on the Pentagon in 1968 to protest the Vietnam War, and got involved on the periphery of the civil rights struggle. He was driving his car when he heard a speech on the radio by the man then running Atlanta Legal Aid. Martin Luther King, Jr., had just been assassinated and this lawyer was talking about using the law to battle poverty, racism, and other social ills. Brennan went for an interview the next day and has toiled in the trenches of legal aid ever since.

Brennan seemed to have a nose for crusades that pit him against people seeking to get rich off the poor. In his first year on the job he exposed a pair of city inspectors who bought apartment buildings on the cheap after citing the original owners for code violations and then jacked up the rent without making repairs. Several years later he took on a former top housing official under Atlanta mayor Andrew Young for demanding under-the-table payments from the Section 8 tenants (those receiving rent subsidies from the federal government) living in properties he owned. The man was sentenced to five years in prison. In 1989, Bill Dedman of the *Atlanta Journal-Constitution* won the Pulitzer Prize for an astonishing series that could be summed up in a pair of nearly identical maps, one showing the city's predominantly black neighborhoods, the other identifying those communities where banks almost never made a loan. Brennan was a key member of the housing group that had first gone to the newspaper with the original idea of an investigative piece exposing the redlining policies of the city's largest banks.

Brennan picked up his first mortgage fraud case at around the same time the *Journal-Constitution* was running its series. And then his second, third, and fourth. Each of his clients told Brennan more or less the same story. All had fallen behind on their mortgages and they heard from a local business, Brown Realty Associates, offering to help. The name of that business rolls easily off Brennan's tongue twenty years after the fact, as if he's been talking about them regularly ever since: the Browns of Brown Realty Associates, a husband-wife team and their adult son. One of the Browns would tell the beleaguered homeowners that clearing everything up was as easy as signing a few papers to make payments to Brown Realty until they were all caught up. "What these folks didn't realize is they had signed a legal document called a 'quitclaim,' transferring ownership of the home to the Browns," Brennan said. "As soon as they missed a payment, the Browns would file to take possession." The Browns had gotten their hands on dozens of homes before he and others with Legal Aid figured out what was going on. Joining forces with a pair of local private attorneys, Brennan and his cohorts won millions in damages against the Browns and forced them out of business.

Perhaps most disturbing to Brennan was the fact that a major downtown bank had granted Brown Realty a $1.5 million line of credit. Without it, he figured, the company could not have accumulated that many

homes in so short a period of time. Brennan didn't care how much the
bank knew about what the Browns were doing with the money. They
were financing scam artists who were "targeting black neighborhoods to
steal people's houses," Brennan said, at the same time they were refusing to make legitimate loans to qualified would-be homeowners in those
same communities. In 1988, with additional funding from the county,
he convinced his bosses to create a Home Defense Program, the first
of its kind in the country. Brennan has served as its executive director
ever since.

Brennan learned from the Brown case that established financial institutions were no longer ignoring the black community entirely. What
he discovered working the next set of cases the Home Defense Program took on was that the challenge was larger than a few rogue lenders working the area's working-class and poor communities. In these
same neighborhoods, larger financial concerns were now aggressively
peddling loans that were so destructive that they left borrowers in a far
more precarious financial position than when they started. "It was incredible," said Brennan. "These banks went from making no loans in all
these black neighborhoods to making loans that were totally abusive."
Jack Long, one member of the group that Brennan assembled to fight
back, gave the phenomenon a name: "reverse redlining."

The first firms to recognize the profits to be made from the neighborhoods that the banks had historically ignored were nonbank lenders
such as Champion Mortgage. A Legal Aid attorney named Ira Rheingold watched in wonder as Champion used redlining as its main selling
point. Its advertising campaign featured the slogan "When your bank
says no, Champion says yes." It was, Rheingold had to confess, devil-
ishly brilliant—and also underscored the shortsightedness of the established banks.

"I don't know if it was because of their own prejudices or because
of the limits of the system they built, but traditional banks failed to
recognize that there was plenty of need and desire in low-income and
minority communities that was going untapped," said Rheingold, who
worked as a legal aid attorney in both suburban Washington, D.C., and

Chicago before becoming the executive director of the National Association of Consumer Advocates. "So companies like Champion moved in and figured out that not only could they make money lending to these people, they could make a lot more money than a bank. These were unsophisticated consumers who didn't know how banks worked, so the Champions of the world came in and said, 'We're going to go in as your best friend and act as your trusted adviser.'" The typical customer, Rheingold said, didn't feel ripped off paying interest rates of 20 percent or more but instead felt grateful that, finally, someone was saying yes.

"It took them time," Rheingold said, "but eventually the banks figured it out."

Annie Lou Collier had been living in the same home since 1953 when a man who could have stepped out of the movie *Tin Men* knocked on her door in 1990. He was a home-improvement salesman who wanted to talk about a new roof. Collier had paid off the house years earlier but she was eighty years old and scraping by on a modest fixed income. She told him she couldn't afford a new roof but the man advised her that given the worth of her home, she could simply borrow the money. He even offered to drive her to a lender who would lend her $6,900 that very day. "She was this wonderful lady," Brennan recalled, "but they gave her this crazy loan she could never afford."

Predictably, Collier quickly fell behind in her payments and by 1991, one year after signing the deal, she was already in arrears on a loan that included 22 percent in points and fees and carried an annual 25.3 percent interest rate. Brennan contacted the lender, who told him that they had Collier's signature on the loan papers and that's all the proof they needed that she understood the terms of her loan. It did not seem to matter to the person on the other end of the phone that Collier had a second-grade education and could not read or that, given her income, she couldn't possibly afford the monthly payments. It didn't matter, either, that the contractor had not completed the job that she had paid for. When the Home Defense Program heard from several more elderly people living in southwest Atlanta who found themselves in a similar predicament to Collier's through strikingly similar circumstances, Brennan figured that they again would be combating a small-time local firm like Brown Realty. The loan terms were "so terribly abusive," he reasoned, there couldn't possibly be a legitimate company behind them. The going rate for a conventional mortgage at the time was around 9 percent, but he had one client who was being charged 29 percent on a home loan. Consequently, he suspected the lender was more interested in seizing homes through judgments of default than in accruing steady profits through regular monthly payments. Brennan would be shocked when he learned that the institution holding paper on all these loans was Fleet Bank, a large, publicly traded firm from Providence, Rhode Island.

For years activists had been lobbying the likes of Fleet to make more loans in the country's less affluent communities. But this was not what they had in mind. These were not loans to first-time homebuyers; they were mortgage refinancings and home equity loans. They were also not conventional loans made through bank branches; they were deals arranged by a subsidiary called Fleet Finance.

While the morality of what Fleet was doing might be questionable, there was no doubting its profitability. Through much of the 1980s, the *Economist* reported in March 1990, banks across the country were posting big losses. One exception was Fleet, which was posting a return on equity (a "spanking 17 percent," the magazine wrote) that made it the envy of the industry. Its "prize performer," the *Economist* wrote—"the jewel in Fleet's crown"—was its "hugely profitable" consumer finance subsidiary. Fleet Finance, with 150 offices in twenty-seven states, produced $43 million in after-tax profits in 1989. Its portfolio would generate another $55 million in profits in 1990. By 1991, Fleet had surpassed the venerable Bank of Boston to reign as New England's largest bank. The financial press hailed Terrence Murray, the company's chief executive and chairman, for transforming a small Rhode Island bank into a regional powerhouse.

Every year, Atlanta Legal Aid gets summer law interns whom the staff is never quite sure what to do with. Brennan sent several to the county deed room in search of any loan involving Fleet Finance. They found more than sixty and then contacted the borrowers in search of people who might talk. Brennan was not drumming up business so much as looking for a discernable pattern of abuse. All the borrowers contacted by the interns were black and they tended to live in the same few neighborhoods. Their homes had been paid off or they had lived in them so long that they had built up considerable equity. Most were older than sixty-five and had little in the way of available cash; almost all had ended up signing a loan with Fleet because they had been enticed by a seemingly helpful contractor offering its services to fix a porch or a roof or some other part of the house in visible disrepair. Fleet never made the loans themselves but used what Brennan called "pass-through companies": local mortgage lenders that would sell the loans to Fleet, often on the same day the loan papers were signed. Typically the repair work would be left unfinished, leaving borrowers with the same problem propelling them to sign the loan—though of course they now had a steep new monthly bill that put further repairs beyond their financial reach.

Brennan knew it would be futile to sue the home-improvement contractors. Annie Lou Collier's roof job might have been only half completed but these were fly-by-night operators who would disappear before he could serve them with papers. Even if he gained a judgment against them, he could be reasonably certain their bank accounts would be empty. He would name two of the intermediary mortgage companies in the suit he filed but he saw them as virtual "shell companies" that were hardly the main culprits. With his boss's blessing, Brennan filed a class action against Fleet itself, charging the bank under the country's racketeering laws. He called a press conference to announce his suit, his first in more than twenty years as a legal services attorney. Then the calls started coming.

Some were from people who believed that they too had been victimized by a Fleet-financed home-repair scam. Several were advocates wanting to join the fight. That's how bankruptcy attorney Howard Rothbloom came to contact Brennan. He had been working late at his office when a woman named Lillie Mae Starr phoned looking for help. Starr was a retired factory worker who had left school after the eighth grade. Now in her sixties, she owned a small home in Vinings, a predominantly black community just west and north of Atlanta. Her financial woes began years earlier when she borrowed $5,000 to fix her windows. She fell behind in her payments and, after two refinancings, she owed Fleet $63,000. Facing foreclosure, she had phoned Rothbloom thinking that bankruptcy might be the solution.

Rothbloom was skeptical as he listened to her story. She claimed to be paying 23.3 percent interest but that seemed too high for a home loan. She brought in her loan documents, which he showed to Roy Barnes, a more senior lawyer working in the same small office building on the edge of the Atlanta metropolitan area. Barnes, who owned an interest in a trio of local banks, was equally incredulous.

But there had been no mistake. That first $5,000 loan had cost Starr more than $9,000, including points and fees. She had paid Fleet more than $19,000 over nine years yet somehow she still owed the bank three times that amount. "She was this real quiet lady who was embarrassed that this was happening to her," Rothbloom said. "I was the one who had to tell her how badly she had been taken." Over the coming months, Rothbloom would meet dozens of Fleet customers. Most were older African-American women living on their own and with a Bible by their bed or the couch. "These were people that trusted other people," Rothbloom said. All seemed more angry at themselves than at Fleet. It struck Rothbloom that just as he had been oblivious to abuses routinely occurring on the squalid edges of the financial system, the victims of this system had little idea of what is fair and what is not in the larger financial world.

Starr had only asked Rothbloom to help her figure out whether or not it made sense for her to declare bankruptcy, but Rothbloom decided to enlist the help of Barnes, who after serving fifteen years in the state senate had recently lost his bid to be the Democrat nominee for governor. "They'd do deed record searches looking for people with high equity," Barnes told me when I asked him why he took on the case. "They had their bird dogs walk a block, writing down those homes in need of repair. These were bad people." Together the two filed a class-action suit against Fleet claiming the bank was conspiring with a cabal of loan originators to defraud customers. Like Brennan, the two lawyers also accused Fleet of violating the country's racketeering laws.

Jack Long, an attorney in Augusta, also sued Fleet. Long was the odd man out in this group, a lifelong Republican who had spent a good deal of his legal career representing corporate clients. "I'm a fairly conservative guy," Long told me, "but I got tired of being the guy who had to go out and screw somebody." Of Fleet he would say, "What those bastards were doing was abuse, plain and simple. They had to be stopped." Long sued Fleet, charging the bank with race discrimination. Another pair of lawyers in Augusta were also suing Fleet, charging that it was in violation of Georgia's usury laws. The group stayed in touch through Brennan and a second Legal Aid lawyer, Karen Brown, a staff attorney with the agency's Senior Citizens Law Project. They spent hours over the phone, sharing scraps of intelligence and batting around strategy. When the group met face-to-face for the first time, Howard Rothbloom was shocked that Brennan was as old as he was. He had pegged Brennan, a legal aid attorney with an excitable voice and a boyish enthusiasm, as a few years younger than he was rather than twenty years his senior.

Yet perhaps the most valuable member of their team was the only nonlawyer among them: Bruce Marks, an activist who was fighting Fleet in Boston. "I'm a real hardball player and no attorney in Boston will work with me," Marks had warned Brennan the first time they spoke over the phone. Atlanta Legal Aid, however, had limited resources and Fleet was the fourteenth largest bank holding company in the country, a publicly traded adversary with deep pockets. "I was happy to get any help I could get," Brennan said. Among other contributions, several people involved in the Fleet fight say, Marks popularized the term "predatory lender." (Marks himself takes credit for the coinage and there is something to his claim. Except for a single use of "predatory lender" in an article in the *Washington Post* in 1983, every other early mention of that phrase, or its close cousin, "predatory lending," appeared in either the *Boston*

Globe or *Atlanta Journal-Constitution* at the start of the 1990s in articles quoting Marks fulminating about Fleet's lending practices.)

"The problem we all faced is that much of the abuse we were seeing wasn't illegal, it was just immoral," Rothbloom said. It was seven local mortgage companies—Brennan took to calling them the "seven dwarfs"—that actually wrote these loans and worked in tandem with the door-to-door contractors. To make their case against Fleet, each set of lawyers would need to demonstrate that the seven companies were in effect acting as emissaries for Fleet. "We knew that a rich corporation like Fleet could afford to litigate this forever in a court of law, which is why we focused a lot of our attention on public opinion," Rothbloom said. "In the court of public opinion, morality is more important than legality." Brennan would describe it as a "multi-faced approach to advocacy." Spokespeople for Fleet would dub it a "media mugging."

The way you get their attention," Marks once explained in a newsletter for housing activists, "is to be in their face all the time." Fleet would unwittingly offer Marks, executive director of the Union Neighborhood Assistance Corporation, a fat opportunity to put this philosophy into action when it announced it was buying the Bank of New England. Marks was a rich kid from Scarsdale, New York, with an MBA who in his previous career had worked for the Federal Reserve. Big mergers meant hearings and press attention and an opportunity to apply pressure on Fleet. "Up until now," he reportedly said at a meeting with Fleet executives arranged by the Fed, "you have dealt with community activists. We are bank terrorists." Data he had assembled showed that for years Fleet had made almost no home loans in Roxbury, Dorchester, and other predominantly black neighborhoods of Boston. At the same time, Fleet was bankrolling smaller lenders hawking high-rate home loans in those same communities. To make his point, he picketed Fleet press conferences and disrupted public speeches by Fleet executives. He infiltrated the company's annual meetings and did what he could to "educate" those in attendance. Protesters dressed in bright yellow shark T-shirts that read "Stop the Loan Sharks" on front and "Sink the FLEET" on back. Between 1991 and 1993, Marks was quoted more than fifty times in the *Boston Globe*, including a lengthy feature article profiling this housing activist with a "beseeching tone in his voice," "flailing mannerisms," and a "red-eyed stare."

Yet there was no denying his effectiveness. Fleet severed its relationship with some of the more unsavory lenders making loans in Boston's black neighborhoods and launched a local marketing campaign to defend itself against Marks's attacks. When that didn't work, Fleet capitulated. It created an $11 million pool to help minority homeowners in Boston receiving what Fleet acknowledged were "burdensome mortgage loans" and then, after more pressure, upped that figure to $23 million.

Atlanta's turn to witness the Bruce Marks Show came when his organization set up a satellite office there in September 1992. "It was Bruce who really stirred things up down here," Rothbloom said, "and it was Bruce who kept things boiling." He dispatched protesters to demonstrate outside the offices of King & Spalding when the news leaked out that this venerable local law firm, whose roster of partners included a former U.S. attorney general and former U.S. senators, was representing Fleet. He set up a phone bank to make sure there would be a good crowd each time they had an appearance in court. One of Rothbloom's more vivid memories from those years was the day at the end of 1992 when a judge agreed to certify Lillie Mae Starr's case as a class-action suit. A packed courtroom responded to the news with a loud burst of applause, and a fervent cry of "Thank you, Jesus!" rang out. If ever he needed a reminder that he wasn't working on just any case, Rothbloom said, that was it.

The battle was fought largely by pulling the public's heartstrings. Annie Lou Collier was granted her fifteen minutes of media fame, as were a number of Brennan's clients, including Frank Bennett, a retiree living on Social Security, and his wife Annie Ruth, who worked as a cafeteria worker for Delta Air Lines. The Bennetts ended up owing Fleet $28,000 after paying a contractor $9,900 for a job that an inspector hired by Legal Aid said was worth barely half that amount. Christine and Robert Hill lost their home after falling behind on a Fleet home equity loan carrying a 23.4 percent interest rate ("I figured if it was God's will, I would get something else," Christine Hill told the Associated Press). James Hogan, a soft-spoken janitor, was $84,000 in debt to Fleet and facing foreclosure in what started out as a $6,200 loan to repair a roof that still leaked. "When my father passed, he didn't have anything to give me," Hogan, the father of five, told a reporter for the Newhouse News Service. "I wanted to give this house to my children."

Fleet's defense was that these stories, while tragic, had nothing to do with them. Fleet had not made the loans; it had merely purchased them from third parties. Holding the company responsible for the business practices of these independent agents, a Fleet lawyer argued, would be like saying Fleet was accountable for the business practices of anyone with whom they worked, including the printer that supplied them with loan documents. "These people may be poor and illiterate, but no one puts a gun to their head and tells them to sign," a Fleet vice president, Robert Lougee, Jr., told the *Globe*. Besides, nothing we do is out of step with the rest of the consumer finance industry, Lougee asserted. The difference, he said, is that Fleet has drawn the notice of a publicity-seeking activist and a small group of self-serving lawyers seeing the potential for a large-dollar judgment.

Lougee was right on at least one point: Fleet's practices increasingly seemed in step with the rest of the industry. There were reports of home repairmen and mortgage lenders working in cahoots to target consumers who were house rich but cash poor in any number of locales. In Los Angeles, a legal aid attorney named Troy Smith might as well have been talking about Atlanta when he told a local reporter about "people going door-to-door, passing out fliers, convincing people to sign up for loans they can't afford and don't understand." In 1991, a jury in Alabama returned a $45 million judgment against Dallas-based Union Mortgage after five black families accused the lender of encouraging fraudulent home repair loans. (Fleet bought millions in loans from Union Mortgage.) Another pair of Alabama juries slapped Union Mortgage with a combined $12 million in verdicts that same year.

Whenever they were talking with the press, Fleet officials insisted that they had nothing to do with the interest rates these loan originators charged or the up-front fees (typically in the double digits) they added. But the *Boston Globe* was able to expose this claim as untrue. Fleet Finance gave its brokers a financial reward (called a yield spread premium) when a lender put a borrower into a higher interest rate loan, the paper reported. There were internal memos showing that Fleet Finance frequently set the terms of these loans. Its people often reviewed the applications of would-be borrowers before a loan would be made. Marc Siegel, owner of Georgia Mortgage Center, one of the seven Georgia lenders that worked most closely with Fleet, told the *Globe* he met several times a week with his Fleet contact. The contact was constantly letting Siegel know he would have to do things Fleet's way or they wouldn't buy any more loans. A former regional manager named Robert McCall went even further. It was no accident that the system evolved as it did, he said. Fleet wanted to give itself plausible deniability and shield itself from charges that it was using high-pressure tactics or in any way violating the loan origination laws. Of these seven companies—the "seven dwarfs"—four sold more than 96 percent of its loans to Fleet, the *Globe* found, and the remaining three sold at least half and as much as 78 percent.

Fleet claimed its lending partners needed to charge so high a rate because of the risk profile of its borrowers, despite the fact that putting up one's home as collateral substantially mitigated those risks. Certainly Fleet didn't prove itself reluctant to go after a person's home if they defaulted. In 1991, Fleet foreclosed on the homes of nearly 13 percent of the residents with whom it did business in Atlanta and its suburbs. That was seven times the rate of the next largest lender in the metro area. A Fleet Finance executive claimed that the company lost money when it was forced to foreclose but a reporter for the *Journal-Constitution* examined the records for the Atlanta area and discovered that while the company lost $17,000 per home on the 101 homes it sold at a loss, it made an average of $32,000 per home on 194 homes. That worked out to a profit of $4.4 million before other expenses.

None of these reports might have made a difference if not for the CBS News program *60 Minutes*. Fleet, the show's Morley Safer told viewers in November 1992, has "set up what amounts to a loan sharking racket." The program introduced the nation to people like Raymond Bryant, who had paid $3,500 in fees on a $11,400 loan—more than 30 percent in up-front costs on a loan carrying a 23 percent interest rate. And they heard as well from Charles Hastings, who spent his days cruising black neighborhoods in Atlanta in search of potential borrowers. "I'm not a salaried person," Hastings told Safer. "I just get up every day and go out and find business." It was Roy Barnes, the lawyer, who offered the episode's most memorable quote and the one CBS used to promote the episode. "I don't know what y'all call it up north," Barnes said, "but down here in the South we call it cheatin' and swindlin'." Shortly after the program ran, the Georgia attorney general announced his office would be investigating Fleet Finance; Bill Brennan's phone again was ringing off the hook.

People who joined Brennan over the years in his crusade to out the country's predatory subprime mortgage lenders speak of him as a living legend. "He deserves a ton of credit for showing the rest of us how destructive this lending was," said Mike Calhoun, the president of the Center for Responsible Lending, the organization that has taken the lead against predatory lending in its various forms. "He got involved before the rest of us, when it was the Wild West of lending and lenders were just grabbing huge amounts of home equity."

Bill Brennan, however, gives credit to a woman named Kathleen Keest. "Keest is the original brains behind all this stuff," Brennan said. "She's our guru. She started figuring out what was going on in the mid-eighties." In 1985, Keest moved to Boston to take a job as a staff attorney at the National Consumer Law Center monitoring the various vehicles that entrepreneurs and large corporations were concocting to get rich off warehouse workers, store clerks, and retirees struggling to make ends meet. "I've watched entire industries grow up," Keest said. "And I've seen a lot of people get hurt." In 1996, she took a posting as an assistant attorney general in Iowa, where she played a key role in exposing Ameriquest Mortgage, one of the more reckless subprime lenders in the first half of the 2000s. In 2006, she moved to North Carolina to take a job as a senior policy counsel at the Center for Responsible Lending.

Keest was running a regional legal aid office in Des Moines in 1984 when she picked up her first predatory mortgage case. This was early in what Keest dubs "wave one" of the subprime debacle, when some of capitalism's scrappier practitioners took advantage of a seemingly sensible set of policy changes. For years many states had a cap—typically around 10 percent—limiting the interest rates banks could charge on a mortgage. Those went by the wayside when the country experienced double-digit inflation through much of the 1970s and the credit markets for people looking to buy a home froze. States were starting to lift those caps and if some locales were foresighted enough to keep in place a floating ceiling on the amount a mortgage lender could charge, those would be wiped out when the federal government, in 1980, passed a law barring the states from imposing limits on the rates a lender could charge on a real estate transaction. Two years later, during President Ronald Reagan's tenure, the federal government would go further, giving lenders the latitude to sell more creative home loans, from balloon mortgages (in which most principal payments are deferred to the end of the loan period) to adjustable rate mortgages, or ARMs, which can see the interest rates a borrower pays fluctuate dramatically over the life of a loan.

The big consumer finance companies such as Household and Beneficial were among the first to jump on this first wave. Traditionally consumer finance firms had specialized in small, high-interest loans in the neighborhood of $500 or $1,500 to customers needing financing to replace a broken refrigerator or to buy a bedroom set for the kids. But this newly deregulated environment meant they could sell larger loans to these same customers at similar rates. "Once these guys moved up the food chain," Keest said of the consumer finance companies, "we started seeing countless examples of people who purchased homes in the prime market"—when home loans were still regulated—"only to lose them in the subprime market." People spoke of a new era of "risk-based pricing," where interest rates were set based on the risk profile of a borrower, but Keest saw it as "opportunistic pricing": charge as much as you can despite the security of a person's home as collateral.

"Who cared if companies were screwing poor people?" Keest asked. "It was the eighties."

With this first wave a new set of terms entered the lenders' vocabulary. A lender was said to be "packing" a loan when a salesperson had been able to load it with points and fees and expensive baubles like the credit insurance Household sold Tommy Myers. "Flipping" was a broker's ability to convince customers to refinance again and again—packing each new loan with additional points and broker fees. Another common gambit was to convince borrowers to consolidate their bills into a single home loan—often not realizing that in exchange for the convenience of a single monthly bill they had suddenly placed at risk their most valuable possession, their home. All of these practices added up to "equity stripping," the fiendish art of siphoning off the equity people have built up in their homes.

Keest spotted other forms of subprime lending creeping into the culture by the end of the 1980s. Deregulation was one cause but broader economics were a factor as well. The country grew more prosperous during the 1980s and '90s but the relative wages of the working class fell, expanding the pool of would-be borrowers desperate for the quick cash that could tide them over between paychecks. It was almost inevitable that a raft of clever entrepreneurs would try to fill the gap—for a price.

Keest struggled to keep up with all the new developments in a bimonthly newsletter she wrote and edited for the Consumer Law Center. Keest, a short, slim woman with a long narrow face framed by a pageboy hairdo, remembers the first time she learned about what she dubbed "postdated check loans." It was 1988 and a reporter in Kansas City called to ask her about the legality of a local company making short-term loans to customers who put up their next paycheck as collateral. To Keest, this was a revival of the "salary buyers" who popped up around the country in the second half of the nineteenth century—the so-called "five for six boys," since people would borrow $5 on a Monday and pay $6 on Friday. The country had outlawed the salary buyers early in the twentieth century but now in state after state, legislatures were providing carve-outs in their usury laws to legalize this new crop of lenders. "Tennessee was the first place to take it big but then plenty of states followed," Keest said.

There were always novel credit schemes to keep Keest busy. One of the more creative was the "auto title loan," which she first heard about in the early 1990s. These were similar to loans made by the country's pawnbrokers except that a lender would take possession of the title as collateral rather than the vehicle itself, allowing people to continue driving while a loan was outstanding. Even businesses that had been around since well before the 1980s, such as rent-to-own and check cashing, provided plenty of fodder for her newsletter as these industries scored legislative victories that fostered further expansion. She felt that she was fighting a losing battle. The gap between the well-off and the less fortunate was widening and a slew of high-interest, high-fee products promised to exacerbate the disparity.

"The first time the issue of subprime had gotten anywhere near the kind of attention it deserved was with Fleet," she said. "Until Fleet, we had never gotten any traction with our issues."

Keest remembers riding the train with Bruce Marks and arguing over his use of the phrase "predatory lender." She was worried that it was too inflammatory, that such a loaded term might turn people off to their cause. She also wondered about the focus on Fleet when she knew they were no worse than the others, only larger and more successful. Years later, she laughed at how little she understood the workings of the media then. It had to be Fleet, precisely because it was so big. While its size gave it strength, it also made it vulnerable to public pressure and outrage.

In the months following the CBS broadcast, both the U.S. House and Senate held committee hearings to probe Fleet Finance's lending practices. Bruce Marks did his part to ensure that the Senate Banking Committee hearing was especially memorable. "Ride an all-expense paid chartered bus to Washington," read the flyers Marks's group passed around poor neighborhoods in Boston, Atlanta, and Augusta, Georgia, in the days leading up to the hearing. Roy Barnes picked up most of the tab for those willing to travel north from Atlanta (meals included) and Marks's organization footed the rest of the bill. So many people took them up on their offer—press accounts put their numbers at between three hundred and four hundred while Marks claimed a crowd in excess of five hundred—that the hearings had to be moved to a larger room. The demonstrators, dressed in their bright yellow "loan shark" T-shirts, broke into chants and song. "It was like a gospel revival meeting," Marks said in interviews afterward. Defending his bank before the committee, Fleet president John Hamill said that the average annual interest rate on a Fleet Finance loan was 15.9 percent and not 20 percent or more as some were claiming. "I've got to tell you," committee chairman Donald Riegle, Jr., told Hamill, "that 15.9 percent . . . bothers me and it ought to bother you. . . . It's very troubling to me and frankly I think it's hurting the country."

The fight lasted several more months. Fleet thought it might outsmart Marks by having a lawyer issue a subpoena requiring him to testify in Boston on the day of its next annual shareholders' meeting in Providence. They wanted it to be a celebratory day as the bank was about to announce a 113 percent jump in its first-quarter profits in 1993. "We just assumed even an ego that size couldn't be in two places at one time," a bank spokesman told the *Globe*. Marks simply ignored the subpoena and marched along with the two dozen people who showed up to picket its annual meeting.

The final straw came in the fall of 1993, when Marks learned that

Fleet's Terrence Murray had been invited to speak at a breakfast for business leaders sponsored by the Harvard Business School. Marks had about thirty-five people planted around the room that morning. "We got the names of Harvard Business alum and started registering in their names," he said. "We just took their names. We didn't ask permission." Marks sidled up to Murray as people were gathering and told him matter-of-factly that they would make sure he wouldn't be speaking that morning. Murray was a working-class kid from Providence who had attended Harvard on scholarship. "In front of everyone, Murray got up there and said he was going to resolve the troubles he was having with Fleet Finance," Marks said. A few days later, the two sat down for the first of a trio of long talks, each lasting three or four hours. "I get a call from Bruce saying he's meeting with Murray, what would it take to settle my suit," Brennan said. When Marks phoned him back a few hours later to tell him that Fleet had capitulated and it was a done deal, Brennan wished he had asked for a larger number.

Fleet paid $6 million to settle the separate class-action suit that Howard Rothbloom and Roy Barnes had filed on behalf of Lillie Mae Starr and twenty thousand other Georgians who had received home loans through Fleet Finance. That was very good news for Starr and the other named plaintiffs and also Rothbloom and Barnes, who (along with two other lawyers) split $2 million in fees and another $150,000 in expenses for their efforts. Jack Long in Augusta fared even better, negotiating a $16 million settlement for himself and his clients. Fleet pledged another $115 million to settle claims filed by the attorney general, a portion of which would provide refunds and other relief to those who had done business with Fleet Finance in Georgia. Fleet set aside $800 million for programs aimed at helping low-income borrowers, $140 million of which would be distributed by Marks's organization. "I want to be the banks' worst nightmare," Marks told *BusinessWeek* in 1993—until they turned into his best friend with a big donation to his group. "What they have put together," Marks said of Fleet in an interview with the *Wall Street Journal*, "is a shining example for the entire industry."

The hearings Congress held to look into Fleet's lending practices led to the passage of the Home Ownership and Equity Protection Act, or HOEPA, which Bill Clinton signed into law in the fall of 1994. The law laid out a series of additional protections for anyone taking out a "high-cost loan," defined by the new law as any mortgage carrying an annual interest rate more than ten percentage points higher than the yield on a U.S. Treasury bill (the trigger point in 1994 would have been around 17.5 percent) or points and fees adding up to more than 8 percent of the loan amount. Among other things, the law banned prepayment penalties on high-cost loans as well as balloon payments lasting less than five years and mortgages that allowed the principal owed to grow rather than shrink. The law also granted new authority to Chairman Alan Greenspan and the rest of the Federal Reserve, deputizing them to serve as the regulatory authority charged with monitoring the practices of the subprime lenders.

Bill Brennan felt ecstatic after their victory over Fleet. He thought the HOEPA triggers should have been much lower but he felt that a very strong message had been sent by both the federal government and the media. "I really thought after *60 Minutes* no bank would dare to target black communities like Fleet did; that no bank would ever do these horrible things," Brennan said. The lending practices of its consumer finance subsidiary had cost Fleet nearly $150 million in fines, wiping out two or three years' worth of profits. The price tag had been almost $1 billion if the bank's other fair-lending commitments were factored in. The bank had taken a huge public relations hit in the view of a banking analyst quoted in an article Brennan faxed to practically everyone he knew. Given the potential for negative publicity and expensive lawsuits, this analyst said, he imagined that other banks would be reluctant to move into subprime. He was wrong.

NationsBank had already plunged into the subprime pool when it spent more than $2 billion in the fall of 1992 to buy Chrysler First, a consumer finance and mortgage company, from the Chrysler Corporation. At the time, NationsBank, based in Charlotte, North Carolina, was the country's fourth-largest bank but its people didn't seem spooked by the potential pitfalls of subprime lending. The potential for controversy might be great—Chrysler First had two hundred consumer lawsuits pending when it was sold—but apparently so too were the profits, because several years later the Charlotte-based giant also bought Equi-Credit, then the country's tenth-largest subprime lender. First Union, Bank of America, HSBC, and Citibank: These were among the name-brand banks that would buy a consumer finance company to cash in on subprime mortgage lending in those first few years after the passage of HOEPA.

The HOEPA legislation wasn't without its influence. Kathleen Keest uses its passage to mark the start of subprime's second wave, or what she calls the "HOEPA evasion model." In Boston, Keest shook her head as she watched the big lenders react to HOEPA. If a high-cost loan was one carrying an interest rate of 17.5 percent, they would loan money at a rate of 17.2 percent and charge 7.9 percent in up-front costs to avoid the 8 percent trigger. To the extent even these small concessions ate into profits, the lenders more than made up the difference pushing overpriced products such as credit life insurance, which pays off a loan in the event of a death.

Fleet exited the subprime mortgage business in Georgia, but the company sold its portfolio to a rival named Associates, so Brennan found himself doing combat with a giant based in Dallas and owned primarily by the Ford Motor Company rather than one based in Providence. If anything, Brennan and Keest said, Associates was more insidious than Fleet. "They just packed loans with credit insurance and other junk, and then flipped people over and over and over," Keest said. Brennan saw the same thing. Whenever he met a new client coming to him because of Associates, they were invariably on their third or fourth refinancing.

In 1998, Brennan would travel to Washington, D.C., to testify about predatory lending at the Senate's Special Committee on Aging. He would fly to the nation's capital again two years later to talk about the same issue, though this time the invitation came from the House. In

April 2000, when Andrew Cuomo, then the HUD secretary, was holding hearings to investigate subprime lending, Atlanta was the first stop
on his five-city tour and Brennan was one of the featured speakers. "Finally, it's our day in the sun," he told a reporter for the *Atlanta Journal-
Constitution*.

It wasn't to be. Instead the dawning of the twenty-first century
marked the start of Keest's third wave. By this time, a wide cast of players had joined the consumer finance companies, including a new crop
of nonbank lenders such as Ameriquest and New Century. Increasingly,
mainstream banks were revving up profits by purchasing or starting a
subprime subsidiary. Unlike during waves one or two, the lenders were
offering first mortgages as well as refinancings. Rather than holding the
loans they wrote, they began selling off the mortgages to third parties
that would in turn bundle and sell them on Wall Street. They were
still frequently selling people loans more expensive than their incomes
could handle, but they gambled that home prices would continue to rise
at a brisk rate. The homeowner wanting a new mortgage could easily
refinance as the home appreciated in worth and, in the event of a foreclosure, the bank would have repossessed a property that had grown in
value. Of course, the gamble would prove disastrous if housing values
were to fall. Brennan's message remained consistent throughout: The
Fed must aggressively crack down on lending that bears no relation to a
borrower's ability to repay. In particular it galled him that Fannie Mae
and Freddie Mac, both created by the government explicitly to foster
home ownership by buying and selling home mortgages, acted as a guar-
antor of some of these alternative subprime products. These twin giants
of the mortgage world lent credibility to the subprime field and could
cost the government untold billions if everything came crashing down.
"Fannie and Freddie, as government-sponsored entities, might very well
turn to Congress for a financial bailout similar to the bailout of the savings and loan industry in the 1980s," Brennan warned when he testified
before Congress in 2000. His words were prophetic but seemed to fall
on deaf ears.

Brennan works out of a satellite bureau that Atlanta Legal Aid maintains in Decatur, just east of Atlanta. The bookshelves in his office are crammed with books on race, and the pictures on the wall include shots of John F. Kennedy and King. Most striking, though, are the souvenirs of his fights, including the many awards he has collected over the years. He has been honored by his fellow legal aid attorneys, the state bar of Georgia, and various national consumer groups. Black groups have honored him for his work, as have religious groups, women's groups, and groups representing the elderly. He has so many plaques and awards that he has room only for a small portion in his modest-sized office. The rest sit in a pile in one corner of the room.

In the fall of 2008, the board of Atlanta Legal Aid honored Brennan with a resolution acknowledging his forty years of service to the poor and working poor. He felt pride that day, but the moment mainly made him feel glum. "I find all the awards discouraging," he said. For Brennan they served as periodic reminders of how hard they had all worked and how little things had changed. "You work on something for twenty years," he said, shaking his head, "and it's been worse than it's ever been."

Three

Going Big

CLEVELAND, TENNESSEE, IN THE 1990s

Allan Jones wasn't seeking to launch an industry in the spring of 1993 as he sat in the cockpit of his single-engine Piper Saratoga on his way to Johnson City, Tennessee. He only wanted to convince a man to come to work for him.

Jones was still in his early twenties when he took over his father's small collection agency and built it into a multi-city behemoth—"the largest in Tennessee," he'll tell you—but it gnawed at him that he had no presence in the northeast corner of the state. "My final plug on the map," Jones recalled in a marbly Tennessee drawl. So when he heard that an old friend of his father's who lived up that way had been let go after years in the business, Jones jumped on the opportunity. He lives in Cleveland, Tennessee, a rural outpost thirty miles north of Chattanooga. He told Steve Hixson, a childhood friend whom he calls "Doughball," to meet him at the small airport where he kept his plane. "We're gonna see ol' James Eaton and see if we can't get him to come work for us," he told Hixson.

Hixson and Jones told me the story after work one day. We were at the bar of the Bald Headed Bistro, a restaurant that Jones opened a one-minute walk from his office. Jones, who has made a couple hundred million from the payday business, was sipping what he calls a "Scotch slushie"—the single malt he drinks over crushed ice in a red plastic cup his bartender stocks especially for the boss—and Hixson was on his feet next to Jones, the better to narrate the story. A small crew of regulars, Jones underlings who seem only too happy to drink his alcohol, laugh at his jokes, and listen attentively as the boss runs through a familiar repertoire of old tales, had joined us. The James Eaton story is apparently a favorite for no other reason than that it offers a chance to showcase the imitations of Eaton that Jones and Hixson have lovingly honed over the years. One or the other will raise his voice one or two octaves and then, adopting a kind of mezzo-soprano hillbilly twang, proceed to make the other laugh.

"Ale-ann. Ale-ann, I shore do i-pree-shy-ate y'all comin' on up he-ya."

Jones had always admired James Eaton. He was a "real stately" fellow, he said, a bespectacled man who smoked a pipe. "He looked to me kind of like Sherlock Holmes," Jones said. That made it all the sadder when they found Eaton working in a shack so shabby the paint was peeling off the walls. It was the office of a dilapidated gas station where Eaton had set up a business he called Check Cashing, Inc. "I guess I've found myself my man in northeast Tennessee," Jones told himself.

Jones was not deep into his pitch that day when Eaton excused himself to deal with a customer. A baffled Jones asked Eaton what he was up to and he explained. "Ale-ann, Ale-ann, I'll tell you what." It turned out he was loaning cash to people who needed a bridge loan until the next payday. The school janitor who needed $100 today would pay him back $120 when he received his next paycheck.

At that point Jones was a successful businessman with around 250 employees. He was wealthy enough to own his own plane but he was also in the debt collection business, which meant he spent his days dealing with unhappy people. The people behind the businesses who paid his bills were constantly bellyaching that his collection agents weren't aggressive enough and he was forever hearing complaints from the debtors that they were too gung-ho. After an hour or so of watching Eaton deal with his customers, he was struck by how friendly it all was. "People would thank him," Jones recalled. "They would thank him and thank him and thank him." The other thing that stuck in his mind was that these were working folk, not poor people. They drove decent cars. They dressed in good clothes.

Jones wondered about the fee Eaton was charging. Wasn't 20 percent too steep for a short-term loan of maybe a week or two? "Ale-ann. Ale-ann," Eaton drawled, and then pointed out that his customers' banks would charge them at least that much on a bounced check.

"That's when the lightbulb went off in my head," Jones said.

Eaton, of course, said no to Jones's job offer. "I sure do appreciate you coming on up here," Eaton told him, "but this is the happiest business I've ever been in. I'm happy, my clients are happy. They just love me."

On the plane ride home, Hixson recalled, Jones was there but not there. "I couldn't hardly say a word to him," Hixson said.

They're happy, I'm happy.

Collections is a tough business. All those hospitals and department stores and credit card companies always on your back.

They just love me.

All those deadbeats demanding to talk with him because his people were rough with them over the phone.

Cheaper than a bounced check.

Jones thought of the grateful look on people's faces when Eaton handed over the money. And Eaton? How could he help feeling anything but ecstatic making 20 percent on his money? He kept thinking about that steep fee and how his customers saw it as a bargain. Jones sat on the board of a local bank; he saw the money they were making on bounced checks. Collections is a low-overhead business but Eaton was essentially running his operation out of a shack.

Jones was pushing forty at the time. He would be getting in on the ground floor of a potential new business. He would be siphoning off money from the banks and make a tidy profit in the process. What was there not to like?

He went over the numbers in his mind. Ten grand, he concluded. He would set aside $10,000 and give it a shot.

The early evening gathering at the Bald Headed Bistro was actually the second time I heard the story of Jones's trip to Johnson City. The first was the day before, when Jones and I were barreling down the interstate in the cab of his shiny new white Ford 4x4 with gleaming mag wheels, heading to Chattanooga for a wrestling match he wanted to see. "I think about that day and all I've accomplished," he said somberly, shaking his head. This version Jones delivered in almost hushed tones, as if sharing something precious, and it ended up making him feel nostalgic and sad. "You work so hard to build something from out of nothing and then watch a bunch of people who don't know anything about business try and take it apart," he said. Payday may have rendered him a very wealthy man but it has also made Jones, the industry's most prominent pioneer and its most outspoken defender, a favorite punching bag of consumer advocates around the United States. "Sixteen years—and all of a sudden what I do has become evil," he says. "I don't know what's changed that suddenly I'm evil." And not for the first time, and also not for the last, he launched into a small tirade about a man named Martin Eakes, the founder of the Center for Responsible Lending.

Jones is bald with a round face and a full beard—Rob Reiner, but more dyspeptic and bulkier and without the liberal politics. He stands about five feet, eight inches tall and has the round shoulders of a former fullback. On our first day together, he wore scuffed cowboy boots and a monogrammed white dress shirt and his large belly hung over frayed jeans. He was likable enough, friendly and self-deprecating; noticing my pages of interview questions, he cracked, "You've done more homework on me than I did at Cleveland High in four years." But mainly he was a man looking for an argument. Where payday's critics such as Eakes live in the realm of theory, he said, his customers live in the real world, where a quick cash advance can mean the difference between the kids going to bed fed or hungry.

"They try and stop check-cashing operations," Jones said of the consumer advocates he's battled over the past few years. "They try and stop the tax refund business. They try and stop the rent-to-own industry. They try and stop the auto title loan industry. I guess as far as Martin Eakes is concerned, it doesn't make a difference if regular people have access to cash when they need it."

In our initial phone conversation, Jones had practically insisted I travel to Cleveland to let him expound on the magnificence of the payday loan. "If you're a'gonna write about payday, you gotta get down here and see me," Jones said. "I created the industry and the rest of 'em just copied me." I was convinced, but then, after dozens of emails and phone conversations with the assistant in charge of his schedule, I received a curt email message from the company's communications director informing me that Jones had changed his mind. I decided to go to Cleveland anyway to see for myself this improbable birthplace of the modern-day cash advance business, a town of thirty-five thousand that had given rise to payday's first two big chains, Jones's and a local who copied his business. A few days before my arrival, I sent Jones an email informing him that I'd be coming to town to talk with people who knew him. An hour later Jones phoned. He'd be happy to make time to see me while I was in town, he told me—and that weekend Allan Jones and I became BFFs.

We attended a wrestling match on the campus of the University of Tennessee, in Chattanooga an hour's drive away, and then had lunch. Back in Cleveland, he showed me the hospital where he was born and drove me by the house where a childhood friend lived who would talk with him late into the night over their CB radios. He pointed out where one of his sisters lived and confided in me that his weight had grown so out of control that he had recently had gastric bypass surgery. He drove me up the hill to show me his house and invited me to watch the Super Bowl with him and his sons, but I declined because we had already spent more than five hours together and had plans to meet the next morning so I could see his operations and then talk again over lunch. Even best friends need time apart.

Destiny, as Allan Jones sees it, was awaiting him even as he exited the womb. The big news in Cleveland in the fall of 1952 was the opening of a new hospital and he was the first baby delivered there. "The day I'm born and I'm already in the newspaper," Jones said shaking his head in amazement. Is it any wonder, he asked me, that he had accomplished "great things" in his life? A few years back he had the idea of building a "First Mother's Garden" on the grounds of the hospital in honor of his mother. "There was all this attention on me," Jones reasoned, "but it was her who gave labor."

Jones figures he was no older than ten when he started collecting dried-out Christmas trees for a giant community bonfire. It became an annual post-holiday tradition in Cleveland, and in time he required kids to be at his house by 8 A.M. sharp if they wanted to participate. He was goal oriented even then, eager to beat his number from the previous year. "I'd get furious at a kid if he didn't show up," he said. He admits to harboring a visceral dislike all these years later for a kid whose mother wouldn't let him start collecting trees until 10 A.M.

"Looking back, there were a lot of firsts in my life," Jones said. "I was the first person to collect all the Christmas trees. I was the first person to buy a fax machine in Cleveland. I was the first to have a cell phone. I was the first in Cleveland to have a Segway."

Jones was never much of a student. He always remembered being kept back in sixth grade but after his mother died he found paperwork reminding him that he had been held back a second time. In high school, his accounting teacher told him he would fail her class if he didn't buckle down. "It doesn't matter," he remembers telling her. "What you can't do yourself, you can hire to get done." He described his family as "regular middle class" but also mentioned a housekeeper who refused to enter his room because of the snakes and other small animals he kept there. By his account, he was a boy's boy, into sports and outdoorsy things. His teacher would describe a fungus or a species of plant—and the next day he would show up with a sample.

"I always wanted to be a biological teacher—or a wrestling coach," Jones said.

Wrestling was his life in high school except during football season. To a certain extent wrestling is still his life. "I was a great high school wrestler," he boasted, second in the state in his weight class by his senior year. He had been a pretty good football player as well, he told me, starting fullback, but then the school was integrated and after that he did nothing but block for a much speedier tailback who was black. He wasn't resentful, Jones said—but he was also sure to mention that his former teammate is on skid row. In high school, he and his girlfriend were named "best-looking couple" but he was disappointed. "I wanted 'most likely to succeed,'" he said.

Jones spent a year at Middle Tennessee State University in Murfreesboro before dropping out to work at his father's credit agency. By then, his father, increasingly incapacitated by emphysema, was only able to work a few hours each day, and a rival credit agency had recently opened in town. "Come home and save the business," his mother asked him, "so we can afford to send your two sisters to college." Jones didn't need much convincing. He had married his high school sweetheart, who was pregnant with their first child. They were living in a trailer near school. Even before his mother's call, he had taken a summer job with a nearby collection agency. That firm had five offices, compared to his father's one—and Jones was already looking ahead to the possibility of going into the family business. "I copied every form," he said. "I got copies of their collection letters. I studied how they hired their lawyers. I studied how they did everything." He was eager to prove to people back home, he said, that he was more than just a star wrestler.

In Cleveland, people know Jones's name if for no other reason than that they see it everywhere. The local high school is home to a million-dollar Jones Wrestling Center and there's an Allan Jones Intercollegiate Aquatic Center on the campus of the University of Tennessee. He seems to own half of downtown, and when one is driving the main highway that cuts through town, it's hard to miss the giant, department-store-sized lettering spelling out JONES MANAGEMENT on the side of his headquarters. Then there are all the smaller reminders, such as the granite marker that stands prominently in the plaza in the center of Cleveland with an inscription: "These Courthouse Trees Are Planted in Memory of W. A. 'Bill' Jones By His Son W. A. 'Allan' Jones, Jr., and Dedicated to All Citizens of Bradley County." The joke in Cleveland is that W. Allan Jones, Jr., has never planted so much as a tree in town without simultaneously issuing a press release and striking a bronze commemorative.

Jones doesn't seem very well liked in his hometown, at least if the sampling of people I met with is any indication. In recent years, Jones has donated property to the city for the expansion of the local public library and he built an attractive white bandstand on the town square to replace the old one. But the city councilman I spoke with didn't seem to care for Jones, nor did the retired publisher with whom I met while in town. Even Jones's generosity served as a target of their derision. Sure, he rebuilt the old bandstand but then he seems to have spent nearly as much money throwing a big party in his honor, flying in Tony Dow, Ken Osmond, and Jerry Mathers (Wally, Eddie Haskell, and the Beav) for the occasion. A woman who has known Jones since grade school brought up that same party when describing Jones as a man "who lives totally and completely in the past."

My companions for lunch my first day in town included a teacher, a local businessman, and a corporate attorney. All of them had been raised in the area and all seemed to share a distaste for Jones. For the teacher it was the secondhand stories she's heard about what it's like to work with Jones and the strings he's attached to the money he's given to the schools. "He's not one to just make a donation," she said. "He puts on all these restrictions." Most of the money has gone to the school's wrestling program. The lawyer was from a moneyed background and seemed to look down on Jones as a man who did not know how to handle his wealth.

The businessman offered perhaps the most interesting perspective. Early in our meal he took a call on his cell phone that he took care of in a rapid, mumbly code like a bookie or a stock trader. After a couple more of these staccato conversations he explained that while he owns a legitimate business, he earns extra money providing cash advances to those who don't have the checking account or regular paycheck a person needs to take out a payday loan from a firm like Jones's. For years he's been watching Jones. He was impressed by what he's accomplished, he said, but not the way he's handled success. It offends him that Jones is "not a man capable of doing anything quietly."

When I told my luncheon companions that I was scheduled to have dinner that night at the home of a local attorney named Jimmy Logan, it provoked laughter. Allan Jones might want to be known around town for his philanthropy and his business accomplishments but he seems most famous for an incident that occurred shortly after he dropped out of college and moved home to Cleveland. Separated from his wife and suspecting she was unfaithful, he spliced into the phone line of his old home to record her conversations. That's how he found out she was carrying on with Logan. Unhappy that Jones was playing tapes of his pillow talk around town, Logan used his influence to get Jones convicted of federal wiretapping charges. Eventually Jones would be exonerated by an appeals court in Cincinnati that ruled that since Jones paid the bill, he could not be guilty of recording a conversation on his own telephone. But that was only the start of the feuding between Jones and Logan that entertained the community for years. From the perspective of my lunch friends, I was stepping into a favorite story line from a popular old soap opera.

"He's a sleaze," Jones would say of Logan the next day. "He's a scum-dog." Logan, however, proved more magnanimous, at least in front of an out-of-town journalist sitting in his study with a tape recorder. His left eye squinted, he curled his lip, he leaned in close as if he were about to impart some great considered wisdom, and said, "Allan Jones has done many fine, fine things for this town."

Logan might not have offered much in the way of insight into Jones but over dinner that night he helped to explain why payday lending had taken hold in the soil of Cleveland. This corner of the world has long been the kind of place that gives a man the elbow room and the ethical leeway to make a living any way he sees fit. Grundy County, to the west, had long been known throughout the region as the car-stripping capital of the South, and there was a time when Cleveland was renowned throughout the United States for a related business. Locally they tended to call them "shade-tree mechanics," men who made their money rolling back odometers for unscrupulous auto dealers looking to jack up the prices of used cars. Dating back to the 1950s and through most of the 1980s, Logan said, you'd see cars up on lifts in front yards and backyards all over town, their wheels spinning backward for hours at a time so that tens of thousands of miles would disappear from the odometer. But don't sell these hardworking souls short, Logan counseled. You'd see them working at 5 A.M. and they'd still be at it until midnight. They would bang out dents and install new upholstery—whatever it took to make a car with 90,000 miles on it plausibly look like one with 40,000 by the time an out-of-town dealer came to pick it up. The dealers got their money's worth, Logan seemed to be saying, but the U.S. Department of Justice didn't see it that way, nor did the state officials who finally beefed up the odometer tampering laws and Tennessee's auto fraud division starting in 1986.

On his first day on the job Jones thought his father might have lost his mind. He had recently hired a new manager but he let him go and announced to Jones, then nineteen years old, "You're in charge, son." But the son gamely settled in and began to crack the whip like an old pro. He figured out the average collection agent made twenty-five calls a day, but by his reckoning a person should reasonably make a new phone call every five minutes. So he imposed a quota of at least one hundred calls per day per person.

"After that the company really took off," Jones grinned.

His father had been a glad-handing, good-time Charlie who had served as the president of both the Kiwanis and the local Chamber of Commerce. It was important to the senior Jones to be well liked. His son, by contrast, was single-minded and impatient, a young bull who muscled his way into an account when he had to. "He was averse to controversy," Jones said of his father. "I wasn't." Angry that they had no share of the collections business at the local hospital where he had been born, Jones, still in his early twenties, demanded a meeting with the hospital's board of directors. He wanted his father to join him to lend his support and the weight of his name, but the old man wouldn't do it, Jones said. "Dad was so nervous, he went home." Jones drove by the family house on his way to the hospital. His father was sitting out front in a lawn chair reading the paper. Jones was twenty-four when he bought out his father for $100,000 and named himself the chairman, president, and chief executive officer of Credit Bureau Services, Inc., a company that in time he would sell for more than $10 million.

Success prompted Jones to start dreaming big. At the start of 1993, shortly before visiting James Eaton in Johnson City, he began accumulating land in the hills just north of Cleveland. After work, he would drive to his property, light a cigar, sip a Scotch slushie, and dream about the grand home he would someday build on his hill. "I was always fascinated with the Beverly Hillbillies' house," he told me. He wanted to build an equally impressive home so that people would remember him long after he had passed.

"Most homes were designed to last a hundred years, maybe," he said. "Mine I wanted to design to last a thousand."

Driving me around Cleveland, Jones was grousing about some of the more ludicrous things people say about him. At the Home Depot he overheard two men talking about him. "I'm telling you," one man said to the other in a voice of utter certainty, "the fixtures are made of solid gold. Solid gold!" Jones shook his head. He has pewter, stainless steel, and perhaps porcelain faucets in his new house on the hill, but none, he assured me, are made from gold.

"There's a price that I never realized I'd pay for fame," Jones said. "People think the worst of me."

His son attends public school. His home number is listed in the phone book. Jones told me both these things the first time we spoke and then repeated them not ten minutes into the start of our two days together. He mentioned this pair of facts a third time during our driving tour. He pointed out that he was driving a Ford pickup. He could afford something much more expensive, he said, but that's not him. He pointed out that his jeans are frayed and his boots scuffed. He buys his suits from a local clothes store. He was intent on convincing me that he's still a regular Joe, despite all his riches.

That is no easy task. His home is still reachable through directory assistance but it also sits behind a locked gate on a hill high above town and includes two working elevators. His youngest child does attend Cleveland High School but while I was there he was driving a $300,000 Maybach, a loaner from his father while his car was in the shop. Jones, a self-described "car nut," had an air-conditioned garage built on his property to house a collection that includes both a vintage Rolls and a vintage Bentley. And then there are the planes and yachts he owns and the $12.3 million he spent in 2002 buying a dude ranch in Jackson Hole, Wyoming, because, he explained, "We really enjoy being out in nature in my household."

People talk about his jets as if they are proof that he's just another nouveau riche entrepreneur who indulges every whim despite the cost. But that's only because "the common person," Jones said, "just doesn't understand business." The three big jets he's bought over the years have been purchased through an airplane leasing company he calls Jones Airways. His payday company leases the jets from Jones Airways (in 1999, Jones was charging himself $360,000 a month for the jets plus extra for flying time), which has allowed him to claim the jets as a business expense. Jones Airways was briefly a three-jet airline but he tells me, "I sold the big one. Had it eight months but sold it for a $10 million profit."

Jones only wishes he could say the same about the 157-foot yacht he bought a few years back after the previous one, a 136-footer originally owned by Spain's King Juan Carlos, was destroyed in a fire. "In the last two years I owned it, I was on it maybe fourteen days," he said. It was a gem, he said—a vessel with "an abundance of exquisite and highly detailed woodwork," marble tiling, and ten big-screen TVs, according to *Yachting* magazine—but also a royal headache given that it required a staff of nine. To pick up extra cash, he would rent it for $200,000 per week but then he sold it in March 2008. "I was lucky," he said. "A guy called me and offered me what I paid for it." Now when he feels like getting out on the water, he uses the forty-four-footer he still owns. "People say I'm making all this money off of payday," Jones said, "but even I'm cutting back."

Jones didn't waste any time once he had decided to jump into the cash advance business. He leased an empty storefront on a busy corner and spent two days fixing it up before he opened its doors. Let MBAs with their fancy degrees waste months writing business plans and modeling alternative scenarios. Three weeks after visiting James Eaton in Johnson City, on the first day of summer 1993, Jones opened a store he called Check Into Cash. His first customer, he said, was a military man who needed $100 to buy a bicycle for his daughter's birthday.

Not long after opening that first store, he opened a second one in a town thirty miles away. As a sort of experiment, he put a childhood chum he was inclined to describe as a "lump on the log" in charge of that operation. It didn't seem to make a difference. That store made money just as rapidly as the first. He consulted with a big firm in Chattanooga whose lawyers advised him that there was nothing in Tennessee law expressly forbidding him from making these high-rate, short-term loans, and he opened another seven stores around the state in 1994. He collected nearly $1 million in fees that year and yet the stores, including salaries and bad debt, cost him only $486,000. That left him with half a million dollars in profits.

He was preoccupied running a statewide collection agency so he hired Steve Scoggins, a man he had known since they were both kids, to help him oversee the payday portion of his business. He gave Scoggins a budget of $1 million and told him to scout for new locations. After doing some research, Scoggins asked him, do you want twenty good-looking stores or sixty that don't look so nice? Jones chose the sixty. In 1995, Check Into Cash generated nearly $1 million in pretax profits on $3.7 million in fees, operating stores in Tennessee, Kentucky, and Indiana, where a quirk in the law exempted small loans from the state's usury provisions. Neither James Eaton or Allan Jones invented the payday loan. Moneytree, a check-cashing firm on the West Coast, had been offering cash advances to its customers since the late 1980s, as had QC Holdings, a check casher that started in Kansas City, Missouri. But Jones was the first to pursue the cash advance as a stand-alone business with blue-sky potential. "It was like we was filling this giant void out there," Jones said.

Jones wouldn't have to look far to find his first big competitor. It was a local man named Steve McKenzie, who was a few years ahead of Jones in high school. McKenzie, who everyone called Toby, had grown up poor in a family whose woes were serious enough to draw the attention of the local authorities. He cut a high profile in town even as a teenager, when, to help support his family, he took a job delivering newspapers in a smashed-up Volvo he had bought for $150. A social worker named Joe Kirkpatrick used to look in on the family and especially McKenzie's younger brother, who had a penchant for getting into scrapes. Kirkpatrick had a theory that people in public housing have no dreams unless they invent a different dream every week. McKenzie was different. "Toby was rough around the edges," Kirkpatrick said, but likable and also a hard worker. Kirkpatrick made sure to keep an eye out for McKenzie because he struck him as one kid whose dreams seemed attainable.

Jones and McKenzie first met in the late 1970s, when both were still in their twenties and McKenzie was looking to rent space for a new business he had recently gotten into called rent-to-own. "You know how stores rent TVs to people?" McKenzie said in explaining the business to Jones. "I'm going to rent them everything. Living room sets. Bedroom sets. TVs. Everything."

"Nobody's going to rent their bed," a skeptical Jones responded.

"Man, you don't know. You just don't know." But even if Jones doubted the business, he recognized McKenzie as his kind of business-man. Buy a television in a store, Jones remembered him explaining, and you might pay a 20 or 30 percent markup over the proprietor's price. But rent out that same TV by the week and you make several times what you paid for it.

Competition was inevitable in a business that lucrative, and down the interstate, just south of Cleveland, a rival had seemingly opened directly across the street from one of McKenzie's stores. The warring between them seemed particularly fierce, with banners that said things like "Don't be ripped off across the street!" Joe Kirkpatrick remembers expressing his sympathies to McKenzie when they ran into one another in town.

"He looks at me with this big ol' grin on his face," Kirkpatrick remembered, "and he says, 'Joe, I own 'em both. The type of person who goes to a store like mine, they get all pissed off because you repos-sess, they get back at you by crossing the street. I'm just givin' 'em a place to go!'"

McKenzie's rent-to-own empire was up to eighty stores when he hired a CPA named Jerry Robinson to put his books in shape for an initial public offering, or IPO. Robinson worked in what he describes as "the bare-knuckles side of banking," lending money to businesses like Mc-Kenzie's while working for a subsidiary of Transamerica, the San Fran-cisco insurance giant, called Transamerica Commercial Finance, which specialized in businesses catering to the subprime market. Robinson, who had grown up poor, thought he had found his meal ticket when Mc-Kenzie asked him to join him in Cleveland. "There was the potential to

make a lot of money doing this," Robinson said of rent-to-own. "There
were millions of people without a checking account and without any
kind of credit who needed some way of financing these small transactions." The only hitch, he discovered, but only once he had moved to
Tennessee, was his new boss. Robinson's eyes began to open during a
trip the two made to Chicago to meet with a banker Robinson knew
there. The banker made a seemingly reasonable recommendation when
he suggested that McKenzie consider slowing down his expansion
plans, at least until he got some of his numbers in order. "Toby says to
the guy, 'You're a fucking order taker; you're lucky I don't beat the shit
out of you right here,'" Robinson said. Maybe more frightening was the
question McKenzie asked him after the meeting: "How do you think
it went?"

"I worked for Toby for two years, four months, nine days . . . ,"
Robinson said.

In the end, though, the problem wasn't McKenzie but bad timing.
Robinson still remembers the exact day in September 1993 that he and
McKenzie were staying in a hotel outside Nashville to meet with people
from J. C. Bradford & Company, the middle-market investment banking firm they were hoping would take the company public. Robinson
was reasonably certain Bradford would green light the offering, until he
took a glance at that morning's *Wall Street Journal*. "Left hand column,
above the fold"—a page-one article casting the industry as one ripe for
reform if not legal sanctions. With Jones, McKenzie had used the example of a television set; the *Journal* focused on the Sanyo VCR that would
cost $289.98 if a customer bought it at a retail outlet—or $1,003.56
over eighteen months if it were purchased through weekly installments
at Rent-A-Center, the industry's leading company. That worked out to
an annual rate of 220 percent. More damning was the new term the
Journal taught its readers: the "couch payment." That was when the
repo man accepts sex in lieu of a payment. Of the twenty-eight former
Rent-A-Center managers interviewed for the article, six admitted that
couch payments had occurred in their territory. The banker passed on
the deal.

At that point, McKenzie was making \$3–4 million a year in profits. He would have grown faster if they had raised \$15 million in an IPO, but he had plenty of cash to plow back into the business. Yet once his boss had been denied the glamour of a public offering, Robinson saw that McKenzie's interest in the rent-to-own business was fading. That's when he asked Robinson to take a closer look at what Allan Jones was up to.

Robinson had already flirted with payday back when he was with Transamerica. On the lookout for entrepreneurs seeking to strike it rich operating on the fringes of the economy, Robinson and his colleagues had flown to Kansas City to talk with the people at QC Holdings, a check-cashing company experimenting with payday loans. They liked the idea of charging a 20 percent fee, of course, but Robinson couldn't understand the logic of offering loans to people with nothing in the way of collateral except their word that they would pay back a loan on payday. "We told them that was the dumbest thing we ever heard and flew home," Robinson said.

Robinson's mind began to change after he spent a few hours doing reconnaissance work outside one of Allan Jones's Check Into Cash stores. He was still nervous even when they opened their first payday lending store. They handed out \$10,000 in forty-eight hours and he wondered if he and McKenzie weren't "the two stupidest people on the planet." An ad of theirs would run on the radio station and he would watch the phones light up—but were they simply reaching a whole new set of people who might be happy to take their money but less eager to pay it back? McKenzie, however, harbored no doubts. He sold his rent-to-own chain for \$15 million and, like Jones, hired people to scour the country looking for fresh business locations. For the two local Cleveland boys, the race was on.

Jones and I were heading up the hill to his home when we passed through a new development of pricey homes and high hedges on the northern edge of town where some of Cleveland's wealthiest residents live. Many of the homes have been built in a style a writer for *Harper's* would memorably describe as "Plantation Revival: columned white monstrosities like something out of *Gone with the Wind*." Jones pointed out one such monstrosity in the making, a half-built multistory brick edifice. That was to be Toby McKenzie's new place, Jones said. There was more than a hint of satisfaction in Jones's choice of tenses. McKenzie had declared bankruptcy a few weeks before I showed up in Cleveland, and the speculation around town was that his home would never be finished. Jones argued that McKenzie's financial woes demonstrate that payday isn't as lucrative as its critics think but in reality it only proved that the business didn't render you so rich that you're inoculated against bad financial decisions. The immediate source of McKenzie's problems, the local media had reported, was the many millions he had committed to real estate deals and especially his investment in a high-end golf development that was an early casualty of the global credit crunch.

The loan shark, who has been a chat-in-the-street friend of McKenzie since both were young men, reached the opposite conclusion as Jones. McKenzie's mistake, he said, is that he got out of a proven market. "You can make more money off the rich but it carries a much bigger risk," he said. In contrast, there's what he calls the "poor people's economy." "The thing about the poor people's economy," he said, "is that basically it's recession-proof. You're always going to have people who need $100 or $200 real quick."

For many, jumping into the payday business would seem barely more plausible than joining Tony Soprano's crew. Yet for people like Jared Davis, a twenty-six-year-old rich kid from Cincinnati casting about for something to do, the lowly cash advance business proved the opportunity he had been waiting for. One year after Allan Jones opened his first store, a friend told Davis about the store his sister was running in Louisville, Kentucky, and Davis, who was working for his father, Allen Davis, the CEO and president of Provident Bank, Cincinnati's second largest, went down for a look. The place had a distinctly backroom feel to it but Davis saw potential. "Loaning people small amounts of money against their next paycheck?" Davis said. "I liked the business. I liked it a lot." His father agreed to stake him money so he could open a store just across the river from Cincinnati, in Covington, Kentucky. He chose the name Check 'n Go.

Davis ran that first store for a few months to get a feeling for the customer and to design a system before hiring a manager and taking to the road. "I was thinking twelve, thirteen, maybe fourteen stores," Davis said. That was before he met Jones and McKenzie in Puerto Rico at his first meeting of the National Check Cashers Association and realized payday lending was bigger than Kentucky. David Davis, his older brother, had recently joined the business, which meant they had the advantage of each other's labor—and a father with deep pockets. "After Puerto Rico, we decided to go big," Davis said.

With each new state Davis would buy a map and book that listed its cities by population. He figured he visited just about every city in Kentucky with at least twenty thousand people before he aimed his Jeep Cherokee toward Indiana and repeated the same routine. "My job was to find the stores," Davis said. "Once I was ready to open one, I would hand the keys over and David would run it."

"I'm not very disciplined," Davis confessed. "I'm not the kind to make eight or nine A.M. meetings. But basically after we built out Kentucky and heard Indiana was available, I started driving and didn't stop."

The more ambitious payday companies had lawyers researching the usury laws of every state. Illinois! Illinois had no cap on the rates a lender could charge. Wisconsin! Oregon! New Mexico! And when they worked their way through this scattering of available states, they explored new frontiers with the help of the lobbyists they put on retainer. "It was necessary to explain to governors and to legislators, 'Here's what we do and here's why it's necessary,'" Jared Davis said. A usury cap that prevented a working stiff from borrowing a few hundred dollars till payday, they argued, was the worst kind of government paternalism. And to reinforce that point of view, these entrepreneurs with a newfound interest in policy debates gave generously to the political campaigns of the right state legislators. "We were very successful in educating them about the usefulness of our product and getting laws passed," Davis said.

J ones parked his truck on a side street a few minutes from the front entrance to his home, which he has given the name "Creekridge." He seemed ready to tell me something meaningful but he only wanted to share with me his vision of a home that would last a thousand years. "I never wanted to live in some subdivision house," Jones told me. "What I was looking for was a big piece of real estate that would let me build a really big house." He paid $1 million for the first two hundred acres and at least $3 million for the next 450 acres. He shaved off the top of the hill and paid for two lakes to be built on the property. He imagined himself fishing with his sons, and his sons fishing with their friends, so he paid a woman $7,000 to drain her lake so he could take her bass. For his kids he had built a regulation-sized football field complete with lights, bleachers, and a fieldhouse and also a three-story tree house. The property is so sprawling that there are little wooden signs pointing visitors in the right direction: "beach," "stadium," "stables," "greenhouse." The property also has an aviary, where he raises birds.

The house itself is modeled on the Biltmore, the stunning 250-room, French Renaissance–style vacation home that George Vanderbilt built for himself during the Gilded Age in the North Carolina mountains. Like the famous Vanderbilt estate, Jones's home is built from stone and stucco and stands several stories high. It has a slate blue roof and a copper dome that had to be flown to the property by helicopter and installed by a crane operator.

"Everyone was laughing when I started buying property up here," Jones told me as we stood in the marble entranceway to his home, a high-ceilinged room with a sweeping staircase. He felt vindicated, he continued, when in recent years Cleveland's moneyed set started building in the new development down the hill, where Toby McKenzie had been constructing his home. "That's where I'm a visionary," he said.

"Now everyone wants to be in this part of town." He invited them to
see his home shortly after it was built. "They saw the estate that I was
capable of building," he said and, as he imagines it at least, "no one is
laughing at me anymore."

They were certainly chuckling back in March 1996, though, when the
big news in town was Jimmy Logan's revenge. Tennessee might not
have expressly outlawed these high-rate short-term loans but state law
didn't permit them, either, and Logan filed a class-action suit on behalf
of several clients challenging their legality. At that point, Jones, in addition to the several dozen Check Into Cash outlets he had in Tennessee,
was operating stores in Kentucky, Indiana, Illinois, and Wisconsin. His
pretax profits for the year would exceed $2.3 million. Yet he faced a
formidable foe in Logan, an ambitious lawyer with a nose for notoriety
who was starting to appear on lists of Tennessee's top attorneys. Jones
opened forty-five stores in 1995, but he would open just seventeen in
1996. "Here's this lawyer everyone is telling me is so powerful," Jones
said, "telling me he's going to put me out of business. I was scared."

Jones saw the suit as an act of revenge. When we met in Cleveland,
however, Logan would claim he sued Jones and several other big payday
chains as a matter of principle. He felt they were operating in violation
of the state's usury and consumer protection laws and he was intent on
seeing them stop making these "loans that were destroying lives." Jones,
the former wrestler, wanted to "drive Logan into the ground," he said,
to "prove to him that I wasn't as dumb as he thought." But after months
of distractions, Jones agreed to a $2.2 million settlement that included a
$600,000 payout to Logan and the lawyers he had enlisted to work with
him. That was on top of the $500,000 Jones had already squandered
fighting the claim and the untold sum he then had to spend convincing
the Tennessee legislature to explicitly legalize payday lending, which it
did in 1997. "They hired a Noah's Ark of lobbyists," a state senator told
a reporter for the Associated Press. "They hired a black lobbyist to get
the black votes. If we'd have had a transsexual, they would have hired

a transsexual lobbyist." Campaign finance records show that Jones and his family donated more than $29,000 to local officials in Tennessee in the months leading up to the vote.

Jones emerged from the fog of those lost months fighting with Logan more determined than ever to grow his expanding empire of payday stores. For that, he needed cash but all the bankers he knew proved to be squeamish about venturing into this shadowy world of fringe financing. He ended up securing the $3.5 million he was seeking from a private equity firm at an interest rate of 14 percent. Check Into Cash opened more than two stores a week through 1997. Jones secured an additional $11 million line of credit from NationsBank at the end of the year, allowing him to open an average of three stores per week through the first half of 1998. Jones promoted Steve Scoggins to president and gave him a 2.5 percent share of the company.

What is there about the entrepreneur who, if he owns two stores, can think of little else but growing his holdings to four or six or ten? Or the corporate executive successfully managing 100 outlets dreaming of running 500 or 1,000? Blame it on Sam Walton, the founder of Walmart, or travel further back in time to the turn of the last century and blame Frederick Winslow Taylor, who might reasonably be dubbed the world's first efficiency expert and also its first management consultant. It was Taylor, a student of the manufacturing process, who championed the notion that a business was nothing but an immense and expandable management-designed machine populated by replaceable cogs whose only job was to learn the processes that the top managers had put into place.

Allan Jones has never heard of Frederick Taylor; nor did he attend any of the symposia put on by those who had rediscovered Taylor's ideas. He is not a man who has much use for management theories, but Taylor would certainly have approved of his approach to growth. Jones established the systems and routines intended to make his business run most efficiently and then ruled over his burgeoning empire with an iron fist. Hiring the best and the brightest was not necessary. With an effective template in place, the only thing that was required was obedience by all those replaceable parts residing in the lower reaches of the organizational chart.

Simplify, routinize, monitor, control—those were the watchwords of Taylorism and they were also the principles that Jones and Scoggins employed as their budding payday loan empire grew. Marketing, payroll, human resources, and other functions that could be centralized were handled by the home office and an expanding core of vice presidents were charged with keeping close tabs on the performance of individual stores. The company would hire a new regional manager every time they added ten to fifteen new stores, depending on the size of the region, and a new divisional vice president would be hired in Cleveland for every five to seven regional managers. Bonuses were granted based on the performance of those directly below them on the organizational chart. If the stores under a regional or district manager saw an increase in fees collected—assuming those financial gains were not washed out by bad debts—they would receive a bonus for that month. If not, well, the disappointed divisional managers chewed out their regional managers, who in turn dressed down the laggards among their store managers, who also were paid bonuses only if their numbers rose.

Store managers tended to have a year or two of college on their résumés; assistant managers typically had high school degrees. The managers were flown to the mothership for four days of intensive training and then, according to a Check Into Cash document, "closely monitored on a daily basis for two to three months." While in Cleveland they were given a policy manual that they were instructed to treat as if it were the word of God handed down from the mountaintop. The manual spelled out in intricate detail the most mundane of tasks, from the proper storage of bank receipts to the number of times a day a manager should phone a bank to see if a customer's postdated check (the check a customer had written when initially taking out the cash advance) was good. There were daily business reports that were to be faxed to the company headquarters at the end of each day and also weekly and monthly summaries.

Study, evaluate, jigger, refine. With time Scoggins and company perfected their system for scouting out new locales. First they would seek out a town's name-brand grocery stores and discount retailers. The Holy Grail was a shopping center anchored by a Walmart, but a shop close to a Kmart or a Kroger was also pretty much a guaranteed winner. The next choice was typically a strip mall because it tended to offer cheap rents and ample parking. Trial and error taught the Check Into Cash brain trust that they should cluster stores rather than renting wherever a scout happened to find a good spot. Clustering meant better oversight and a more efficient use of marketing dollars. It wasn't uncommon for Check Into Cash to open one store in an area and then open a bunch more, even if that meant opening branches no more than a few miles apart. On average a new store would start showing a profit less than five months after opening. By its ninth month, it had typically generated enough cash to cover the initial start-up costs.

The new stores all looked exactly the same. Uniformity meant expediency—the ability to move in quickly and cheaply while also helping to build a brand. By 1998, a Check Into Cash team could open a new store in less than two weeks at a cost of $20,000. The new look conjured up something like a bank branch, though one outfitted by the local Office Depot. The walls of each new store were painted the same pale yellow, its floors covered by the same industrial-strength tufted mauve carpeting, the furniture made of particleboard finished with the same cherry wood veneer. Male employees were instructed to dress in a starched blue or white cotton shirt and tie; female employees were told to wear similarly professional attire. Clothing expenses would be borne by the employees, who were paid salaries in the high teens or low twenties.

When Jones first got into the payday business, he was cautious about how much Check Into Cash would lend a borrower, but he gradually loosened those guidelines and by the late 1990s the company established the lending standard that it still uses today: A person can borrow as much as one-quarter of his or her monthly paycheck. Predictably, that increased the proportion of people unable to pay back the money they had borrowed (the percentage of loans the company wrote off doubled from 2 percent in 1993 to 4 percent in 1998) but the company's financial statements from that period show that the change made economic sense. The increased revenues more than made up for the jump in people who failed to pay back a loan. Profits soared.

Jones, as well as McKenzie and the Davis brothers and others, moved into Ohio. They competed out in California and in Missouri, North Carolina, and Washington state. In 1997 Check Into Cash generated $21 million in fees; it brought in that same amount through the first six months of 1998. By then, the average store in Jones's growing archipelago of shops was generating $46,000 in profits. The only thing stopping him, Jones concluded, was a shortage of money. He sold his collections business. He started meeting with investment bankers about a possible public offering. It was time, Jones decided, "to really throw the hammer down."

Four

Confessions of
a Subprime Lender

DURHAM, NORTH CAROLINA, 1980–1998

When conservatives defend the Bush administration against the charge that its devotion to deregulation helped bring about the 2008 global economic collapse, they like to talk about the past. The real culprit wasn't unbridled capitalism as it was practiced in the early years of the twenty-first century; it wasn't missed opportunities to rein in strange new creatures, such as credit default swaps and collateralized debt obligations, that had been birthed by Wall Street. Instead, fault lies with all those inept if well-intentioned liberals who forced otherwise sober bankers to extend credit to marginal borrowers to buy houses they couldn't afford. They blame legislation like the Community Reinvestment Act, or CRA, a Jimmy Carter–era law that forced banks to make loans in every neighborhood in which they had branches.

Allan Jones, though, is more specific. He blames the evaporation of trillions of dollars of global wealth in only a few months' time on just one man: Martin Eakes.

It's easy to see why Jones might name Eakes. It was Eakes who, in the mid-1990s, convinced the Federal National Mortgage Association—

Fannie Mae—to help his organization, the Center for Community Self-Help, create a first-of-its-kind secondary market to buy and sell subprime mortgages. With Fannie's backing, Eakes and Self-Help were able to buy up billions of dollars' worth of subprime loans from banks across the country and repackage them into mortgage-backed securities sold on Wall Street. It was the failure of so many subprime loans buried in mortgage-backed securities that accelerated the global credit crisis.

There's no doubt that Eakes possesses a revolutionary's desire to change the world. Eakes and Self-Help started making home loans in the mid-1980s to African-American families and others of modest means. As if targeting the kinds of neighborhoods other banks expressly avoided weren't enough of a challenge, Self-Help deliberately sought borrowers with a credit score below 620 "because we wanted to prove that this number says as much about the lack of wealth in a family as it does the lack of character, which was the dominant stereotype at the time," Eakes said. Over the years, nearly half the homebuyers who have received financing through Self-Help have been black or Latino and nearly half were single mothers at the time they took out a loan. Its borrowers paid an interest rate around a percentage point above the going conventional rate and a fixed 1 percent in fees and points. That was more than enough, he found, to compensate him for the additional risks he took lending to those of modest income.

Eakes himself never put up much of a fight when someone dubbed him a subprime lender. "It used to be, we were happy to describe ourselves as subprime lenders," said Eric Stein, a top Eakes aide until taking a post inside the Obama administration as deputy assistant Treasury secretary for consumer protection. "We would say, 'We've been subprime lenders since 1984,' or whatever." Self-Help has dropped that sobriquet but Eakes is unapologetic about making loans to all those single mothers with tarnished credit and meager savings. If he harbors any disappointment about his years as a subprime lender, it's that Self-Help never made nearly enough loans and that the secondary market didn't grow larger than it did. "I'd rather put my faith and my money in a person who knows what it means to work hard,"

Eakes told me when I visited him, more than a year after the start of the subprime meltdown, "than someone who has paper credentials."

In person, Eakes seems an unlikely candidate for bringing the worldwide capitalist system to its knees. He's on the short side, about five feet, five inches tall, a wiry and good-natured man in his fifties who seems more jokester than master of the universe. He has an old woman's cackly laugh and a tendency to playfully propel his eyebrows into a dance to punctuate a point. He certainly hasn't grown rich off subprime mortgage lending. When I visited with him, he was driving a sixteen-year-old Chevy Corsica with a moldy backseat that for years had a crack that ran the length of the back window. Eakes's foes, and they are many—"half the people I know would take a bullet for me," he likes to joke, "and the other half want to fire the gun"—work hard to blacken Eakes's name so I feel obliged to check: His is among the bigger homes on his block but that's only because he lives in a working-class neighborhood in Durham, North Carolina, where homes sell for $150,000 to $250,000. He meets frequently with bankers, politicians, and regulators yet owns a single suit, and his wife, Bonnie Wright, still cuts his hair to save money. He claims, and Wright confirms, that he has never had so much as a sip of alcohol in his life.

Eakes had tried warning others about the coming collapse in subprime as early as 2000. That's when he stood up at a meeting convened by the Federal Reserve to report that overpriced subprime loans were a growing problem across the country. If anything, he made a pest of himself trying to sound the alarm about what he saw going on around him. He is not a man without connections. He has met a president (Clinton) and I heard him speak at a one-day conference sponsored by the Federal Deposit Insurance Corporation (FDIC) that also featured appearances by Ben Bernanke and Henry Paulson. He has testified before Congress at least a dozen times. Yet to Eakes these appearances only underscore how little clout he truly has. "If they had listened to me up in Washington, we wouldn't be in this mess," he cackled. In 2002, he created the Center for Responsible Lending (CRL) to fight predatory lending in all its forms, whether overpriced and destructive mortgage loans or any of a long list of products entrepreneurs had devised to grow rich off the working poor over the previous decade or two. If anything, people inside Self-Help chide themselves for having taken so long. "We were way late to this fight," said David Beck, a longtime Self-Help staffer who handles media and policy for Eakes. "Some people here thought we were embarrassingly late."

It's an interesting question whether Martin Eakes was a culprit in the Great Crash of 2008, but his creation of the CRL seems a more reasonable explanation for how Allan Jones came to blame him for the subprime meltdown. The payday loan has taken a close second behind the predatory subprime mortgage as the CRL's top issue. Eakes and his organization were behind the payday lending industry's first big political loss in the late 1990s and they would play a critical part in every big loss payday would suffer in the ensuing years. Unsurprisingly, Eakes was involved in the Ohio fight over payday lending that preoccupied the industry through most of 2008.

At his home, Eakes has a framed photo of himself in Ohio, posing in front of a roving billboard that his payday foes had leased specifically to discredit his organization as a "predatory charity." It's one of Bonnie Wright's favorite photos of her husband, who is smiling happily despite the smear. The attacks help to sustain him, Wright said—and on occasion cause him even to betray the memory of his beloved mother. A few years back, Eakes told me, someone inside the payday industry tried scaring him with the news that they had created a $10 million fund not just to counterbalance the CRL's attacks on the industry but also to destroy his reputation. "My momma raised us that any level of pride is a sin," Eakes said. "But that got me pretty close to making me feel real proud."

His mother was the bleeding heart in the family. A demure college graduate from the mountains of western North Carolina, she would make sure to show up at the polls if for no reason other than to cancel out the vote of her husband, a Jesse Helms Republican. "You could say I grew up genetically confused in terms of my politics," Eakes said. It was more than just politics. His mother, with her simple adages and generous heart, was frequently described as a "living saint." His father, by contrast, was a tobacco-chewing farm boy who taught himself the heating and air-conditioning business and then grew rich installing systems for businesses around Greensboro. The elder Eakes was outspoken and opinionated, a real brawler. "He makes me look tame," Eakes said.

Allan Jones saw his birth as a sign he was destined for greatness. Eakes's birth seemed a testament to his determination. His mother had tied her tubes after having her first two sons but then gave birth to this one, a so-called "blue baby" whose very survival required an immediate blood transfusion. Eakes's friend Gordon Widenhouse recalled when the two played Pee Wee football together. Eakes was scrawny and small but, Widenhouse said, "Martin always insisted on playing nose tackle." The position normally calls for someone beefy and wide but "that was Martin; he wanted to show you how tough he was." Marshall Eakes recalls the time a bigger kid challenged his brother to a fight— and the bigger kid got the living tar knocked out of him. "What sums up Martin," Marshall Eakes said, "is a refusal to give up, a refusal to give in, a refusal to lose."

Eakes was around eleven years old when his parents moved into a white brick mansion with a two-acre farm on the southwestern edge of the Greensboro metro area. His father wanted to teach his sons a love for working on the land but the move seemed to have had the opposite effect. "All that experience taught us is that none of us would ever want to be farmers," Eakes said. The senior Eakes miscalculated on a second front as well. "What he didn't realize," Eakes said, "is that the community he moved us to, like many rural communities in the south, was ninety-five percent black." And so this red-haired son of the Old South with a love for basketball spent much of his time running with a largely African-American crowd, and a housing activist was born. He saw how hard the mothers and fathers of his friends worked and how modestly they lived. "The people I grew up with would do anything they could to pay back their loans if ever anyone gave them a chance to borrow money," Eakes said. "I know that on a gut level."

Over lunch Eakes chose to tell me three stories from his childhood, all relating to race relations in Greensboro in the second half of the 1960s and early '70s. These three events shaped his life, Eakes told me. The first took place when he was eleven or twelve, in the office of the preacher of his church. Eakes had a good friend from the neighborhood and he was there to ask to let his friend join the congregation so they could both play football in the church league. His friend, an African-American, had accompanied him. Eakes remembers the preacher being kind about letting them know the friend couldn't join their whites-only church, but he also remembers the tears that welled up in his friend's eyes. "He says, 'I don't understand,'" Eakes said. Neither did Eakes. "Little kids don't understand why we have to tolerate inequity—which is a pretty good trait," he said.

The second event happened during the integration of the Greensboro public schools in the late 1960s. Eakes was fifteen at the time and in the ninth grade. There was one black student on their bus and it bothered Eakes to watch the way the other kids taunted and abused him. After several weeks Eakes stood up next to the kid and declared, "I'm not going to let you pick on this person again." That prompted a bigger boy at the front of the bus to walk straight at him and, without a word, smack Eakes to the ground. Yet what sticks most with him, Eakes said, was the reaction of the kid he was standing up to protect. "He pulls me up to the seat beside him and says to me, 'You can't fight hate with anger, you can only show people who you are by how you live your life.'"

The third event occurred a couple of years after that when a kid named John Rogers proposed the idea that the two of them run on a black-white student government ticket. Only around 10 percent of the student body was black in a school that had been 100 percent white only three years earlier, but Rogers had practically dared Eakes to run. "You're a big shot here," Rogers had said to him—and if you run with me, I might be elected school president. Eakes couldn't say no. "He was so charismatic I used to think this was someone who could be the first black president someday," Eakes said. "He would speak and send chills up and down your spine." If nothing else, he was struck by Rogers's boldness. "I realized it took so much more courage to ask me to be an ally than it took me to say yes," Eakes said.

Somehow the pair won. Eakes claims to have no idea how Rogers had been elected president and him treasurer but Gordon Widenhouse said a lot of it had to have been Eakes, a top student (Eakes was his school's valedictorian) from a well-off family who was nonetheless liked by pretty much everyone. "Martin always had this charm about him," said Widenhouse, now a death penalty defense attorney living in Chapel Hill. "Male or female, everyone liked Martin. He got along with everyone."

Tragically, Rogers died shortly after graduating from high school. He had volunteered to coach at an area playground and was shot and killed when he called out someone for bringing a gun to a place where children play. "When I get really tired, I try to remember that my friend would not stop fighting for what he thought was right, so I don't feel like I have the choice to do that, either," Eakes said.

Eakes was attending Davidson College, a small, elite liberal arts school just north of Charlotte, when he learned that his friend had been murdered. At Davidson, an oasis for idealists and big thinkers, Eakes fell in with a brainy, eclectic crowd that included Tony Snow, who would go on to be a conservative commentator and regular on Fox News and served briefly as press secretary to President George W. Bush. Eakes drove a beat-up bread van that he had fixed up after buying it for next to nothing, and, said his friend Gordon Widenhouse, who went to Davidson and roomed with Eakes, the two spent the bulk of their free time either trying to meet co-eds or debating solutions to the big social ills of the day. "Martin and his friends were different than anyone else I had ever met," said Bonnie Wright, who was a freshman when Eakes was a senior at Davidson. "They could be a lot of fun but they were already interested in poverty and housing and all these other big issues." Wright met Eakes while he was wrapped in a blanket and tied to a flag-pole in the center of campus, retaliation for the elaborate pranks he had been pulling on his friends. The pair started dating shortly thereafter. Eakes would move to New Haven, Connecticut, to attend Yale Law School and then Princeton, where he earned a master's in public policy studying economics at the Woodrow Wilson School, before the couple settled, after much debate, in Durham in 1980.

Eakes was still in law school when he, Wright, Widenhouse, and several others rented a house in Washington, D.C., so they could spend a summer trying to figure out how they were going to save the world. The goal was to pick a single locale where they would all live after graduation, so they could collectively have an impact on the life of the dispossessed and downtrodden of that community. "The idea was that it'd be unanimous, whatever we decided, and so basically you had to beat everyone into consensus," Bonnie Wright said. That served as this small band's first big lesson in the limits of idealism. "By the end of the summer," Eakes said, "we were spending less time talking about revolution and more time arguing over the schedule for washing the dishes." Eakes and Wright ended up choosing Durham because it was only an hour's drive away from Greensboro and his parents but "far enough away so that if I fell flat on my face," Eakes said, "I wouldn't embarrass them." They would move there alone.

In 1980, Eakes and Wright created an organization they earnestly, if not redundantly, named the Self-Help Center for Community Self-Help. The idea, at least initially, was to foster the spread of worker-owned cooperatives around the state. Cheap imports, automation, and corporate takeovers were causing plant closures at textile mills and furniture factories around North Carolina. Self-Help, the pair hoped, would provide legal and technical advice, along with moral support, to workers seeking to retain their jobs by buying threatened factories from departing owners, hiring a manager, and running it themselves. There was one year, Eakes recalled, when his fledgling organization had a staff of four and a budget of only $4,000. The first Self-Help employee to receive anything resembling a living wage was Thad Moore, a local activist who shared Eakes and Wright's faith in the potential of worker-owned cooperatives (when he met Eakes, Moore was toiling away at an employee-run scrap metal yard despite a degree from Wake Forest)— and he remembered being paid a salary of maybe $10,000.

"I don't think Martin paid himself a penny until 1985 or 1986," Moore recalled. In time, Moore said, he came to realize he was in the presence of a virtuoso workaholic—a man who approaches the job as if it were an extreme sport. To save money and keep Self-Help going, Eakes and Wright lived in a wreck of a home that was so cold in the winter that ice would form in the toilet. His office was the backseat and trunk of whatever car he had bought at a salvage yard and fixed up so he could crisscross North Carolina looking for potential worker cooperative sites. "I've worked with some crazy, crazy committed activists in my time," said Moore, who was still working for Self-Help more than twenty years later when I visited Durham. "But Martin took it to a maniacal degree, beyond normal even for people who were abnormal in their commitment. He brought an intensity and devotion to his mission that I don't think I have ever observed even in the activist world."

Eakes and Wright initially lived off Eakes's savings. When that money was gone he opened up a small legal office in downtown Durham, but then, as if seeking to undermine his goal of bringing in extra money while building Self-Help, he announced that his hourly rate for his services would be whatever a client earned for an hour of his or her time. Why should an hour of his time, the former philosophy student posited, be worth any more than that of another human being? The problem with that logic was that he was spending most of his time with unemployed textile workers. "It turned out my first four or five clients were out of work," Eakes chuckled. Adding to their financial pressures, Wright had returned to school to earn a graduate degree at the Yale School of Management.

Eakes added a law partner a year or so later: Wib Gulley, a tall, blue-eyed man with sandy hair and a Dudley Do-Right chin. Gulley was another committed soul, a man who had taught at a school for the mentally disabled and then ran the North Carolina chapter of the Public Interest Research Group before going to law school, but even he had to roll his eyes over the novel sliding scale Eakes had devised. "It was wonderful what Martin was doing," he said. "Except textile workers were making $8 an hour, $12 an hour, maybe $15—and our overhead worked out to like $25 an hour." So by fiat Gulley initiated a new billing policy that Eakes would later dub "unjust but pragmatic": Clients were still charged based on their hourly wages but then hit with a $25 hourly surcharge on top of that rate. "We were hardly getting rich off that plan," Gulley said, "but at least we were no longer losing more money with every new client." A longtime legal aid attorney named Mike Calhoun would join the firm in 1985. Legal aid societies are notorious for lousy pay, but Calhoun figured he took roughly a 50 percent pay cut when joining the firm of Eakes and Gulley. "In seven years there I don't think I ever got back up to my legal aid pay," Calhoun said. To supplement his income, Calhoun would do side work for Self-Help until going to work there full-time in 1992.

This first incarnation of Self-Help as a consultancy providing advice to fledgling employee-owned cooperatives was not without its successes. They helped a group of unemployed textile workers in a coastal town a couple of hours from Durham convert their old mill into a bakery, and they provided critical assistance to a sewing cooperative of around seventy workers, most of them black women, struggling to make payroll each month after buying the bankrupt cut-and-sew operation where most of them had worked. But mainly they learned the world was more complicated than they had imagined it to be during their late-night bull sessions. It turned out there were other reasons for plant closings beyond the heartlessness of management. Sometimes there was no longer a market for the goods a mill produced; other times the costs of upgrading a facility were prohibitive. Moreover, they discovered that the main impediment workers faced was a lack of working capital. Self-Help could provide all the expertise and encouragement in the world but it meant nothing if a lender refused to finance a deal, even when the employees could offer a mill and pending orders as collateral. "For some reason," Eakes says, "bankers wouldn't give these people a loan, particularly if they happened to be African-American, female, or from rural Carolina." The answer, Eakes and Wright decided, was to get into the lending business themselves.

That would be Wright's job. For a class project at Yale, she had written a business plan for a credit union, and she put the plan into effect after returning to Durham in mid-1983. (The couple would marry the next year "once both of us were done with schooling," Wright said, and have two children.) Wright would run the Self-Help Credit Union until the early 1990s. "It was time," she said, "for me and for my family." One all-consumed activist in the family, it seemed, was more than enough.

Raising money so they could start making loans proved easier than they thought. Their first benefactors were several Catholic orders that together put up well over $1 million in working capital during that first year. "We were paying them better than zero interest but not by much," Eakes said, "but they wanted to put their money to use to help working people." Eakes was so touched by their generosity that he vowed that, if necessary, he would work the rest of his adult life to pay back the Catholic orders should Self-Help lose any of their money. He would strike a lighter note when around that time he joked in an interview with the local Durham daily, "We make money the old-fashioned way. We beg for it."

At first the credit union stuck to financing worker-owned cooperatives. When, for instance, an out-of-state owner shut down a mill in the center of the state, laying off more than one hundred people, Self-Help loaned money to thirteen former employees so they could reopen the plant and get back into the business of making men's and women's socks. It helped another 150 workers buy a nearby sock factory after the children of the former owners made it clear they had no interest in running a struggling textile mill for the rest of their lives. Self-Help tried to use its money as leverage to help these fledgling cooperatives pry money from the local banks or agencies like the federal Small Business Admin-istration. "People really had to make their case to us," Wright said. "We needed to see a viable business plan." But that didn't make the ventures any less risky. Self-Help wrote off the first three loans it made, for a total of $90,000, and Eakes had to acknowledge that he probably knew a lot more about eighteenth-century philosophy and nineteenth-century economics than twentieth-century financing. "I had to confess my banker friends were not as dumb as I liked to think," Eakes said. Over time, the credit union expanded its loan profile to women and people of color seeking capital to start or expand a business, even if those en-trepreneurs had no intention of creating a worker-owned cooperative. Self-Help continued to grow, and by 1986, with $4.5 million in deposits that had been harvested from churches, labor unions, foundations, and socially minded individuals, the credit union moved into home loans.

Over lunch at a restaurant in Durham in 2008, Eakes wondered what had taken them so long. Self-Help is now housed in an old bank building it bought and rehabilitated more than a decade earlier. In the fashion of a big bank, it has put the Self-Help name on top of the eight-story building in letters large enough to read from the highway. It owns several more buildings downtown to house its various operations, in-cluding the Center for Responsible Lending, and employs more than 250 people. "When we started Self-Help, we felt jobs were the key to making a difference in the life of poor people," Eakes said. Then he came across statistics showing that where the median white family had a net worth of $44,000 in the mid-1980s, the average black family had a net worth of under $4,000. The difference, he knew, was the equity people built up in their homes. Dating back to his undergraduate days, he and his friends had been debating whether jobs or education or health care or poverty eradication programs were the most effective way of bringing about a more equitable world. He now had his answer. "I guess we were very slow learners, because it took us six or seven years to figure out that the real issue was equity. We became preachers for the importance of owning a home." They opened branch offices around the state and focused on helping the working poor grow their wealth through what he liked to call "bricks-and-mortar savings accounts."

It was never easy. "If we had known what kinds of loans you intended to make," Eakes quotes an early regulator as saying, "we'd have never let you get started." Self-Help was deliberately seeking out those with the poorest credit rankings getting by on meager wages; its typical borrower in the early 1990s had a family income of $22,000. (A household wasn't eligible for a Self-Help loan if its occupants earned more than the area's median income.) But Self-Help's borrowers were purchasing $30,000 or $50,000 homes and receiving loans almost as favorable as their prime counterparts. The key, Eakes said, was to find people who had proven themselves to be hard workers and then make sure they weren't buying a home beyond their means. In a 1993 interview with a publication called *Business/North Carolina*, H. Allen Carver, who ran the Atlanta office for the National Credit Union Administration, declared himself a convert. His agency, he said, watched Self-Help "like a hawk" but Eakes's organization had proven "they've got their act together."

The local media seemed equally impressed. The editorial board at the *Raleigh News & Observer* dubbed Self-Help "heroes of high finance" and the *Winston-Salem Journal* heralded the organization as "the bank of last resort." All around the state newspapers were running Self-Help profiles featuring single mothers and people who had known mostly bad luck and misfortune until Self-Help boosted them out of a trailer park or public housing and into a modest home of their own. President George H. W. Bush designated Self-Help one of his "thousand points of light," and in 1993 President Clinton singled out Self-Help as a model when announcing a $382 million revolving loan fund to help bring economic opportunity to neglected communities. By that time, the Self-Help Credit Union had thirty-five full-time employees and $40 million under management. Over the next few years, the United Nations would honor Self-Help as one of the United States' twenty most successful economic development projects and the MacArthur Foundation would bestow on Eakes a $260,000 "genius" grant for "helping the rural poor, women and minorities obtain $90 million in loans to start businesses and buy homes."

His shoes were a pair of scuffed, dirt-smeared Reeboks that might raise an eyebrow at a backyard barbecue. They looked even more out of place given the rest of Martin Eakes's ensemble. He wore a pair of pinstriped gray dress slacks that matched the suit jacket draped atop a box in the corner, and a wrinkled white dress shirt that was frayed at the cuffs and collar. Later that day, he explained after shaking my hand to welcome me to his office, he would be flying to New York. So he put on the pants this morning and wore the sport coat to the office so he wouldn't have to carry a garment bag on the plane.

"Martin," said Keith Corbett, who has worked with Eakes since 2000, "is not a man who wastes a lot of time thinking about things like fashion." His old law partner's manner of dress, Wib Gulley told me, caused bemused smirks even on the basketball court. He's deceptively quick, said Gulley, who played in a regular pickup game with Eakes. He's smart and tough on the court and he's certainly not opposed to throwing the occasional elbow. But it was also like playing with Will Ferrell in the movie *Semi-Pro*, headband and tight shorts included. "He'd show up wearing these fat knee pads and thick Clark Kent glasses—all taped up, of course, because Martin isn't going to buy new glasses when he can fix them with a little tape," Gulley said.

He's lean and fit, despite his age and what Gulley described as Eakes's "very narrow approach" to food groups. "It's a wonder he can operate as efficiently as he does," Gulley said, "on a diet of chocolate chip cookies and ice cream." For twenty-five years Eakes was a vegetarian but it was causing too many headaches in his family. "I decided I'd be the accommodating one," Eakes said. He has hazel eyes, a ruddy complexion, and a proud, stubborn chin that he thrusts out and clenches, Bill Clinton–style, when conveying sincerity or defiance. With a razor tongue and reedy Southern accent, he is constantly cracking jokes, offering wiseguy asides, and making self-deprecating remarks. He tends to smirk a lot, as if constantly amusing himself with private jokes, and more often than not he seems to share those lines. For fun the former physics major reads science journals.

His office has a temporary look to it, as if he's only just moved in. Picture frames and plaques lean against one wall; several cardboard cartons sit on the floor. The walls are practically bare. The first time I saw it, late in 2008, I asked if he'd recently switched offices. He cocked his head and looked at me confusedly. He has had the same office, he told me, for nearly a decade.

Since its inception, Self-Help's bylaws have dictated that no employee can earn more than three times the pay of the lowest-paid person on the staff. At the end of 2008, some Self-Help workers made $23,000 a year, so that meant Eakes, despite the size of Self-Help and his fancy credentials, was earning a salary of $69,000. "He's a guy who could have made a bazillion dollars on Wall Street if he didn't have these social goals," Calhoun said. "Martin is a hard-nosed businessperson. Make no mistake about it."

Despite its inability to pay big salaries, Self-Help has never had trouble filling its headquarters with young graduates with advanced degrees from redoubts like Harvard and Princeton. Its halls are filled with Eakes clones, nerdy and smart and over-degreed and seemingly indifferent to their clothes and their cars. Some years back, when the maximum salary at Self-Help was $32,000 a year, a potential funder came to visit. He took one look at the employee parking lot and shook his head. Never in his life, he said, had he seen such a collection of junkers in a single place. "Basically you could describe Self-Help as a bunch of misfits," Eakes said. New initiatives seem to be born at night, when people find Eakes in his office and sit to spend an hour or two puzzling through a problem. Eakes describes himself as an introvert but friends and even subordinates scoff at that characterization. Being around other people seems to enliven him, and he certainly doesn't seem an introvert during staff meetings when he's acting like the class clown.

Yet Eakes seems to have mixed feelings about the limelight. I've seen him speak and he's a natural, playful and chatty and entertaining, yet he says, and people around him confirm, that he genuinely would prefer to remain at the office and let others take the podium on Self-Help or CRL's behalf. "He probably turns down ten requests to speak for every one he accepts," said Mark Pearce, who worked as a top Self-Help executive between 1996 and 2006. "To Martin, testifying before Congress or a state legislature—any kind of public speaking—is a necessary evil that he'll do only if he can convince himself he has no choice."

That's not to say Eakes lacks a robust ego. At times he can come off as supremely confident—even cocky. Within the first few minutes of our first meeting, he mentioned an email he had just written to the chief of staff of an important congressman and then dropped the names of two senators with whom he'd recently spoken. "We're going to get the mortgage industry cleaned up over the next year," he said over lunch, "and then we'll be able to take care of these other issues like payday loans and credit card overdraft fees." He said this matter-of-factly, as if these vexing national issues were just chores his wife had asked him to do on the way home from the office. Given Self-Help's modest roots, I asked Eakes, was he astonished by its soaring success? "Not really," he said with a shrug.

With the recognition and the acclaim, the deposits flowed in, and with more capital to work with, Eakes and Self-Help were able to get more ambitious still. A fund was established expressly to loan money to people wanting to get in the day-care business and the credit union got in the charter school financing business as well. Self-Help financed a homeless shelter in Durham and a large home that served as an early sanctuary for people with AIDS. Self-Help even acted in the role of a developer, buying landmark buildings in cities around North Carolina where it had a branch, rehabbing the properties, and then leasing offices to local nonprofits at a discount.

Self-Help's boldest move began when Eakes started to think about the limits of what he had built. By the mid-1990s, Self-Help was up to seven branches around the state, but in ten years the organization had helped maybe one thousand families buy a first home. Some might have been impressed with Self-Help and its pace of growth but Eakes was struck with how slowly they were moving. That was what propelled him to make the drive to Winston-Salem, ninety minutes from Durham, to meet with Leslie "Bud" Baker, Jr., then the president of the Wachovia Corporation, one of North Carolina's largest banks.

"We knew we were never going to be big enough to have the kind of impact we wanted to have," Eakes said. "But Wachovia had branches all over the state. If we could get Wachovia to make loans to single African-American mothers, it would have a much bigger impact than we ever could."

In Baker's office, Eakes offered Self-Help's clients as Exhibit A. His borrowers might not seem loan-worthy at first glance but they also realized this might be the only chance in their lives to own a home. They had less of a financial cushion than those in higher income brackets and were more likely to fall behind in their payments, Eakes conceded. But by that point, Eakes and Self-Help had been in the home loan business for nearly a decade. They had foreclosed on only three homes, and in all three cases the credit union had recouped its original investment. In almost ten years, they had yet to write off a single loss.

Eakes didn't persuade Baker to start loaning Wachovia's money to low-income families that first time they met. He failed to convince him a few months later when they met again or when he visited him for a third time several months after that. It might have been the right thing to do, and also judicious given the Community Reinvestment Act, but it also meant breaking with the established benchmarks of lending and Wachovia was a traditional, old-fashioned bank. When Baker finally relented, he told Eakes, "We'll give it a try. We'll make $10 million worth of these loans. I think we'll lose half that money but it's worth it to get you out of my office so I don't have to hear you talking anymore." As Eakes likes to tell the story, he walked out of Baker's office without another word.

As Baker had promised, Wachovia wrote $10 million in home loans to those with solid work records but tarnished credit ratings, and

Wachovia would write another $10 million in similar loans after that. But though people inside Wachovia assured Eakes the loans were performing well, they also told him that was more or less it. The bank didn't feel comfortable carrying more than $20 million in nontraditional, subprime loans on its books.

That was when Self-Help decided to take the truly revolutionary step of creating a secondary market for subprime loans. As Eakes saw it, Self-Help could help so many more people if they had more than just a dozen or so loan officers scattered around a single midsize state. That was Eakes's pitch to Bud Baker and the other bank presidents with whom he would meet. "I said to them, 'Most people covet your money but I covet your delivery mechanism. You have branches all over the state. You have twenty thousand loan officers all over kingdom come. You can reach every little neighborhood we can't.'" And if joining in his cause wasn't reason enough to play in the secondary market he was creating, there were more concrete advantages as well. "I would tell them," Eakes said, "'We'll pay you a fee, you'll make your money, and you get to be the hero and get your CRA credits.'"

Again Eakes started with Wachovia, whom he approached with a unique offer. We'll buy all the $20 million in loans you've made to low-income clients, he told Baker, if you promise to use the proceeds to make more loans to people of modest means. The catch was that Self-Help was going to borrow most of that $20 million from Wachovia itself. They'd put up $2 million as a down payment and the $20 million loan portfolio would serve as the collateral for the loan. "We were taking all the credit risk," said Mike Calhoun. "If the mortgages went bad, we were out our reserves and the entire portfolio with a book value of $20 million reverted to them." They would pay market rate on the loan to Wachovia but Calhoun and others had done the math: Self-Help would still come out ahead if all went as planned. Wachovia said yes and, Calhoun said, "We knew we were in business."

Eakes was anxious to approach other banks with what he called his "godfather proposition"—a deal too good to refuse. Holding him back was a lack of cash. To make that first $20 million deal work, Self-Help needed to make a $2 million down payment, and it wasn't as if the organization had that kind of money lying around to write more checks of that size. As luck would have it, one of Self-Help's biggest financial backers, the Ford Foundation, which had aided Self-Help dating back to its worker-owned cooperative days, was confronting a unique challenge: the need to spend a lot of money and spend it fast.

By law, a foundation must pay out at least 5 percent of the total worth of its holdings each year, and in 1998, with dot-com fever fueling the stock market, the Ford Foundation's portfolio ballooned. "I have a really big idea," Eakes began when contacting his liaison at the foundation, and his timing couldn't have been better. Ford gave Self-Help $50 million to help underwrite this new secondary market for subprime real estate loans, and with the commitment from Ford, Self-Help was able to convince Fannie Mae to guarantee the loans. Self-Help's money would still be on the line—the company had to indemnify Fannie for 100 percent of any losses—but the mortgage giant's imprimatur meant that this relatively anonymous, relatively small, Durham-based nonprofit could package and resell mortgages to Wall Street.

The process was called "mortgage securitization."

Five

Freddie Rogers

DURHAM, NORTH CAROLINA, 1999

The staff of Self-Help was so focused on their mission of expanding access to mortgage credit for the working poor that for a long time—despite some high-profile warnings—they didn't notice they had competition. One of the most prominent was the investigative piece that ABC's *Primetime Live* did on a company called Associates. It featured an interview with a former Associates loan officer who claimed he could barely live with himself while he worked there, given the gimmicks he was taught (talk fast, turn the pages fast) by higher-ups to trick people into signing for loans they couldn't possibly afford. A second former employee told of the "tremendous pressure" every loan officer felt to pack loans with expensive extras, and both confessed to witnessing fellow agents forge signatures. The *Wall Street Journal* ran an equally unflattering piece about Associates focused on a single customer, a retired quarry worker named Bennie Roberts living in Virginia on $841 a month in Social Security and retirement benefits. The *Journal* found that Associates, a subsidiary of the Ford Motor Company, had refinanced, or flipped, Roberts' loan ten times in four years, costing him $19,000 in fees on what had originally been a $1,250 home equity loan. Associates would even earn its own chapter in a book called *Merchants of Misery*, edited and largely written by a reporter named Mike Hudson. But who had time for books or the *Wall Street Journal* or TV when inside Self-Help they were busy saving the world? "It's a tough act to run the business we do," Mike Calhoun said.

Then a man named Freddie Rogers, a widower in his fifties raising a daughter on his own, walked into Self-Help's offices. "I think we're basically self-honest about where we're making a difference and where we're not," Eakes said. And Freddie Rogers, earning $8.24 an hour driving a bus for the Durham public schools, showed Self-Help "that just one predatory lender like Associates was doing more harm than all the good we were doing."

Lanier Blum took an instant liking to the tall black man who showed up in her Self-Help office in the fall of 1998 interested in talking about a new home loan. Borrowers at Self-Help typically seem to arrive wearing whatever they happen to have on, but Freddie Rogers had dressed smartly in nice slacks, a button-down shirt, and a stylish hat worn jauntily on his head. "I had business to take care of," he would later explain. He was outgoing, warm, and chatty, and he showed Blum pictures of his daughter and spoke lovingly about his wife, who had died some years earlier. "He was a very, very charming guy," Blum said.

Self-Help had always focused on first-time homebuyers. But Blum had recently been put in charge of a new product Self-Help was experimenting with called the "fix-it loan." Borrowers seeking a mortgage on a home that needed extensive repairs were eligible for a fix-it loan but so, too, were homeowners who needed money to make the basic repairs so a property holds its value. That was Rogers, who years earlier had bought a home with his wife in a semirural neighborhood on the southern outskirts of Durham. Drainage problems caused the basement to flood, and the flooding, along with a lack of proper ventilation, was causing mold to form on walls inside the house. Worse, there were no sewer or water lines in that part of the city and the septic tank they used for their waste had developed a leak, which was fouling the water of a well they relied on for their drinking water. It had gotten so bad, Rogers explained to Blum, that he and his daughter had been forced to move out until he could find the money to make the repairs.

Blum was familiar with the community where Rogers lived, an historically black section of town not far from a large regional mall that had recently opened near the interstate. Subdivisions were popping up all around that part of town, and, though Rogers still lived in a neighborhood with gravel roads and few amenities, his was a potentially hot property. Already there had been noise about rezoning the area to encourage outside investment. "I really wanted to help him stay where he was living," Blum said. "He was obviously very attached to the house because he had bought it with his wife. But I also thought he could be in a position to do very well if the area was developed."

Rogers had served in the army when he was young and then taken a job with the Durham schools, where he had worked since the early 1960s. "He seemed a real stable guy," Blum said. "He had some credit issues but nothing too terrible. I thought, Let's get a payoff quote and see what we're dealing with." She phoned Irving, Texas, where Associates had its headquarters—and then she phoned and phoned and phoned some more. "We absolutely harassed those people," said Blum, whom Eakes has nicknamed "the Pest."

At first the sticking point was the payoff figure. The person on the other end of the phone refused to give it to her, though refusing a payoff quote for a borrower is akin to a credit card company declining to tell a customer the total amount he or she owes in back charges. When finally someone provided Blum with the dollar figure, that only served to confuse the issue further. Rogers had records showing that while he was often late in paying his mortgage, he had never missed a payment, yet Associates was claiming he still owed the company nearly as much as he had borrowed ten years earlier. In all those years he had managed to pay down the principal by only a few thousand dollars. That must be a mistake, Blum told herself, so she asked someone to fax over a copy of his payment history. That seemed no more complicated than making a few taps on a keyboard but a company representative claimed that information wasn't available. The Pest persevered until eventually somebody in Irving faxed over pages of records that Blum was convinced had been fabricated, and she handed the file off to Self-Help's loan servicing department.

At that point, Blum wasn't suspicious so much as curious. Sure, the people on the other end of the phone couldn't respond in a straightforward manner to a routine request, but she figured they were some fly-by-night operator staffed by incompetents. "I had never seen a loan like this," Blum said. "I really wanted to know what these other lenders knew that we didn't know." More borrowers came in seeking a fix-it loan and they too had loan terms similar to Rogers's. At Self-Help, they required down payments of at least 5 to 10 percent, yet Associates and other lenders proved willing to write loans valued at 100 percent of the assessed worth of the property. "I was thinking, Why are we being so conservative? What have these banks figured out that we haven't?" said Blum. These other lenders were charging interest rates four, five, or six percentage points higher than Self-Help's, if not more. That struck Blum as a steep premium but she also had to ask herself if Self-Help was taking more risk than people inside the organization realized.

"We always saw ourselves as the high-risk lender of last resort," said Blum, who had a degree in city planning, not finance. "We thought we were the ones out there providing loans to our customers where no one else was doing it. It came as a surprise that there were even these other players in the communities we were serving."

The truth would emerge once Blum, with the help of others inside Self-Help, was able to piece together the details of Rogers's loan. Years earlier, he and his wife had borrowed $29,000 through the Veterans Administration to buy their home, but then they had allowed themselves to be talked into refinancing with Associates. Under the new loan terms, they were paying 13.7 percent in interest and now owed $47,500, including thousands in fees and thousands more for a credit insurance policy. Associates hit Rogers with a penalty fee every time he was late with a payment, as any lender would, but the company would also tack on extra interest charges, treating his account as if it were perpetually in arrears. The bottom line was that Rogers was stuck. His home was not worth enough to justify the size of the loan Self-Help would need to pay off Associates and still have enough money left over for Rogers to make the necessary repairs on his property. And even if Self-Help were inclined to take the risk, Rogers, with a salary of around $17,000 a year, didn't make enough to reliably cover the monthly payments.

"It took us some time," Blum confessed, "but we eventually realized this wasn't just an issue of one guy. This was a big company out there and they were lending a lot of money to a lot of people."

Blum stopped by Eakes's office one night when both were working late. She told him about Rogers's predicament and Eakes pulled out his calculator. Had Rogers refinanced his loan through Self-Help and made the same monthly payments he had been making to Associates, Eakes found, he would have paid off his loan in full and even built up a modest-sized savings account. Instead he still owed Associates nearly as much as he had borrowed. Freddie Rogers's only crime was that he, like much of the populace, wasn't financially sophisticated. It had ended up costing him tens of thousands of dollars and it might well cost him his house. "This is scandalous," he declared. He promised Blum he would call Irving, Texas, the next day.

Pretty much any housing activist or consumer advocate who has heard Martin Eakes speak in public in recent years has heard the story of the phone call Eakes made to Texas on behalf of Freddie Rogers. The woman on the other end of the line accused Eakes of being a competitor out to steal a loan away from her company. She was evasive and dodged basic questions that a lender was legally obligated to answer. "I just snapped," Eakes said. "I just started making a lot of threats." We're going to get this borrower out from under your thumb, he told the woman. We're going to drive your company out of our state. "You've picked a fight with the wrong guy at the wrong time," he told her. It was only after he hung up the phone that, with the help of his staff, Eakes realized he had threatened to boot from North Carolina one of the two or three largest consumer finance companies in the world.

Eakes is intense when he's angry but he's not the demonstrative kind. The signs that he is steeling for a fight are more subtle. His normally ruddy complexion turns a darker, more splotchy red. His jaw gets a fierce set to it and his jaw muscles start working. Those who have been at his side for a long time notice that his language changes as well. The more pragmatic Eakes, the physics major turned lawyer and banker, is replaced by the philosophy major who orates about right and wrong and the moral imperative everyone at Self-Help should feel to confront injustice when they see it. When Eakes is in that mode, Thad Moore, who has worked with Eakes for more than twenty-five years, hears a lapsed Baptist channeling the sermons of his youth. "He gets in this preaching mode about why we do what we do and why it's important and how we're taking on these pressing issues in our society that demand to be dealt with," Moore said. "When I hear him power up and get going, I feel like I'm hearing the Baptist within."

The Self-Help way is to meet, analyze, and dissect, and then meet some more. Every time Self-Help contemplated venturing into a new area, whether it was loaning money to charter schools and day-care centers or the move into the refinance business, their modus operandi was to gather in small groups and as an organization debate the new initiative. Eakes might have been hell-bent on action but they were a credit union, not a public interest advocacy organization. With everything else going on, were they going to devote the money and the energy that would be required to see them through a fight that would invariably land them in Raleigh, the state capital, if not Washington—all because the boss had lost his temper during a phone conversation with another lender? Mark Pearce, who had started at Self-Help in 1996, was among those arguing forcefully for them to take the fight to Associates. But Pearce, who would serve as the Center for Responsible Lending's first president before leaving in 2006 to take a posting as North Carolina's deputy commissioner of banks, also saw why some, especially those working in the business loan department, might disagree. "It was a real challenge to our mission," Pearce said. "Self-Help was working so hard to get people into homes, and it's not like we were anywhere near to meeting our goals on that front."

In the end, though, the sheer size of Associates left the Self-Help executive team feeling they had no choice. Associates had started its life nearly a century earlier as an auto finance company aimed at helping people buy a Model T. Where Self-Help had a half dozen offices around the state and had made around five hundred home loans in North Carolina in 1998, Associates had eighty storefronts scattered around North Carolina making or buying thousands of home loans each year. Self-Help relied largely on word of mouth and a network of nonprofits; Associates had Terry Bradshaw, the former football great, pitching its loans on television and booming, "We make loans that make life better!" At Self-Help they felt like they were really something when in the late 1990s they were making more than $25 million in home loans each year. When, in 1998, Ford spun off Associates First Capital, as its subprime lending unit was called, through an initial public offering, it was generating nearly $1 billion a year in profits.

"It really hit us in the face," Mike Calhoun said. "We recognized that if we don't do something about predatory lending, we're kidding ourselves that we're really achieving something by putting people in homes." This organization that had always viewed its core mission as helping families build wealth had come to the conclusion that it was equally as important to help families protect the wealth they had already attained. The solution, as they saw it, was for North Carolina to become the first state in the country to pass an anti–predatory lending bill aimed at reining in the most audacious practices of its subprime lenders.

In downtown Durham, an activist named Peter Skillern heard from Martin Eakes and told himself that it was about time. For years, Skillern, the executive director of the Community Reinvestment Association of North Carolina, or CRA-NC, had been organizing protests against subprime lenders at home and in Washington. He had even been known to don a rubber shark's nose to underscore his point that these lenders were a dangerous breed to avoid. Skillern admired Eakes and all that he had accomplished but Self-Help had declined to take part in CRA-NC's actions. "Martin is a remarkably effective leader," Skillern told me when I visited with him in Durham—but that only made Eakes's lack of engagement in the fight that much more maddening.

Skillern's bête noire wasn't Associates but a lender much closer to home, NationsBank, based in Charlotte. To him, NationsBank, one of the country's largest, offered a stark example of what he saw as the country's "parallel banking system." "It's like NationsBank has two doors, side by side," Skillern told me. If you were white, middle class, and had good credit, you were ushered into one door. If you were low-income and had imperfect credit, you were shuffled into the door for either NationsCredit or EquiCredit, Nation's two subprime subsidiaries. And if you were black your economic class or FICO score didn't seem to matter; according to studies, you were far more likely to end up with one of the subprime lenders and one of their high-interest loans just by virtue of the color of your skin. The subprime lenders claimed they needed to charge higher interest rates and steeper fees to offset the increased risk they were taking with subprime borrowers but Skillern thought that was bunk. The big consumer finance companies, *Forbes* reported in 1997, were enjoying returns as much as six times greater than those of the best-managed banks. Neither NationsCredit nor EquiCredit was nearly as large as Associates, but by the late 1990s the two units were generating around $400 million in profits each year.

Skillern would prove to be one important Eakes ally against Associates, Bill Brennan in Atlanta another. Eakes could rely on Rogers to help put a human face on predatory lending and there were others from among the fifty people who had complained about Associates to the state authorities over the previous year. Brennan, however, provided video, much of it starring Bill Brennan and all of it powerful. Brennan had played a key role in the making of the *Primetime Live* episode, providing some of the piece's rhetorical fire (he described Ford Motor as "the worst predatory lender in the country") and also its heart. It was Brennan who pointed a producer to the couple who would give the exposé its emotional anchor, the Iveys of Atlanta, who almost lost their home of twenty-five years after a broker with Associates talked them into consolidating some credit card bills in a preposterously expensive home equity loan that included 24 percent in up-front charges and a payment schedule this couple of modest means couldn't possibly afford.

Then there were all those television pieces Brennan was able to orchestrate in the Atlanta area using his local contacts. Abusive and predatory loans weren't necessarily illegal, and so when he was getting nowhere with a case, he would give a heads-up to a friendly TV reporter. In short order, a story would air about an elderly black woman living on meager means who had been ruined by Associates, or the short-order cook with diabetes who struggled to stand on his feet all day, or the hardworking couple with two young children, and there would be Brennan, eyes moist, bathing the viewer in sincerity, decrying the terrible injustice that had been done. With the heat turned up high, negotiations would commence and an accord would be reached contingent upon everyone's future silence. Brennan's friends dubbed it the "media-induced settlement." Brennan copied several of these local broadcasts onto a video and, along with the *Primetime Live* piece and a few other choice offerings (including snippets of depositions with two former Associates employees, who spoke of the lengths they would go to lard deals with expensive extras), sent it along to Self-Help.

In the hands of most advocates, Brennan's tape would have been a useful tool. In the hands of Martin Eakes it took on a life of its own. Inside Self-Help they made jokes about what they called Eakes's "teletubby"—the stout combination TV-VCR that the boss brought with him everywhere during the months they were lobbying for an anti–predatory lending law in Raleigh. There were fifty state senators in North Carolina and 120 members of the state assembly and Eakes, intent on showing the tape to every last one of them, rolled his teletubby door-to-door in the manner of an old-fashioned vacuum cleaner salesman. If a reception or some other staffer was reluctant to allow him inside to see a legislator, he would show it to that person, hoping after viewing it he or she would feel compelled to pass the tape he left behind on to their boss. One news account had Self-Help distributing seven thousand copies of the videotape around the state. By that time, Eakes had testified no fewer than eight times in favor of an anti–predatory lending bill. "People say I work hard," Mike Calhoun said, "but he put me to shame in that fight." The initiative was supported by a group calling itself the Coalition for Responsible Lending. The coalition included such mainstream advocacy groups as the NAACP and AARP but the political establishment in Raleigh could be forgiven for thinking this legislative battle was brought to them and sponsored by Martin Eakes and the people of Self-Help.

Calhoun, whom Bill Brennan described as "the smartest lawyer I've ever worked with," was the resident expert on consumer law within Self-Help, so it fell to him to type out a draft of the legislation. ("You're not going to see a lot of clerical staff at Self-Help," Calhoun sighed.) The aim of the bill was to impose limits on what a subprime lender could charge its customers. Roy Cooper, the senate majority leader and a Democrat, agreed to sponsor the bill. "We were beginning to see complaints filed by consumers and we began to hear concerns voiced by lawyers seeing these unfair terms at closings," said Cooper, who had been elected to his second term as North Carolina attorney general by the time I visited him in the fall of 2008. "So we realized we needed to put some bright-line limits on the amount of charges associated with the loans." Years later Cooper still remembered Freddie Rogers—not just his name but also his exact hourly wage and other details of his case.

Initially a long list of senators joined Cooper as co-sponsors, but after the lobbyists weighed in, Cooper ended up as its sole sponsor in the Senate. "North Carolina is the second-largest banking state in the country, so the banking industry is a significant economic engine here," Cooper said. "They had a significant influence over the legislature and government process." The key was to bring the banks around, or at least convince them to remain on the sidelines. That would be no easy task given the hundreds of millions in profits a local giant like NationsBank was booking selling subprime loans.

A year after the predatory lending fight was over, Eakes asked Keith Corbett, an executive at North Carolina Mutual, the nation's oldest black-owned insurance company, to join them at Self-Help. "We don't pay a lot in salary," Eakes told Corbett. "But if we see someone who's been mistreated, we're willing to spend two to three million dollars to right that wrong." Corbett was sold.

That's exactly what happened in the case of Freddie Rogers. Mike Calhoun was among those working out an out-of-court settlement with Associates that allowed Rogers to refinance with Self-Help under terms he could afford. A few years later, a developer seeking to gentrify Rogers's neighborhood paid him a substantial bounty for his home. By that time he had remarried.

Over the years Eakes had made his share of political enemies in Raleigh. "Imam" or "ayatollah" were among the less flattering nicknames given to him inside the state capitol by those resenting his sermonizing and righteousness, but there was also no denying his effectiveness. "He got along with a lot of my Republican colleagues, maybe better than I did," Wib Gulley said. To his activist allies he might have been the accidental banker who was still one of their own, but for political purposes he was a subprime mortgage banker horrified by the lending practices of some of his more unscrupulous rivals. He was also a man on a first-name basis with the CEOs of some of the state's largest lending institutions. He made the same pitch to each: The bad practices of the worst subprime lenders hurt the reputations of all in the mortgage business. Eventually even the North Carolina Bankers Association supported the reform bill. "That was Martin," Roy Cooper said. "Working and working and working to bring the industry into the fold."

The political fighting over the anti–predatory lending bill raged for the better part of a year. The bill was modified, for instance, to allow a lender to charge a borrower as much as 5 percent in up-front fees. "If your parents paid five points on a loan, you wouldn't be very happy," Calhoun said. But the legislation banned prepayment penalties on any mortgage less than $150,000 and made it illegal to roll into a loan the cost of credit insurance (credit insurance itself, with separate monthly payments, was still legal). Lenders could charge interest rates well above the rates enjoyed by prime customers but anyone wanting to sign a deal that would have them pay rates more than ten percentage points higher than a Treasury bill would be required to meet with a credit counselor. The bill was signed into law in July 1999.

Even with its limitations, consumer advocates hailed the law as a significant breakthrough. Inside Self-Help's offices, the phone was now ringing with activists from places such as New Jersey, Chicago, and Dayton eager to pass something similar in their locale. "Initially we thought we passed this predatory lending bill, okay, good, we're done, now we can go back to our day jobs," said Mark Pearce. "But people wanted to know how we did it, especially as North Carolina wasn't exactly seen as the most liberal, consumer-friendly state in the country."

Six

The Great Payday Land Rush

SPARTANBURG, SOUTH CAROLINA, THE LATE 1990s

Allan Jones parks in front of his old office building and a sly smile appears on his face, like someone anticipating the punch line of a favorite joke. He points his chin at a drab, low-slung cement bunker of a structure sitting in the corner of a shopping center parking lot. This is where he played host, he tells me, when all those investment bankers flew south to see him in the late 1990s to talk about taking Check Into Cash public. They would arrive dressed in Bill Blass and Brooks Brothers and Armani. He would be wearing an off-the-rack suit he bought at a discount place in town. He would then usher them into his "conference room"—maybe ten metal chairs around a banged-up, folding banquet table—where he would make his presentation. Check Into Cash's revenues were on pace to more than double in 1998; its profit margins were well above 20 percent. At that point, Jones said, they could have cared less had he been naked and standing in a cave: "Them numbers are all they ever noticed," he said.

CIBC Oppenheimer agreed to serve as the lead underwriter on Check Into Cash's IPO. CIBC wasn't Goldman or Morgan but it was a large bank, respectable and legitimate. He even got to New York and rode the subway, where he saw a man with a hairdo he later learned was called a Mohawk. For months he entertained Doughball and the rest of the boys with stories about life up north. I must have arrived, he would say mockingly, because now I have me a real-life lawyer with a Park Avenue address.

Jones claims to have been relieved rather than disappointed when CIBC put the IPO on hold. They told him it was temporary, a short-term setback while the market recovered from a financial crisis every-one was calling the Asian flu, but the competition was heating up and he was anxious for his money. In Cleveland (Ohio), an old-time bank called National City was awakening to the profit potential of subprime and he convinced officials there to loan him the $50 million he had planned to raise through a public offering. The IPO would have meant $50 million in the bank while borrowing from NatCity meant paying back the loan with interest, but remaining private had its own rewards. He was not a man who liked answering to anyone but himself.

"We have board meetings at Check Into Cash," Jones likes to joke, "but I win every vote one to nothing." He mentioned a competitor named Billy Webster, whose company, Advance America, has traded shares on the New York Stock Exchange since 2004. "How much of his company does Billy own?" Jones asked. "How much of my company do I own? Go ask Billy and I'll bet he'll tell you: His shareholder meetings are a lot longer than mine."

William M. Webster II lost everything during the Depression. His son, William M. Webster III, started from scratch, turning a single gas station in Greenville, South Carolina, into a modest-sized empire of twenty stations that he would sell to Marathon Oil in the 1970s at a handsome profit. Yet in the eyes of his son, William M. Webster IV, whom everyone called Billy, his father could have accomplished so much more. Billy Webster spent a good part of his teen years working for his old man, pumping gas and thinking how he would be different.

His father had inherited his grandfather's skittishness and worry about taking risks. He vowed that would never be him.

While he was still in college Billy Webster bought a laundry and charged other students a fee to wash their clothes. A Fulbright scholarship took him to Germany to spend a year studying Romantic poetry, but it was while he was studying law at the University of Virginia that his father started talking about the long lines of people queuing up at the Bojangles chicken shack near one of his old gas stations. That spelled the end of his legal career. "I graduated law school on a Saturday and Monday night I'm in the back of a Bojangles, learning how to fry chicken, being taught by a sixteen-year-old black guy from Frogmore, South Carolina," Webster said. Ten years later, Webster and his father sold their holdings back to Bojangles; the pair were operating two dozen stores generating a combined $24 million in annual sales. By almost any standard, though not his own, Billy Webster was a rich man.

For a time Webster got into politics. Again his father proved the catalyst. He had grown up with Dick Riley, who would serve two terms as South Carolina's governor (the elder Webster had served as chairman of Riley's first political campaign). Riley introduced Billy Webster to Bill Clinton, and when the new president appointed Riley to serve as education secretary, Riley brought Webster to Washington to serve as his chief of staff. Webster resigned after two years, intent on returning to the private sector, but then Clinton invited him for a run around the Mall. My scheduling office is a mess, the president told him, and I think you're the man to help me straighten it out. So Webster spent one more year in Washington before returning to South Carolina to figure out what he would do next.

"I'm not an engineer," Webster told himself. "I'm not a software guy." It was the mid-1990s but starting a technology company was out. This man who had made his money selling fried chicken and washing other people's clothes reminded himself to keep it simple. He thought of his father's friend, George Dean Johnson, Jr. He had gotten into the garbage collection business before selling it to Waste Management and then jumped into the video rentals market, opening more than two hundred Blockbuster stores before selling them back to the parent company for $156 million. The key was to find a field before it came under the control of its Blockbuster or Home Depot and then aggressively attack it with money, MBAs, and an all-or-nothing aggressiveness.

Webster went to visit Johnson, who by that time had moved back home to Spartanburg. Johnson, who had served three terms in the South Carolina legislature when he was younger (the first as a Democrat, the second as a Republican, the third as a declared Independent), was already on to his next business, Extended Stay Hotels, but he told Webster he would be happy to provide him with financial backing. You find a business that you think you can run, he told him, and I'll take care of the money.

Webster mulled a return to the food business. He contemplated starting an automotive supplies company and thought about creating a competitor to the Sylvan Learning centers. Sometimes he would drive around town looking for businesses that had lines of people wanting to buy what they were selling. The idea for getting into the payday lending business came when George Johnson suggested Webster go talk to someone at Stephens, Inc., a boutique investment bank based in Little Rock, Arkansas, that had staked out the "specialty finance" sector as its own. There Webster spoke to a junior banker gung-ho about the moneymaking potential of the cash advance business. It was Jerry Robinson, who had moved to Tennessee to help Toby McKenzie take his rent-to-own company public but ended up helping him get into payday loans. We have a relationship with one of the industry's top players, Robinson told Webster. He'd be happy to make the introductions.

Webster didn't know what to think about payday when he first heard about the idea in 1996. He was intrigued, though, so he flew to Tennessee to spend the day parked outside one of McKenzie's stores. He was struck by the sheer number of people visiting this one small outpost on the outskirts of Cleveland and asked Robinson to approach McKenzie about letting him see the operations from the inside. If that first trip to Tennessee left him eager to learn more, then the three weeks Webster worked the counter at a National Cash Advance storefront convinced him he had found what he was searching for. "I didn't see an unhappy human being in my three weeks working there," Webster said.

Back home Webster worked the phone. There were budding chains of 100 or 200 stores, he discovered, "but there was no dominant national player who could leverage efficiencies over hundreds and hundreds, if not thousands and thousands of operating units." Those who had arrived before him in these low-rent credit fields hardly struck him as invincible. Jones and McKenzie, from what he could tell, were payday's "Hatfields and McCoys," two men with high school degrees building their businesses with one eye on the other and by the seats of their pants. In Cincinnati, the Davis brothers, with access to their father's connections and his millions, could prove a more formidable team but already Webster was picking up reports of strife inside the family. "It didn't take too much to figure out everyone was distracted," said Webster, who then dryly added that "distracted" is "an understatement." The opportunity seemed that much more bright given the sorry state of the typical payday outlet—"storefronts with a hole cut in the wall," he said.

It didn't take much effort for Webster to sell George Johnson on the idea, nothing more than two lines on a piece of paper. One line was the cost of a payday loan and the other depicted the rising costs of a bounced check or credit card late fee. "When those lines crossed," Webster explained for Johnson, when the penalties a bank charged started costing more than these short-term quick loans, "the industry just grew and grew and grew." Both put up money (Johnson invested the lion's share) to start a company they called Advance America. Using their connections, the pair secured sizable lines of credit at Wells Fargo, Wachovia, and NationsBank. "We basically borrowed forty or fifty million dollars before we made anything," Webster said. "We had an infrastructure for five hundred stores before we had even one."

Advance America opened 300 stores in 1997 and then opened another 400 the next year. In 1999, Webster started calling competitors to see who might be interested in selling. Jones turned him down, LBJ-style, while soaking naked in a tub in a summer home he owned outside Cleveland, but McKenzie jumped at the chance, selling to Advance

America for $150 million. Advance America opened 300 more stores in 1999 on top of the 450 or so they had bought from McKenzie. By the start of 2000, Advance America was operating more than 1,400 stores, including 250 in California, 150 in Florida, and another 120 in Ohio, each looking identical.

In the early days, payday could sometimes seem like something out of a Quentin Tarantino film rather than a burgeoning industry. Those touting the business had been excited when the *Wall Street Journal* sent a reporter to Tennessee to do one of the first big profiles of payday lending—and then Jones hooked up the guy with a store manager who, when asked if he was worried about people paying him back, pointed over his shoulder to the baseball bat he kept prominently displayed behind the counter and said, "I like to call that an attitude adjustor." McKenzie could be even more of a loose cannon. When an Indiana legislator floated a bill that would have lowered the rates lenders could charge (back then, at least, Indiana allowed lenders to charge as much as $33 for every $100 they loaned out), McKenzie rushed north to lend a hand—and then handed his foes a fat gift when he was caught boasting in front of a meeting of his employees that "I've never seen a legislator I couldn't buy." The jobs of all those working to promote payday would be easier with George Johnson, a former state legislator, and Billy Webster, the friend of a sitting president, atop the industry's largest company. "You would hear people say, 'Payday can't be too bad if Billy Webster is involved,'" Martin Eakes said.

"You don't normally want competition," Jared Davis said, "but in this case, we think Billy's been a big help to the industry. From a lobbying perspective. From a legitimacy perspective."

For a year or two it was enough for Advance America to build in states where others had gone before them but a company that ambitious could play fill-in for only so long. Before the end of that first year Webster was already staffing up a government affairs office. "There was always an overt business objective—to broaden the geography," Webster said. In 1998, South Carolina legislators welcomed payday lenders into their state, as did elected officials in Mississippi, Nevada, and the District of Columbia. By the end of 2000, twenty-three states had legalized payday lending, and the likes of Advance America and Check Into Cash were operating in eight more because there was no law specifically forbidding them from doing so. Where a traditional lender was earning a return on investment of between 13 and 18 percent, Jerry Robinson, the investment banker who had worked for Toby McKenzie before taking a job with Stephens, Inc., told Business Week that the average payday lender was earning an average return of 23.8 percent.

At first reporters scratched their heads over this odd new business. "I don't know how someone who just does payday advance is going to make it," a local check casher told a reporter with the *Sacramento Business Journal* who was trying to figure out how a South Carolina–based company had opened twenty stores in the greater Sacramento area in a matter of months. Each would need to attract a "high volume" of customers, the check casher posited, just to cover the rent and labor costs; otherwise more than a few would be closing their doors as suddenly as they had opened them.

But quickly a new story line emerged: the payday client who had gotten him or herself into deep financial trouble availing themselves of a product pitched as requiring no credit check. Reporters never seemed to have much trouble finding unhappy customers. Readers of the *New York Times* would meet three when the paper turned its attention to the payday loan in 1999, including a thirty-nine-year-old woman named Shari Harris who earned $25,000 a year working computer security in Kokomo, Indiana. Harris had borrowed $150 from the Check Into Cash store near her home after the father of her two children stopped paying child support—six months later she owed $1,900. An Associated Press article that appeared around the same time featured a woman named Janet Delaney, a $16,000-a-year hospital food worker from Cleveland, Tennessee, who borrowed $200 from a Check Into Cash after falling behind on some bills. One year later, Delaney had paid nearly $1,000 in fees but had yet to pay back the original $200. "I'm just lucky," that same AP article quoted Allan Jones as saying. "I hit on something that's very popular with consumers."

One theory offered to explain the immense and sudden popularity of payday loans was that ours is an instant-gratification society where almost anything we desire is only a few clicks away. Others pointed to a society at once comfortable with, and addicted to, debt; in a country where so many middle-class people were willing to mortgage the future for a new bathroom or a large flat-screen TV, was it any wonder that those of modest means might likewise avail themselves of these corner lenders? But there were deeper structural reasons for payday lending's popularity, financial in nature rather than cultural, starting with the widening gap between the haves and have-nots. A full-time worker at Walmart, the country's largest private employer, might make $15,000 or $16,000 her first year on the job, and polling showed that nearly one in two Americans was living paycheck to paycheck. The problem was particularly acute among the bottom 40 percent, whose income growth was flat in terms of real dollars throughout the 1990s while the cost of everything from health care, heating oil, and housing soared. For those living on the economic margins, payday offered a simple solution they could squeeze in after work, between the grocery shopping and making dinner for the kids. "Our motto is 'quick, easy, and confidential,'" Jones had told the *Wall Street Journal*. "We can get people in and out in thirty seconds."

Opposition was inevitable, of course. Before Martin Eakes there was Jean Ann Fox at the Consumer Federation of America. Fox's first assault on what she originally called "delayed deposit check loans," or "check advance loans," was called "The Growth of Legal Loan Sharking." This report, released in 1998, and subsequent ones provided an early chronicle of an industry largely getting its way in state legislatures around the United States. But Fox's main contribution to the debate was adding an element of math. As she read it, the Truth in Lending Act, passed in 1968, required any business to express the cost of a loan not only in dollar terms but also as an annual percentage rate, or APR. The $15 per $100 that payday lenders could charge in stricter states like Ohio and Washington worked out to an APR of 391 percent. In

Arkansas, where payday lenders could charge as much as $21 for every $100 borrowed, the APR was 546 percent, and in Colorado, where the going rate was $25 per $100, 650 percent. Borrowers in Indiana, with its $33 per $100 cap, were paying the equivalent of 858 percent on a two-week loan.

In Spartanburg, Webster tried not to get angry as he read Fox's reports. Instead he flew to Washington to meet with her. Webster prides himself on his ability to get along with anyone but he confessed Fox proved the exception. "A person says stuff like 'legalized loan-sharking,'" he said, "and it's hard not to take this stuff very personally." But he had to agree with Fox on at least one point: the need to state the cost of their loans as an annual percentage rate. That was what Advance America's general counsel had concluded after researching the law. Webster could have overruled her, but he figured people didn't care about the APR, they only cared that they could have $300 today and what they would owe in two weeks. And so Advance America, alone among the big chains, started posting its rates not only as a dollar figure but also as an APR.

It bothers Webster when people think there's a taint to the way he's made his money. People don't say anything directly to him, he told me when I visited with him in Spartanburg in early 2009; they are too polite for that. But he hears things secondhand and he always addresses it immediately when it comes up. He prefers to give someone a tour of an Advance America store but, if they're not willing to do that, all he asks for is a bit of their time. "I have to say that virtually to a person, if I have thirty minutes to explain the business to them, they'll let me know that it makes perfect sense: 'I didn't understand that.'"

The hallways of the handsome postmodern brick building that Advance America has built as its headquarters in central Spartanburg are lined with posters that express good feelings in words and images. The self-affirming artwork justifying what everyone inside does for a living seems a staple of the big Poverty, Inc. chains. More typically they are more wholesome and upbeat, leftovers from old advertising campaigns that depict a veritable Rainbow Coalition of handsome, extraordinarily happy young people ("They showed me the money!" the young Latino man with the smoldering brown eyes and thousand-watt smile exclaimed in an ad for a company called Instant Tax Service) but at Advance America, at least in the winter of 2009, they were more playful and droll, a series of small testimonials to some of its archetypal customers. For the postal worker, the payday loan is for when "the mail bag's heavy but your pockets are light." The working mom needs Advance America for "those times when your eyelids weigh a little more than your wallet."

Webster is a slight man, with angular features and a tiny pug nose. Dressed in jeans and running shoes, he bobbed his foot incessantly through our few hours together. Webster had served as chief executive through Advance America's first nine years but several years ago, when he was in his late forties, he stepped down because his wife was sick and he wanted to take care of the couple's four children. He had recently returned, replacing George Johnson as board chairman, but he started by telling me that he had been reluctant to meet with me, despite being back at the helm. It was the APR. "Most journalists stop at the 391 percent interest rate, and the only question is, 'How on earth can you charge so much?'" he said. He had his answers, just like the other payday lenders did when I visited them. But to him, it's a meaningless number—like saying salmon costs $15,980 per ton or advertising a hotel room as costing $36,500 per year. A flat fee is not an interest rate. Webster shakes his head. He had been the first to post the APR and had to confess, "It has been a millstone around our neck ever since."

Webster listed his decision to post the eye-popping, three-digit APRs as one of his "two gross misjudgments." The other was his failure to anticipate the hailstorm of criticism that would rain down on the payday lenders. "If there's an irony to all this, it's that we both should have been more politically aware that there was a political dimension to this business," he said of himself and Johnson. "It's hard to imagine but back then there was little controversy about payday lending." Sure, there were companies overly aggressive in their collections and lax about post-ing their fees. But Advance America, Webster said, was trying to clean things up. They refused to criminally prosecute anyone who failed to pay them back and unilaterally announced that they would give people twenty-four hours to change their mind about a loan. Along with the other big chains, Advance America, in 1999, formed a trade association they called the Community Financial Services Association, or CFSA, so they could offer a narrative that might serve as a counterforce to the shock of a three-digit APR. "With a trade association in place," Jared Davis said, "we thought we could actually get back to doing what we do, which is create new jobs and give people access to credit when they need it."

As the 1990s turned into the 2000s, worried payday lenders told themselves to relax. Theirs was a young industry experiencing a bit of turbulence but that was to be expected. The rent-to-own furni-ture stores had gone through a similar boom period in the late 1980s and early '90s; their brethren in the check-cashing business had been fighting with regulators and their critics for more than a decade. Leg-islatures around the country had implemented caps on the fees check cashers could charge and regulators frustrated the more aggressive rent-to-own entrepreneurs by dictating new business practices that cut into their profits, but both industries adjusted and both were post-ing big profits.

For all the bad publicity the industry was receiving, the payday lend-ers were also thriving. The check cashers would hold workshops at their annual meeting about getting into the payday loan business and the ses-sion would be standing room only. For many it was a no-brainer given it required no special expertise. Small-time pawnbrokers might resent the intrusion of payday as an option for those with bad credit seeing quick cash, but the bigger pawn chains were now seeing only opportunity in these quick, unsecured, cash loans that earned triple-digit interest per year, and they jumped. "It was an easy way to add rocket fuel to the bottom line," said Jerry Robinson, the former Stephens, Inc. banker. The industry passed the 10,000-store mark by 2001 and entrepreneurs with national ambitions were still lined up at the industry's door, hoping to get in.

"It got unbelievably competitive," Jared Davis said. "It was literally a race from space to space." It was, Davis said, like all those horses and wagons lined up on the Oklahoma border in 1889 for the great land rush. And, oddly, probably the most frantic opening of a new market took place in 2003—in Oklahoma. "If I could do anything differently," Billy Webster told me, "it would be to spend more time telling our story to journalists, editorial boards, and opinion leaders." But who had the time when there were still great stretches of the country to conquer?

Seven

Subprime City

DAYTON, OHIO, 1999–2000

D ean Lovelace first focused on all the payday lending shops sprouting up around Dayton. It was the second half of the 1990s and to Lovelace, who had served on the Dayton City Commission since 1993, it felt like his hometown was under attack. It was no wonder. By 1999, Allan Jones and Billy Webster had each opened seven stores in the greater Dayton area and Toby McKenzie had opened six. Jared and David Davis, the brother tandem behind Check 'n Go, had added another four. It was as if the demographics from this one unprepossessing blue-collar city in the heartland had been poured into a database and bells started clanging and lights started flashing JACKPOT! on computer screens in the corporate development offices of payday chains across the country. Closer to home, there was Lee Schear, a local entrepreneur whom Lovelace was inclined to describe as a "profiteer." For years Schear had been making plenty off the working poor, cashing checks (for a fee) and selling lottery tickets at the small chain of grungy grocery stores he ran in Dayton's poorer precincts. But with the legalization of payday, he was now operating two dozen of these storefronts in and around town. By the end of the 1990s, Dayton, a city of 150,000, and the surrounding suburbs were home to more than fifty payday shops.

Lovelace had grown up in Dayton, born to a single mother who raised three children largely on her own. It was only after his mother died during his senior year in high school that he learned that she never earned more than $200 a week. Looking through her papers he finally realized why they had moved every year he was in high school; his mother had fallen behind on the rent and each time they had been evicted. Lovelace would go on to earn an undergraduate degree in business from the University of Dayton and a master's in social economics at Wright State University. He then worked as a planner inside city hall until taking a job as the director of neighborhood development at the University of Dayton, a post he would hold for more than twenty-five years. He won a seat on the Dayton City Commission (its equivalent of the city council), a part-time position, on his third try. He lives in a nice-size, handsome house in a modest middle-class community in Dayton but there could be no dismissing Lovelace as a silver-spooned elitist who has never been desperate for quick cash. He knew what it meant to be broke.

The payday lenders started showing up in 1996 shortly after the Ohio legislature, after intense lobbying from the industry, voted to exempt small, short-term loans from the state's 28 percent usury cap, thereby legalizing payday lending. As a commissioner, Lovelace had championed a living wage ordinance (but had to compromise on an $8.80 an hour minimum wage that applied only to those doing business with the city) and to him shutting down the payday lenders was the flip side of the same coin: Making sure people earned a better wage would mean little, he reasoned, if they only spent that extra money borrowing money at usurious rates from these new shops. The issue really hit home when his niece phoned him one day. "They got me," she told him. She barely made minimum wage but after frittering away hundreds of dollars in fees that she couldn't afford, she was now in a deeper mess. "They're calling me at work," she told Lovelace. She was scared she might lose her job.

Lovelace didn't know what a city commissioner could do about a statewide law that had only just passed a few years earlier, but he felt compelled to do something. Using his limited clout, he held a series of community meetings around the city. "I just figured at that point I needed to raise awareness," Lovelace said. "I at least wanted to start a dialogue." He wanted to alert people to what he saw as a growing menace to the city's economic health.

Only around thirty people showed up at that first meeting. A couple of consumer advocates were enlisted to explain why high-interest, short-term loans were very seldom an effective answer to a customer's cash flow crisis and a local legal aid lawyer told the group about the hundreds of payday-related default judgments clogging the local courts. A few payday customers stood to voice their displeasure over these new neighbors taking over empty storefronts in strip malls throughout town. You borrow to "bridge a gap," a woman named Pam Shackelford explained, "except there's no way you're gonna bridge a gap if the gap keeps getting bigger." But then a woman named Suriffa Rice, a home health-care worker, took her turn at the microphone. "I can't go to my mama," Rice said. "I can't go to a bank. I can't go to my church. Where am I supposed to go if I don't have payday [loans] anymore?"

Dean Lovelace is a short and stocky black man with a mustache and silver-framed glasses that always seem to be sitting slightly askew on his face. When his turn to speak came, he had to confess to Rice that he didn't have much of an answer for her. A couple of credit unions around the state were experimenting with what they were calling "stretch pay loans" but that was about it. An economist by training, Lovelace recognized that the real issue was better financial education and other reforms. Whether or not the payday lenders were greedy would be a moot point if banks actually offered products aimed at the working poor. In the end, his meetings generated a few articles but added up to little more than some high-profile hand-wringing.

Lovelace was hardly done, though. He has a mild-mannered and pleasant disposition yet by nature he is a battler and a crusader and not one who goes along just to get along. Early in his career, C. J. McLin,

Jr., the godfather of black politics in Dayton, took him under his wing but Lovelace proved incapable of serving the gofer role he was expected to play. He ran the Dayton chapter of the Rainbow Coalition for Jesse Jackson's two presidential bids in the 1980s and led the local fight against police brutality. He had also spearheaded a coalition formed to pressure the city's big banks over their lack of lending in Dayton's low- and moderate-income communities. In fact, at around the same time he was organizing his hearings into payday lending, a local activist named Jim McCarthy, the executive director of the area's Fair Housing Center, invited him to join a committee they were putting together to figure out what was happening on the home ownership front. Businesses were starting to lend in the city's lower-income communities but it wasn't turning out to be a good thing.

Ever since its frontier days, Dayton had always been a place that devoted itself to making things: steam pumps and water wheels in its earliest history, stoves and solvents, tool-and-die machines, cardboard boxes, and a goodly portion of the country's cash registers well into the twentieth century. "The city of a thousand factories"—that's what Dayton, once home to 260,000 people, dubbed itself.

But then a sizable portion of those thousand factories shuttered their doors, moving south or overseas, in search of lower taxes and weaker unions, or simply going out of business. The city lost more than one-fifth of its people through the 1970s and more kept leaving. By the time *Forbes* dubbed Dayton one of America's fastest-dying cities in 2008, it had lost 40 percent of its people. A few months later, the magazine singled out Dayton again, placing it in the top five of the country's "emptiest cities." *Forbes* had a point. The city's rental vacancy rate stood at 22 percent, which was more than twice the national average and second highest in the country. Nearly 4 percent of the city's houses sat unoccupied. Was it any wonder that those in the poverty industry saw Dayton as a place rich with possibilities?

Jim McCarthy can remember pretty much the exact moment when

he realized Dayton was being aggressively targeted by a new kind of business. It was 1999, he was thirty-three or thirty-four years old, and, as the newly installed head of Fair Housing, he was a member of an advisory board the county had created to oversee an affordable housing fund. Fair Housing routinely heard from people claiming they had been denied a loan because of their race, but in recent weeks several people, all of them African-American, had contacted his organization making something like the opposite assertion: They were about to lose their home because of a refinancing. When he mentioned this during a meeting of the advisory board, someone offered that he too was noticing something strange. Over the years the federal government had set aside billions of dollars to make low- and no-interest home loans available to people living in areas that had designated community development zones, yet now people were coming to his office with large checks in hand to pay off these loans. "These are the kinds of loans you basically don't pay off until you die," McCarthy said. "It made us all ask the question, 'What the hell is going on?'"

The advisory board decided to form a group to look into the matter. Dean Lovelace joined them and so did Beth Deutscher at Consumer Credit Counseling Services. Like Lovelace, Deutscher didn't need any convincing. She oversaw a Consumer Credit project created to help first-time homebuyers but in recent months she seemed to be spending as much time aiding existing homeowners who had fallen into trouble. Where her organization had typically heard from maybe one or two people a week seeking mortgage default counseling, the call volume had jumped to four or five per day. She grew more alarmed, she said, once the agency's counselors started meeting with people. "These were loans designed to bring maximum profit to the lender and minimum benefit to the borrower," Deutscher said. Rounding out the group were executives with KeyBank and Fifth Third, two of the bigger banks in town, along with representatives from the local board of Realtors and the home builders' association.

The industry representatives were initially defensive. You beat us up for failing to make loans to these customers and now do you see what happens? "There was a real 'I told you so' attitude around the table," McCarthy said. But they dug deeper and even the bankers had to concede the point: The problem wasn't the people but the product they were being sold. The staff in the county clerk's office told of brokers and lenders rummaging through residential tax records, looking to see who had fallen behind in their property tax payments. They were poking around the ownership records as well to determine how long people had owned their homes. "It was like they were focusing on elderly African-American ladies, mostly widows, who all lived within a few miles of each other in west Dayton," said Stan Hirtle, a legal aid lawyer in Dayton.

Dora Byrd was ninety years old, a widow for the previous thirty-five years, when a man knocked on her door to talk about some home repairs. "'He was a nice, clean-cut young man'—she kept saying that to me over and over," McCarthy said. "'He was so nice he'd even read my mail for me.'" Byrd, who had owned her home outright for twenty-seven years, had made a modest living running a small beauty salon out of her home. She had been enough of a businesswoman to recognize it would be unwise to let her home fall into disrepair, and this nice young man talked her into financing several home-improvement projects, all in the name of maintaining a property that ended up in foreclosure. Byrd died before the issue would be settled in her favor.

"She was this little bitty, tiny, frail woman who sat on her front stoop with her head in her hands and just cried," McCarthy said. "She said she was so embarrassed this had happened to her." Others would feel equally foolish—people like Gloria Thorpe, who was living on a monthly Social Security check of $354 when a lender sold her a $5,000 home equity loan. With fees, the deal ended up costing Thorpe $12,000 and so, at the age of seventy-two, she found herself working once again, a security guard on the second shift at a local factory. "They're sitting there talking to you and making it sound so good," Thorpe told the *Dayton Daily News* in 2000. "And me, my stupid self, I signed. But it was too much paper to read." One study showed that in a three-year period, from 1997 to 1999, subprime home equity loans had quadrupled in the Dayton area. Another found that at least one in three refinancings had been initiated by the lender, not the borrower.

Even those in McCarthy's working group were stunned when, at the start of 2000, the county government agreed to fund what they called the Predatory Lending Solutions Project. They had asked for $350,000—but county officials gave them that much plus another $600,000 to educate the public about these loans based on the worth of someone's home rather than a person's ability to pay. "It really worked in our favor that most of these people were senior citizens," McCarthy said.

Those behind this new project tried everything they could think of to spread the word. They leased billboard space along busy thoroughfares warning people about predatory loans; they took out ads in the *Dayton Daily News* that employed arrows and circles to teach people to decipher the gibberish of the HUD-1 disclosure form that by law is part of every home loan. They ran ads on the sides of buses and ads inside those same buses. An advertising agency was hired to develop a series of radio and TV ads warning people against signing deals that sound too good to be true ("If you're not careful," a baritone-voiced narrator intoned, "you can end up with huge payments, even lose your house"). Glossy brochures were handed out to real estate agents ("Help your clients avoid predatory loans"), and another set explained terms like "origination fee," "balloon payment," and "prepayment penalty" for potential borrowers. They established a hotline and stamped its phone number on everything from refrigerator magnets to plastic water bottles to lawn signs. They used yellow and black for everything because the agency had taught them that these colors suggested caution and hazards ahead, like police tape and road signs.

The Miami River cleaves Dayton in two, and the vast majority of the city's black citizenry lives to the west of it. The Predatory Lending Project focused mainly on the city's west side because that's where the lenders were focusing their efforts. Its people, mostly volunteers, set up a booth at the Dayton Black Cultural Festival and did Saturday blitzes in west side neighborhoods, borrowing a replica trolley from the regional transit authority and showing up eight, ten, or twelve strong, dressed in yellow-and-black T-shirts that read DON'T BORROW TROUBLE: ANTI–PREDATORY LENDING SOLUTIONS. They distributed door hangers and brochures and trinkets stamped with their hotline number and spoke with thousands—8,578 residents in their first full year, according to the report they submitted to the county. Yet while they were busy spreading the word in one part of town, lenders were working the other side of the river.

"Apparently they started to reach a saturation point in the inner city so they moved into the rest of the city," McCarthy said. So in 2001, its second year of operation, the Predatory Lending Project added the Appalachian Mountain Days festival to its list and dispatched the trolley and its teams of volunteers into white working-class neighborhoods.

But they remained perpetually one or two steps behind the lenders. In 2001, Richard Stock, the director of the Center for Business and Economic Research at the University of Dayton, released a study offering the first snapshot of subprime lending in Dayton. The first surprise in his study was the steep rise in foreclosures. There had been barely 1,000 foreclosures in 1994 but the county registered nearly 2,500 in 2000. The city's deteriorating manufacturing base could explain some of the rise but Stock's numbers also revealed an eightfold spike in foreclosures involving subprime home loans.

The second surprise involved the names of the most active subprime lenders. Those behind the Predatory Lending Project were pleased that the county had been so generous in providing them funding yet it turned out they were fighting large corporations with millions to spend on marketing and millions more to invest in sales teams. They included H&R Block, which was one of the area's most aggressive subprime lenders through a subsidiary called Option One, and a list of large banks as impressive as it was disturbing. Bank of America, Bank One, First

Union, and Washington Mutual ranked among the top subprime lenders in the Dayton area, but topping Stock's list were Household Finance
and Citigroup, the New York–based giant that promoted itself as the
world's leading bank.

The final surprise—and perhaps the biggest—was how widespread
the problem had become in so relatively short a period. Stock and his
team of researchers found that a large portion of those default judgments involving subprime loans weren't occurring on the west side or
even in the white working-class enclaves on the city's east side but instead in first-ring suburbs that had fallen on hard times. Zip code and
the color of a borrower's skin, it turned out, wouldn't make a difference
to subprime lenders seeing nothing but opportunity in Dayton's economic decline. They were, McCarthy concluded, "equal opportunity
predators."

In 1998, Senator Charles Grassley of Iowa, the Republican chairman
of the Senate Special Committee on Aging, held a one-day hearing
into subprime mortgage lending. The title he chose for the event left
no doubt about his sympathies: "Equity Predators: Stripping, Flipping,
and Packing Their Way to Profits." Among those testifying on Capitol
Hill were Ormond and Rosie Jackson, an elderly Brooklyn, New York,
couple living on Social Security, whose loan had been "flipped" so many
times that, six years after a salesman knocked on their door promising
that new windows could be theirs for just $43 a month for fifteen years,
they owed $88,000 and were facing foreclosure—the "stripping" of their
equity. Helen Ferguson, a seventy-six-year-old widow from Washington,
D.C., living on a monthly $504 Social Security check, told a similar
story, except that in her case it wasn't a knock on the door but an ad
she saw on television pitching low-interest home-improvement loans.
Prior to that, her mortgage payment had been $229 a month, but—in
part because her loan had been "packed" with an expensive credit insurance policy that a woman living alone did not need—five years later
she had a house payment of $810 per month. "My perfect customer," a

former salesman for several subprime lenders told the senators, "would be an uneducated woman who is living on a fixed income—hopefully from her deceased husband's pension and Social Security—who has her house paid off, is living off credit cards and having a difficult time keeping up with her payments."

People in Dayton reached out to their congressional delegation hoping for help in Washington. They did their homework, and Jim McCarthy made contact with Martin Eakes and Bill Brennan. They were fighting national banks and other publicly traded companies with a broad geographical reach. This was a problem best fought in Washington, D.C., not Dayton city hall.

Those hoping to warn the rest of the country about the threat posed by the subprime lenders had their successes. Andrew Cuomo, in his final days as HUD secretary under Bill Clinton, spoke out publicly against the problem and Cuomo, along with Larry Summers, the Treasury secretary, created a short-lived task force in April 2000 to examine predatory lending in the United States. That same year Congress would again turn its attention to the subprime lending industry when Congressman Jim Leach, a Republican from Iowa and the chairman of the House Committee on Banking and Financial Services, held a hearing to look at the situation. But it was the misfortune of those advocating reform that in the 1950s, a woman named Florence Gramm managed to buy a small bungalow home in Columbus, Georgia, despite the risks inherent in extending her credit.

There's no doubting Florence Gramm's grit and fortitude. Her husband, Kenneth, suffered a stroke shortly after she gave birth to their son Phil. That left him partially paralyzed and unable to work. But Florence Gramm, a nurse, convinced a finance company to loan them the money they needed to buy a home, even though that meant she would need to work double shifts. Throughout his political career, which included three terms as a U.S. senator, Phil Gramm spoke frequently about the subprime loan that enabled his mother to become the first person in her family to own a home.

Gramm wasn't just any senator; he was determined to serve as his party's resident expert on the financial industry—once he settled on a political party. He held a Ph.D. in economics and had taught at Texas A&M, while running an economic consulting firm on the side, before deciding to get into politics in the 1970s. The surest route to victory in Texas back then was to run as a Democrat, and that was what Gramm did when he was first elected to Congress, but he had switched to the Republican Party by the time of his election to the Senate in 1984. He is probably best known for his co-authorship of the landmark Gramm-Rudman-Hollings Act, which in the 1980s established deficit reduction targets for the federal budget. More recently, he was the primary sponsor of the Gramm-Leach-Bliley Act, the bill that undid the post-1929 crash reform mandating that banking, brokerage, and insurance businesses remain separate. There was no denying his power through the 1990s and into the 2000s. Any federal legislation curbing the behavior of the country's subprime lenders would need to first pass muster with the powerful chairman of the Senate Committee on Banking, Housing and Urban Affairs, and Senator Phil Gramm of Texas was not about to meddle with this corner of the free enterprise system that had played so exalted a role in his family's history.

"Some people look at subprime lending and see evil," he said on the Senate floor during debate over a bill to clamp down on subprime lenders in 2001. "I look at subprime lending and I see the American dream in action. My mother lived it as a result of a finance company making a mortgage loan that a bank would not make." And if nostalgia were not enough to ensure his gung-ho support, then there was also the generosity of these lenders who helped to keep him in office year after year. Between 1989 and 2002, commercial banks were more generous with Gramm than with anyone else in the Senate and he received more from Wall Street than all but a few colleagues. In 2000, the National Association of Mortgage Brokers praised Gramm for killing an anti–predatory lending bill that was gaining momentum in Congress.

There's a difference, of course, between a subprime loan that costs a borrower a couple of percentage points above standard mortgage rates and those costing five or ten percentage points more. Gramm told of the 50 percent premium his parents paid in interest rates because she was a higher credit risk, but Tommy Myers, Freddie Rogers, and Dora Byrd could only dream that they had been paying interest rates only 50 percent higher than the conventional rate. There were no doubt other differences between the mortgage that Florence and Kenneth Gramm received in the 1950s and the high-fee, high-interest-rate loans that some of Gramm's colleagues wanted to curb. The Gramms received their loan prior to the deregulation of the 1980s, when lenders were still prohibited from charging more than 1 percent of the loan amount in up-front fees. It's also doubtful that Florence Gramm's loan would have been saddled by lump-sum credit insurance policies, giant balloon payments they couldn't possibly afford, or any of the other practices critics were trying to curb.

"We wanted to go for a federal fix," McCarthy said. "Because that was really the way to deal with predatory lending. [But] basically, Senator Gramm's view was, 'Over my dead body,' and so we said fine, we'll start from the bottom up."

Maybe the biggest surprise following the success of Martin Eakes and his allies in North Carolina was that their victory didn't inspire copycat bills in states across the country. Their victory had inspired people in Ohio, but the activist leading the charge in favor of an anti–predatory lending bill, Bill Faith, the executive director of a group called the Coalition on Homelessness and Housing in Ohio, was telling people it wasn't time. "The banks and mortgage brokers and these other characters have the place completely locked down," Faith told them. "We're trying everything—and all it's meant is our heads are bloody from hitting them against a wall." California passed a watered-down subprime lender bill in October 2001, more than two years after North Carolina, but mainly the fight fell to a few cities like Chicago, Philadelphia, and Dayton.

The Chicago legislation came first, but it was a largely symbolic law, a bill that claimed jurisdiction only over those banks already doing business with the city. "We have very limited power as a city," Mayor Richard M. Daley told the *Chicago Sun-Times*. "It's basically building a groundswell."

Philadelphia's law, passed in April 2001, was anything but symbolic. Tougher than even North Carolina's, Philadelphia's dictated that lenders operating inside the city limits could not charge more than 4 percent in up-front costs or interest rates more than 6.5 percent higher than a long-term Treasury bill. Philadelphia, a city with a population greater than that of twelve states, had its own Bill Brennan: Irv Ackelsberg, an attorney with Community Legal Services who as far back as the mid-1990s was talking about subprime lending as a "public crisis." It's as though society has dealt with the problem of inadequate credit among low-income people, Ackelsberg would say, by drowning them in destructive debt that only increases their chances of reaching financial ruin. Access to credit wasn't necessarily a positive thing.

The next locale to draw the industry's attention, improbably, was the country's 152nd-largest city, with slightly more people than Joliet, Illinois, but not nearly as many as Amarillo, Texas, or Newport News, Virginia.

Dean Lovelace had never been the most popular fellow inside Dayton city hall. For starters there was the way he was elected, running against the political establishment in tandem with a white man who would be elected Dayton's first Republican mayor in twenty-five years. And if that were not enough to earn the ire of his new colleagues, he ensured their antipathy by voting against the emergency measure they sponsored to grant themselves a raise. Lovelace would begin his crusade to champion an anti–predatory lending bill with the activist community at his side as well as the town's main newspaper ("a striking jump in unscrupulous lending," the *Daily News* wrote in a 2000 editorial, "[is] putting more low-income homeowners at increasingly higher risk of losing their homes"), but no solid allies among his fellow commissioners.

Lovelace gave me a funny look when I asked him how his modest-sized city came to occupy so prominent a position in the fight against some of the nation's biggest financial institutions. He had constituents complaining, he said with a shrug, and advocates asking him for help. Anyone doubting that Dayton was experiencing a widespread problem only had to read the reports the Predatory Lending Project was submitting to the county. Its hotline was receiving so many calls that, despite having hired extra staffers to answer the phones, they simply stopped advertising the number. "It got to the point where there was such a backlog that people would have to wait six or eight weeks even to be seen," McCarthy said. "We felt we were doing people a disservice."

Lovelace introduced his bill at the start of 2001, sparking an immediate backlash. In the suburbs a firm called Ohio Mortgage Funding had just set up shop. What critics don't understand, its branch manager told the *Daily News,* is that the people who will be harmed by this legislation are the very people whom subprime's critics are seemingly trying to help. "They're going after predatory lenders," he said, "and all they'll do is make low-income people unable to get loans." The title companies came to the defense of their brethren in the lending business, and even the mainstream banks lined up against Lovelace. "That was one of the big surprises," Lovelace said. As he saw it, the mortgage products the town's established banks were selling were a world apart from the predatory lending he was aiming to stop. To win their support, he agreed to amend his bill so it exempted any bank scoring at least a "satisfactory" on the CRA test used to measure their level of lending in low- and moderate-income neighborhoods. The banking establishment continued to oppose him nonetheless. "We have seven big banks in Dayton," Lovelace said. "I can't say all seven came out against us but most of them did." Only in time did he realize that the corporate parents of most of these banks had subprime affiliates and that their affiliates were the problem.

Lovelace made other compromises. He had originally proposed capping the fees a lender could charge at 3 percent of the loan total but he agreed to raise that to 5 percent. Similarly, he bumped the cap on the permissible interest rate from six percentage points above the going rate on a thirty-year Treasury bill to nine points. Some of its strongest provisions were left intact, though, like its prohibition against prepayment penalties and its ban on any loan with monthly payments that exceed 50 percent of a borrower's income. The measure was unanimously passed into law in the summer of 2001.

Elected officials and others from around the country phoned Lovelace with their congratulations but their praise was premature. Lovelace might have stopped the worst excesses of the subprime mortgage business but his ordinance only applied to Dayton proper, not the suburbs. The poverty industry may have first taken root on the city's west side but they had crossed the river and were spreading into the first-ring suburbs and even to the more rural communities along Interstate 75 on the fringes of the metro area. As its industrial lifeblood continued to drain, Dayton, it seemed, was becoming a subprime city.

Then the American Financial Services Association, a trade association representing the consumer finance companies and other lenders, challenged the bill's legality in court. Instead of taking effect thirty days after its passage, as written, it would remain on hold pending a trial. That would give the industry time to turn its attention to the Ohio state legislature, which had the power to preempt Dayton's ruling.

Eight

An Appetite
for Subprime

Martin Eakes confesses he didn't really know Sandy Weill's name when a congressional staffer called his office asking if he could be in Washington the next day. Weill was a man editors put on the covers of their magazines, but apparently those weren't magazines that Eakes read. Now Citigroup, the company Weill bought and transformed into the world's largest financial titan, had announced it wanted to buy Associates—officially Associates First Capital—for $31 billion. They were holding a press conference the next day. Eakes was livid that a financial giant would lend its brand and its reputation to a company like Associates. Of course he would come.

His hosts the next day were Congressman John LaFalce of Buffalo, then the ranking Democrat on the House Banking Committee, and Senator Paul Sarbanes of Maryland, then the ranking Democrat on the corresponding Senate committee. LaFalce and Sarbanes spoke and then, at least the way Eakes likes to tell the story, the two exchanged alarmed glances as he took his turn at the podium. Eakes casts himself in high dudgeon that day, telling the story of Freddie Rogers, declaring

Associates a moral cancer eating away at the body of American communities. "I was up there saying, 'We can't allow this to continue any
longer, we must stop it and we must stop it now,'" Eakes remembers. "I
went up there with my normal, all-guns-blazing style."

A few weeks later, LaFalce, a fourteen-term member of Congress,
sent a letter to Weill and also to Robert Rubin, the chairman of Citigroup's executive committee and Bill Clinton's former Treasury secretary, expressing his dismay that Citigroup intended to purchase a lender
"that community advocates have for some time placed among the worst
predatory lenders in the country." Congress didn't have the power to
prevent the acquisition but a couple of committee chairs could make
life miserable for a company; toward that end LaFalce named Eakes
as his and Sarbanes's emissary. To drive home the point, LaFalce and
others sent a separate letter urging banking regulators to "closely scruti-
nize" the deal because of some "disturbing allegations." Sanford I. Weill,
tireless and driven, a man of relentless ambitions who had transformed
Citigroup into what the *New York Times Magazine* dubbed "the world's
biggest money machine," would have to deal with the likes of Martin
Eakes.

"Sarbanes and LaFalce basically deputized me," Eakes said. "They
told Weill and Rubin that they had no choice but to deal with this young
punk. They couldn't ignore me even if they wanted to." With charac-
teristic bravado, Eakes announced at his first meeting with Citigroup's
representatives, "You will change these practices. Or we will bring you
to your knees."

Sandy Weill had attained great heights, but that only made his fall
in the spring of 1985 seem that much more spectacular. He had
arrived on Wall Street fresh out of Cornell, his finance degree in hand
and ready to conquer the world, but instead he felt snubbed. A Jew from
Brooklyn, born to Polish immigrants, he felt like an outsider in a world
that favored the blue-bloods and WASPs. He started as a runner on
Wall Street and was quickly promoted to broker, but after a few years

he quit his job to help start a brokerage firm that eventually Weill and his partners sold to American Express for nearly $1 billion in stock. "The Jews are going to take over American Express and they'll never know what hit them," Weill boasted to a friend, according to one of his biographers. But American Express was run by men of lineage. Weill, by contrast, was brilliant and cunning but also plump and ill-mannered. He chewed his nails and wore rumpled suits and propped his scuffed shoes up on the furniture while smoking fat, pungent cigars. He ultimately attained the president's post at American Express, but finding himself on non-native soil, he was out within four years of his arrival. At fifty-two and with a net worth north of $50 million, Weill leased a pricey set of offices in the Seagram Building on Park Avenue, hired a personal assistant, and waited for the phone to ring.

All the well-wishers offering their sympathies kept Weill busy during those first weeks. His wife thought the two of them would travel the world together, but Weill was impatient and hyperactive; he was not a man to ease into the comfortable life of the rich gentleman farmer. The most she got from him was a fortnight in Europe. "The prospects of being away for more than a few weeks from whatever action might arise," wrote Monica Langley, author of the Weill biography *Tearing Down the Walls*, "was more than Sandy could bear." Back in town, he sifted through newspapers and business magazines in search of inspiration. He put out feelers about any number of companies. He played golf and gave generously to Carnegie Hall and other charitable causes if for no other reason, Langley wrote, than to remind the world that he was still here. He made a clumsy public play to take over Bank of America, then a financial giant going through a rough patch, but his bid was rebuffed and then exposed. The "definition of chutzpah," sniffed *Fortune* in an article that appeared under the headline SANFORD WEILL, 53, EXP'D MGR, GD REFS.

Who knows what Weill might have said to the two junior executives traveling to New York to pitch him on a business called the Commercial Credit Corporation, had they visited him shortly after he resigned from American Express rather than one year into his exile. Commercial

Credit was a consumer finance company whose owner, Control Data, the computer maker, had been trying to sell it for at least a couple of years. Weill, in fact, Langley reports, was among those who had passed on a deal while he was still at American Express. But back then he was serving as president of a credit card giant with dreams of one day taking over as chief executive. Now he was a man trying to keep sane in search of a platform that would let him rebuild his empire. And if his vehicle had to be this ailing, grubby competitor to Household Finance, so be it.

The woman Weill had hired as his personal assistant tried to talk him out of Commercial Credit. It's the loan-sharking business, she chided him—and he barked back that she was being a snob. Regular people have the same right to capital as Wall Street rich guys, he told her. He would be like a Walmart or a McDonald's, selling to ordinary Americans. A friend from his American Express days was equally incredulous. Weill had reached the pinnacle of the corporate world and Commercial Credit was a third-rate company with a mangy reputation. It's beneath you, he counseled. But Weill had looked at Commercial Credit's numbers and if nothing else he was a pragmatic businessman. The publicly traded giants like Household and Beneficial were reporting double-digit profits but Commercial Credit's profit margin was 4 percent. Commercial Credit had 600,000 customers and he wondered why it couldn't have 5 million. There seemed a huge upside in operating a business that made small loans at high rates to blue-collar customers, and especially this one, which by Weill's standards had not come close to reaching its potential.

On Wall Street they call it "the spread." In short, it's the difference between what money costs a company to borrow and the rate at which they can loan it out to others. The loan sizes inside Commercial Credit were minuscule by Weill's standards—a thousand dollars plus fees to buy a new dining room set—but they were loaning money at a spectacular interest rate of 18, 20, or as much as 23 percent. If Weill could whip the company's finances into shape and improve Commercial Credit's lousy credit rating, he could further widen that spread. Everywhere Weill looked he seemed to see only upside and so he decided to move to Baltimore to take over a company so sleepy that he had nicknamed it "Rip Van Winkle." By dangling generous stock option packages in front of old friends from Wall Street, he was able to lure more than a few of them to Baltimore to join him.

For years, Commercial Credit had been run by a CEO who had started in the business as a repo man thirty-five years earlier. The company hadn't opened a new branch in years but perhaps more offensive to Weill and the A-team he had assembled was Commercial Credit's compensation system. Bonuses weren't based on performance, as they are on Wall Street, but instead every branch manager throughout the company was given an automatic increase of 5 percent a year. One of Weill's earliest changes was a new bonus system to inspire managers to think more entrepreneurially about the small office under their charge. Those who ran a branch whose performance ranked in the company's top 10 percent would receive double their salary for the year; those whose stores ranked in the bottom tenth would be out of a job.

Among those eager to accept the new boss's challenge was Henry Smith, a Commercial Credit branch manager in Hazard, Kentucky. That's what he told a *BusinessWeek* reporter whom Weill, anxious to show his former compatriots back home that he was still on the hunt, had invited inside the company to profile the turnaround. Commercial Credit peddled a high-priced, potentially dangerous product designed expressly for people living on the economic margins. Yet as Smith described it, the brilliance of Weill's system was that he turned the company's business model on its head: Where once the branch manager and his sales team spent their days deciding whether to extend credit to those who applied for it, they were now aggressively soliciting new business. Smith had lived in Hazard his whole life and his plan, he told *BusinessWeek*, was to tap into his extensive network of families, friends, and acquaintances in search of extra revenues. To save costs, Weill had fired most of the company's human resources department and given the individual branch managers responsibility for hiring, training, and disciplining their staff. That meant one less check on the branch manager operating in the hinterlands, determined to run a top store. To no one's surprise, profits inside Commercial Credit soon reached into the double digits. Eventually, Weill would declare that it was Commercial Credit, more than any other enterprise he had ever owned, that had rendered him a very, very wealthy man.

It didn't take Weill long to expand his focus beyond consumer finance. He had purchased Commercial Credit in the middle of 1986; in 1988, he bought Primerica, the parent company that owned Smith Barney, and in 1992 he snapped up a 27 percent share of Travelers Corporation, the insurance giant. In 1993, he paid $1.2 billion to buy his old brokerage house from American Express, and that same year he bought the remainder of Travelers for $4 billion in stock and changed the name of his company to the Travelers Group. In 1996, he paid $4 billion for the property and casualty division of Aetna Life & Casualty, and in 1997 he traded more than $9 billion in stock for control of Salomon Brothers, another Wall Street giant. Weill's signature deal took place the next year, in 1998, when he brokered a merger between Travelers and Citicorp. That meant tearing down the wall that for seventy years had existed between commercial banking, investment banking, and insurance but Weill and his minions were able to do just that with passage of the Gramm-Leach-Bliley Act.

As the new millennium dawned, Citigroup, a $250 billion behemoth, was being described by the *New York Times* as the most powerful financial institution since the House of Morgan a century earlier and its CEO and chairman was being richly compensated for his efforts. Weill owned tens of millions of shares in Citigroup, and already his net worth was tied to his company's fortunes. But that was the advantage of handpicking your own board of directors and having a close relationship with people on the executive compensation committee. Weill would pay himself $15.5 million in 1999 and then grant himself nearly twice that amount the next year: $1 million in salary, an $18.5 million bonus, and $8.7 million in restricted stock. In short order, he would make the *Forbes* 400 with a net worth of more than $1 billion.

Still, does a Sandy Weill ever lose his appetite for the profits generated by a subprime lender? Years later Weill would declare Commercial

Credit the single best investment he had made during a career marked by smart deals, and it was the bushels of cash Commercial Credit was spinning off, especially in the early years, that allowed Weill to launch his ambitious buying spree. And Commercial Credit continued to be a robust if not minor producer within Citi throughout the 1990s. Under Weill, the company had tripled to 1,200 the number of consumer finance stores under its control by the time it renamed them CitiFinancial in 2000—and each new branch more than pulled its weight on the ledger sheet. Where Commercial Credit was earning about a 2.5 percent return on its assets inside Citigroup, the conventional banking side of things was generating close to a 1 percent return. A year before the proposed Associates deal, Citigroup snapped up the assets of a relatively small failed lender called IMC Mortgage in Tampa, Florida. Sandy Weill was not a man to turn up his nose at a rough-style lender like Associates, not when the company was spinning off $1 billion in profits each year.

CEOs love talking about their "vision." For Weill that was the dream of creating a full-service global supermarket of financial products. That provided Weill with another rationale for pursuing Associates. The very rich could avail themselves of the advice offered in the well-appointed offices of Citigroup's Private Wealth Management. Citi sold any number of products to the country's professional class, including insurance, standard banking, and the brokerage services offered by the hundreds of Shearson and Smith Barney outposts that Citigroup owned. But what about those of modest means who had bounced too many checks in their lives or who didn't carry a credit card?

If Weill was always on the prowl for his next deal, his target in this case, Associates, was a battered company eager to find a suitor. North Carolina had proven a blow to Associates and the bad news only seemed to pile up in the intervening months. Even the *Dallas Morning News*, the hometown newspaper, got into the act, reporting on a leaked memo, "The Roadmap to Continued Record Profits in 1995," that showed that flipping loans wasn't happenstance but company policy. Older loans are far less profitable than new ones, the memo pointed out, so it was crucial to continued success to convince existing customers to refinance. "Your controller can provide lists to you of aged personal loans to target for renewal," the memo suggested. Not surprisingly, the paper found, half of all customers had refinanced with the company and one in four had refinanced with Associates two or more times.

Credit insurance products were another huge source of profits for the company. Sixty percent of all loans included some kind of credit insurance, according to the "Roadmap" memo, but that apparently wasn't a high enough penetration rate. The key to selling more credit insurance, Gary Ayala, a former assistant branch manager at Associates in Tacoma, Washington, said in a deposition, was to never use the word "insurance." Call it a "payment protection plan," his bosses instructed him. Use phraseology like "Just so you know, that includes a payment protection plan if anything happens to you." Anything to make it sound like a policy came automatically with the loan and hide the fact that it could add as much as 20 percent to the amount of principal owed.

Negative news accounts, however, might have been the least of the worries inside Associates as 1999 turned into 2000. The U.S. Justice Department, the Federal Trade Commission (FTC), and the North Carolina attorney general's office were all investigating its lending practices, and the economy, suffering a brief recession following the collapse of the tech bubble, was putting a big dent in its earnings. They were in the mobile home financing business but what had once been a lucrative field had blown up once people realized that the thirty-year loans companies were typically writing were outlasting the trailers themselves. The market was beset by defaults. Even one of the company's great strengths, its place as a top-five lender in Japan, had turned into a weakness by mid-2000, when that country lowered the cap on allowable interest rates from 40 percent a year to 29 percent for the type of loans Associates made, forcing the company to warn its investors that the change would hurt their profits there.

"They were in any number of businesses that basically blew up on them," a Credit Suisse First Boston financial analyst told the *New York Times*. Associates' stock price sagged and Sandy Weill, a bargain hunter with a nose for weakness, pounced.

The first batch of articles reporting Associates' acquisition focused on Weill's deal-making acumen. The financial analysts seemed especially impressed by the deal's potential to spin off huge profits for Citi overseas. Through its various subsidiaries, they pointed out, Citigroup had $77 billion in overseas deposits. What better way for a burgeoning global colossus to put that money to work than loaning money to the working class the world over? Buying Associates meant Citigroup would be the fifth-largest consumer finance provider in Japan, which Weill described as the second-largest market for consumer lending, behind only the United States. "I really think Sandy scored," a money manager named Robert Albertson gushed in a *Times* article announcing the deal. The piece ran on page one, but made only glancing reference to Associates' reputational troubles.

The trade press seemed to know better, though. "If there has ever been a deal that community and consumer activists would want to block," *American Banker* predicted a few days after the announcement, "it is Citigroup Inc.'s planned acquisition of Associates." The article quoted at length a spokesman for Associates who said there was no doubt that "certain groups" would use the merger "to draw attention to their cause." Citigroup, however, had nothing to worry about. "Associates regards predatory lending as an abhorrent practice and is committed at every level to treating customers fairly," said the spokesperson, who was left nameless in the article.

The first time Martin Eakes was set to meet with someone at Citi he thought he was going to have a private session with Chuck Prince, the company's general counsel and chief operating officer, at a Washington, D.C., law firm. But apparently Prince sought to send a message at that first meeting. "It was me and twenty Citibank lawyers," not just Prince, Eakes said. Eakes delivered his change-or-else threat and Prince just leaned back in his chair and with a bemused smile said, "You know, we're not accustomed to having anyone tell us what we have to do."

Their next meeting was held six weeks later in Durham. This time it was Eakes's turn to flex his muscle. Eakes assembled a posse of around fifty activists and community leaders, including Bill Brennan, who had flown from Atlanta for the occasion. They dubbed themselves the Coalition for Responsible Lending, just as they had done during the 1999 North Carolina predatory lender fight. To drive home his point, Eakes had arranged for the testimony of a half dozen homeowners who believed Associates had defrauded them. Those in attendance described Chuck Prince as genuinely moved by what he had heard. He gave the group his fax number and asked them to send him the details of specific cases. He also designated one of the aides who had flown down with him, a top Citigroup lawyer, as his point person in charge of all Associates-related complaints.

"He tells us, 'We're going to fix everything,'" Bill Brennan recalled. "He assures us, 'We're going to straighten this company out.'" Brennan ate up every word Prince said—and then felt like a fool after doing some research. Commercial Credit might have been smaller than Associates but that only meant they had been less successful following more or less the same formula. Gail Kubiniec, for instance, who ran a CitiFinancial branch just outside of Buffalo, sounded like she was reading from Associates' playbook when she told FTC investigators about her secrets for boosting revenues by packing loans with unnecessary insurance policies. "The more gullible the consumer appeared," Kubiniec said, "the more coverage I would try to include in the loan." By "gullible," she explained, she meant the very young or very old, minorities and those who "appeared uneducated, inarticulate." And then there was Prince. For years Chuck Prince had served as the general counsel at Commercial Credit. He had risen to the top of Citigroup in no small part because of the deftness with which he helped Weill take care of political messes like the one he faced with his planned purchase of Associates. "Chuck Prince didn't know what Associates was up to? He was blindsided by all these subprime mortgages? What a joke," Brennan said.

Martin Eakes was similarly disgusted. "Citigroup has stated that they would solve the problems in Associates by bringing Associates up to Citigroup's standards," Eakes told a *New York Times* reporter around the time of the Durham meeting. "But it's not totally clear that Citigroup's standards are any tighter." During the conference call announcing the deal, Weill had told analysts that he thought that Citi could squeeze much more profit per customer once Associates was under his control. "I remember thinking," Eakes said, "More per customer? You need to extract much, much less from every customer."

In 1998, when First Union, then the country's sixth-largest bank, announced it was buying the Money Store, then the nation's third-largest subprime lender, for $2.1 billion, a monthly magazine called *Mortgage Banking* ran a cover story expressing its shock. Bankers, after all, were "the staid elder statesmen of the financial world." The "go-go entrepreneurs of sub-prime" operated "out of nondescript strip malls [and used] veteran sports celebrities as TV spokesmen" (Terry Bradshaw for Associates, Phil Rizzuto for the Money Store). There would be some occasional intermingling between those *Mortgage Banking* dubbed the "odd couple of financial services," as when NationsBank bought Chrysler First and EquiCredit, but then people concluded that NationsBank was a different breed of bank. But it was becoming increasingly plain that NationsBank hadn't been an outlier but instead a trailblazer.

The motivator, of course, was the same thing that had first drawn Sandy Weill to subprime: the spread. At its core, banking is a pretty straightforward business. A bank pays a depositor an interest rate that's not as high as the interest rates a bank charges those who borrow money—and the Money Store was charging its customers as much as 14.95 percent on a home equity loan. "These two sectors of the financial world rarely crossed paths until recently," *Mortgage Banking* reported, "when the profit potential of the sub-prime industry convinced banks this might be a business opportunity." Was it any wonder, then, that a man named Hugh Miller, the president of Delta Funding, a large New York–based subprime lender, boasted, "my phone has been ringing hot and heavy," though his company was under federal investigation. The "profit potential" of players in this "promising sector," the magazine reported, were making such deals "irresistible."

Yet never before had there been a deal of this magnitude, and never before had it involved a player like Citibank. The *Times* may have put Weill's blockbuster announcement on page one because of the flabbergasting price tag—$31 billion for a lender whose name few readers of the *Times* even recognized—but more likely it was because of the star power of Citigroup and its flamboyant CEO and chairman. Under Weill's direction, Citigroup ranked among the most valuable corporations in the world.

There was opportunity for Eakes and his allies in the business press's interest in all things Sandy Weill and Citigroup. Citi offered both a big target and a large stage; the same bright light that shined on this Wall Street giant might also help expose the predatory lending spreading within working-class enclaves across the country and finally make subprime part of the national dialogue. There was also the potential to make an example of Citigroup. If they could force reform on a corporation powerful enough to steamroll its way over one of the key reforms enacted following the 1929 crash, then maybe other lenders would fall into line.

Yet Citigroup's might and its prodigious reach also raised the stakes. Citi had burnished and polished its brand through hundreds of millions of dollars' worth of advertising, building up trust. If the deal with Associates was consummated, Weill and his team would be running nearly two thousand storefronts in forty-eight states, all carrying the

CitiFinancial name. Weill, when announcing the deal, promised the Street that the addition of Associates to his holdings would add at least ten cents a share in additional earnings, or about $500 million. Everything from the stock price to the size of next year's bonuses depended on hitting that number. "The Citi Never Sleeps": Citigroup was large and ravenous, and if the activists were to fail, there might be no stopping the company and its copycats from treading unrestricted through a deregulated landscape in search of new profits.

Bill Brennan remembered the early 1990s when he was fighting NationsBank's purchase of Chrysler First. "[If] there [have] been problems with prior business practices, this acquisition may well be the most effective way to fix them," a spokesman for NationsBank told the *Charlotte Observer*. In Brennan's view, the opposite happened. NationsBank was a scrappy regional player striving to show Wall Street what it could do, and as a consequence, complaints against NationsCredit, Brennan said, had skyrocketed. Over the years he kept hearing the same story. A bank would say it was bringing integrity to the subprime enterprise it had just purchased, but invariably the opposite happened. "The problems always got worse," Brennan said flatly. Citigroup's purchase of Associates seemed destined to turn out the same way. Citigroup was a company carrying too much debt and run by a CEO anxious to demonstrate for the Street that his company, despite its size, was still a top-pick growth stock—a company, in other words, always on the lookout for ways to jack revenues.

Hoping to avoid a generic we'll-bring-them-up-to-our-standards kind of statement, in advance of the Durham meeting the Coalition for Responsible Lending had worked up a list of specific business practices they wanted changed. The boilerplate language of an Associates contract included a prepayment penalty and a provision that waived a person's right to sue in case of a dispute. The activists called on Citigroup to drop the prepayment penalty and the mandatory arbitration clause. They also wanted Citi to cap up-front fees at 3 percent of a loan and to stop the noxious practice of charging borrowers the full price of a credit insurance policy and then financing it as part of the loan. They also said there should be some limit on the interest rates CitiFinancial could charge. Lenders deserved a healthy return on their investment, Eakes and his cohorts acknowledged, but a signature of the subprime market was the unmooring of interest rates from any calculation of risk. "Risk-based pricing," it seemed, had become an excuse for whatever a lender could get away with—demonstrated by the sky-high profits the subprime industry was producing.

But Citigroup had no intention of agreeing to a sweeping set of concessions certain to dampen profits. Instead the company, in a letter addressed to regulators, made some vague promises about better training and an improvement in their compliance review procedures. They promised, too, to review CitiFinancial and Associates loans that had ended in foreclosure during the prior twelve months to see if any should be reversed. They would also disappoint activists on the issue of credit insurance. A study released by HUD and the Treasury Department in the final months of the Clinton administration concluded that the consumer finance companies often employed "unfair, abusive and deceptive" techniques to sell lump-sum credit insurance products that were, more often than not, "unnecessary." Citigroup said it would offer people the option of making monthly payments rather than financing the entire sum at once but it would continue to sell the lump-sum product. Citigroup agreed to cap its up-front fees at 8 percent (the HOEPA trigger) and not 3 percent, as activists wanted, and while it wouldn't drop prepayment penalties altogether, they shortened the penalty period from five years to three years. The company also promised not to target borrowers with a no-interest or low-interest loan written by a government entity or a nonprofit such as Habitat for Humanity, and to at least experiment with the idea of treating people more fairly. One might have thought it was already Citi policy to give a customer the best rate possible given a person's credit history but Citigroup announced it was testing a pilot program called "referring up," whereby CitiFinancial employees would let those with good credit know they could get a conventional loan at a significantly lower interest rate with Citibank.

"Their proposed changes are generally consistent with the stringent policies and procedures that have long been in place at Household," Household Finance said in a statement expressing its support for the Citigroup plan. This was near the end of 2000, just about one year before Tommy and Marcia Myers would step into a Household office just outside Dayton and two years before the company was forced to pay a $484 million fine for its bad loan practices.

Martin Eakes dismissed Citigroup's concessions as "baby steps" on the path to reform and then, in a Q&A in the *New York Times*'s Sunday business section, seemed to be talking directly to the people inside Citigroup's executive offices. "I have been in meetings where black ministers made the statement that this will become the civil rights movement of this decade, the confronting of the systematic destruction of wealth by abusive lenders," Eakes said, turning up the heat considerably. "Will it take street demonstrations? Boycotts? I hope not. But many of us are prepared if necessary to spend the next 15 years battling Citibank."

Eakes might have known how to push all the right buttons inside Citigroup, but in that same article he proved himself an awful prognosticator. Subprime, he said, seemed a "fad" unlikely to gain momentum. "Is it a trend that will be picked up across the banking industry?" Eakes asked himself. "I rather doubt it. I think that Citigroup will find itself somewhat isolated."

Weill, for his part, chose to ignore the activists. He and his staff had met with any number of community groups, Weill wrote in a letter to regulators. They had spoken with elected officials and their representatives. They had listened to everyone's concerns. And he felt satisfied that the company had reached a good balance between its responsibilities to its investors and the communities it served.

More than seventy community lenders and advocates had signed a letter addressed to the FDIC and Office of the Comptroller of the Currency asking the two agencies to hold hearings into the Citigroup-Associates deal. Regulators were limited in the conditions they could impose on a company but by holding hearings and threatening to withhold their approval they can often extract reforms. That's what the Clinton-era Office of the Comptroller did when First Union bought the Money Store. It approved the deal only after First Union pledged that its new subsidiary would not sell subprime loans to borrowers who qualified for conventional financing. In this case, though, representatives from both the FDIC and Office of the Comptroller complimented Citigroup for voluntarily agreeing to change select policies inside Associates. Both agencies declined to hold hearings.

In the end, only the New York State Banking Department held a hearing to review the proposed merger. Dozens of critics spoke against the deal, including Sarah Ludwig, executive director of the New York City–based Neighborhood Economic Development Advocacy Project. For years she had joined others in criticizing Citibank for its lack of branches in low-income and minority neighborhoods. If you allow Citi to buy this high-priced and unscrupulous lender, Ludwig argued, "you're giving Citibank a perverse incentive" to stay away from the communities most in need of traditional banking services. Citigroup claimed that it had significantly increased lending to blacks and Latinos since 1997 but the activists countered with studies of their own, including one that showed that more than 80 percent of the loans Citi had made in the greater New York City area over the prior year had been small, unsecured, high-interest loans of $1,000 or less. Regulators in New York state managed to wrangle from Citigroup several written concessions, including a promise that it would at least temporarily stop selling single-premium credit insurance—but only inside New York's borders.

Activists were disappointed, but Eakes and others told reporters they were not about to quit. With its acquisition of Associates, Citigroup ranked as the country's largest subprime lender. "Look, if Citigroup thinks we're going to go away, they're in for a big surprise," Eakes told the *Raleigh News & Observer*. "We're just getting warmed up." Among other tactics, Eakes and his allies took to inundating Weill with thousands of emails each week and ultimately would try confronting Weill more directly in New York.

Martin Eakes worried that he was spreading himself and his organization too thin. But he also saw himself as having no choice, given the nature of the Citigroup fight, just as he felt he didn't have the option to say no when people asked him and Self-Help to join in the pending battle over the future of the payday advance business in North Carolina.

The Tar Heel State had opened the door to the payday lenders in 1997. "They had a compelling story," said Wib Gulley, Eakes's old law partner, who voted in favor of the original bill authorizing payday lending in North Carolina. "Times were tough here back then. People needed access to credit and payday seemed a reasonable way of offering poor people quick emergency loans." But to make sure they weren't institutionalizing something they didn't fully understand, Gulley and his allies included a sunset provision in the bill. If new enabling legislation were not passed by July 31, 2001, then payday lending would no longer be legal in the state. "Within two or three years," Gulley said, "it was clear we were not getting what we thought we were getting."

Gulley helped enlist Eakes in the anti-payday cause, as did Eakes's old ally from the predator mortgage fight, Peter Skillern. Skillern and his staff had even written a small book about the payday loan industry in North Carolina called *Too Much Month at the End of the Paycheck*. At that point, North Carolina was home to more than one thousand payday stores and, if nothing else, Skillern thought lawmakers should at least have a better understanding of what was going on. The book included interviews with store owners and industry representatives but its emotional heft was in the stories of North Carolinians who went to a payday lender for help but ended up feeling trapped. One woman had borrowed $300 after falling behind in her car payments. She ended up paying $2,000 in fees over a two-year period before she finally caught up. A second borrower said he was paying rates so high it's "pretty much impossible not to get in a cycle there" and a third was quoted as saying, "It's worse than crack." The book wasn't written specifically to engage Martin Eakes in the fight against payday lending but it might as well have been.

"The time wasn't right for us," Eakes said. "But we knew if we didn't take it now, we might never have another chance again." There are a thousand ways to kill a bill, he reasoned, and passing one is always difficult. It was the spring of 2001 and he was barely six months into Associates' fight but Self-Help would add its considerable muscle to prevent the payday lenders from obtaining a majority for the legislation they would need to continue operating legally in the state.

Allan Jones and Billy Webster said they felt blindsided by the North Carolina fight. Maybe so, but then they had only themselves (or at least their government affairs people) to blame and it didn't seem to take them long to recover. There were so many lobbyists running around the state on behalf of the payday lenders, Wib Gulley said, that it was as if each legislator who hadn't yet committed to the payday side had his or her own personal lobbyist—if not more than one. When the first two lobbyists sent to talk with Gulley couldn't convince him to support the payday lenders, they sent a young and attractive woman to see if she could be more persuasive. "I could almost hear them saying, 'Well, we tried the policy approach with Gulley; let's go this other route,'" he said. Gulley described the ensuing political fight as probably the hardest-fought donnybrook he had witnessed in his twelve years serving in the state senate.

Defeating a bill may be easier than passing one, but the payday lenders had collected more than $80 million in fees in North Carolina during the previous year. It wasn't until July 31 came and went without a new bill that the foes of payday could be confident they had won. "We thought we were having a debate over what changes might have to be made in the law," Billy Webster said. Would the legislature give borrowers the right to rescind a loan within twenty-four hours? Would they put restrictions on the steps lenders could take to collect on a bad debt? "But all of a sudden, it was over and we were out," he said. At the time Webster thought the defeat, while significant, was a mere "speed bump," but Allan Jones worried it might be a portent for the future. During the North Carolina battle, Jones said, he first heard the name Martin Eakes. "I learned about who he was and I got nervous," Jones said. "I realized we were up against a zealot."

"To think that a bunch of people who don't know the first thing about business or how we operate just ups one day and says they've changed their minds, 'We're not going to let you do business here any-more, we're going to put all these people out of work,'" Jones said. Was it any wonder, then, that Jones, Webster, the Davis brothers, and several others kept operating in North Carolina even after the enabling legislation expired?

The payday lenders would lose that battle as well—eventually. They tried to talk to the new attorney general, Roy Cooper, but it was their bad luck that he was the former Senate majority leader who had proven so critical to passage of the predatory mortgage bill back in 1999. "He did everything he could," Jones said of Cooper, "to make sure no matter what we tried, we couldn't make a go of it as a business there." Cooper's office sued, as did the state's Division of Banking. Advance America operated for another four years before they were finally ousted from the state, and Check Into Cash, Check 'n Go, and a third company called First American Cash Advance lasted for nearly five years. That trio would pay a collective $700,000 in fines but only after collecting multiple millions in fees in the intervening years.

Defeat in North Carolina had been a bitter pill for the payday lend-ers to swallow, but practically speaking it had not proven much of a setback. North Carolina had been a good market, not a great one, and there was still plenty of room for growth. At that point there were per-haps ten thousand paycheck advance stores in the country and analysts were saying the country could handle more than twice that many. "We probably should have taken [Eakes] more seriously earlier on," Webster said, "but we also were growing our businesses and looking for better ways to compete."

Federal bureaucrats had refused to intervene to stop Citigroup's acquisition of Associates but the lender did not fall off the regulatory radar screens entirely. Eighteen months after Citi was permitted to acquire Associates, the FTC took action. Citigroup might have hoped they could acknowledge Associates' past abuses and quietly pay a modest fine, but the FTC was seeking a settlement in the hundreds of millions of dollars. Citi balked at the cost, negotiations stalled, and the agency filed suit, naming not only Associates in its complaint but also Citigroup and CitiFinancial.

The lawsuit was probably an FTC negotiating tactic. If so, it was a particularly effective one. The *Wall Street Journal* reported the news deep inside its second section but the *Times* reported it on page one, under the headline U.S. SUIT CITES CITIGROUP UNIT ON LOAN DECEIT. It was not the kind of publicity a big bank wanted on the front page of its hometown newspaper. Loan officers for Associates, the FTC charged, routinely employed trickery to lure customers into costly loan refinances, often promising people they would save money by refinancing when the opposite was true. They regularly sold overpriced credit insurance policies, generating an extra $100 million in profits over five years. Customers who objected to an insurance policy, the agency charged, were told that removing it would mean delaying the closing and therefore waiting longer for the check they were typically anxious to receive. The suit also accused Associates of training employees to rush people through a loan closing to minimize questions, and alleged that the company engaged in abusive methods when pursuing delinquent accounts.

"What had made the alleged practices more egregious is that they primarily victimized consumers who were the most vulnerable—hard working homeowners who had to borrow to meet emergency needs and often had no other access to capital," Jodie Bernstein, the director of the

FTC's consumer protection bureau, told the *Times*. The agency's five commissioners—three Democrats and two Republicans—had voted unanimously to file the twenty-six-page complaint, which accused Associates of violating four federal laws.

Citigroup held its annual shareholders meeting one month later. At his behest, a group that owned large positions in Citigroup, including Warren Buffett and Bill Gates, Sr., invited Eakes to present a resolution on their behalf that, if passed, would link Weill's compensation to Citi's record on social responsibility. Eakes flew to New York to confront the CEO directly and see if he might be able to increase the pressure on Citigroup at a time when it might already be reeling from negative press.

The meeting was held in Carnegie Hall. Eakes's first shock was the stagecraft of the day. "Little plebeians like me," Eakes said, lined up in the hall's center aisle, awaiting their turn at the microphone. The theater was dark so that each presenter was a disembodied voice over a PA system. Weill, meanwhile, stood center stage, a spotlight trained on him, "as if he were God himself," Eakes recalled. Eakes refused to be intimidated. Citigroup, he said when his turn came, had "steadfastly refused" to adopt standards of responsible lending. The company had "aggressively opposed" legislative efforts to rein in predatory lenders. And then he turned up the heat on Weill himself. "Any CEO who will cheat his customers," Eakes boomed, "will eventually cheat and lie to his shareholders." Eakes claimed that his remarks won him an ovation from the crowd, but if so, that was about all he got. The resolution was soundly defeated.

It may have been easy to dismiss Eakes or any dissident shareholder. No one usually pays much attention to what goes on at a company's annual meeting, especially back then. But Citigroup was a large consumer company whose caretakers were skittish about more negative press, a fact driven home for Jim McCarthy in Dayton when he lost his temper with a roomful of Citi lawyers while trying to negotiate on behalf of a client he believed had been trapped in a predatory loan.

McCarthy didn't hesitate when I asked him to name those he considered the worst subprime lenders operating in Dayton. "CitiFinancial has to be at or near the top of my list," he blurted. In part that was due to the volume of loans CitiFinancial wrote and the terms of those deals. But McCarthy confessed he felt a special enmity for the New York–based giant in no small part because of the attitude of the Citi lawyers he mixed it up with while attending mediation sessions on behalf of people about to lose a home. "They were so damn arrogant and condescending," McCarthy said. He and his allies were activists and couldn't possibly understand how a business works. "And because we didn't understand, that's why we were asking for these ridiculous things like a reasonable interest rate that might actually let the people stay in their home and continue to pay on a mortgage." Citi would send eight or nine people to every mediation session, McCarthy said, "and then they wouldn't offer a thing."

By that point McCarthy was spending his days listening to old people frightened about losing homes they had owned for thirty years, angry at themselves for making the mistake of walking into the wrong office door. His pent-up frustration and anger boiled over during a meeting on behalf of several CitiFinancial customers. "I'm telling them, 'I'll get in front of the television cameras and just blast you for what you're doing to these people. I'll put them in front of the camera so they can tell everyone what you did to them. I'll bully you in every way we can think of in front of the media.'" McCarthy had no idea whether he could back up any of these threats, but to his amazement, the gambit worked. Citi agreed to write off the loans, essentially letting the three borrowers off the hook. "These were the early days of all this stuff," McCarthy said with a laugh, "so it was still possible to talk about hurting the reputation of one of these lenders."

Citi followed with other concessions aimed at appeasing its critics, including the announcement in June 2001, ten months after its purchase of Associates and six months after the FTC announced its suit, that it was phasing out its single-premium credit insurance product. It would continue to sell credit insurance, Citi said, but it would be sold separately from the mortgage and be paid for with regular premiums through the life of the policy. Perhaps Citigroup was motivated by a sense of moral responsibility but an alternative explanation was that the financial giant wanted to avoid additional criticism. The Democrats had recently taken control of the Senate, and Paul Sarbanes, the new chairman of the Finance Committee, had just announced that he would hold hearings to look deeper into predatory lending.

Another year would pass before Citigroup agreed to pay $215 million to settle its suit with the FTC. At the time it stood as the largest consumer protection settlement in FTC history. Citigroup also agreed to pay up to $20 million to settle an investigation into Associates that Attorney General Roy Cooper of North Carolina initiated shortly after he took office.

Citigroup would set another record in 2004, when the Federal Reserve hit the company with a $70 million penalty—the largest fine the Fed had ever imposed for a consumer lending violation. This wasn't for misdeeds committed by Associates pre-Citigroup but for newer improprieties that dated back to 2001. CitiFinancial, the Fed claimed, was routinely converting personal loans into equity loans secured by a person's home without regard to a borrower's ability to pay. The Fed also charged CitiFinancial with trying to mislead regulators once they started to investigate.

Eakes, meanwhile, had never stopped trying to convince Citigroup to change. In May 2005, five years after Citi announced it was acquiring Associates, Eakes stood at a podium and publicly praised Citigroup. The company had finally agreed to drop a clause from its subprime contracts requiring borrowers to agree to mandatory arbitration. The lender also greatly reduced the penalties it charged for early payment on a loan. "It only took them five years to do the right thing," Eakes said. Goliath had not been killed, but he had also not emerged from the competition unscathed.

Among those noticing Eakes as he fought with Citigroup while simultaneously doing battle against the payday lenders were Herbert and

Marion Sandler, who ran the World Savings Bank, one of the country's largest savings and loans. In 2002, Herb Sandler started phoning Eakes in the hopes that he could convince him to create a national organization to build on the work he had been doing fighting Citi in North Carolina.

The Sandlers were hardly the first to broach the idea, but Eakes always offered the same stock answer when anyone proposed this idea of broadening Self-Help's scope beyond the state's borders. "We'll look at other places," he would say, "when the job has been completed in North Carolina."

Yet the Citigroup fight had forced Eakes onto the national stage, and Self-Help's fight against first the predatory subprime mortgage lenders in North Carolina, and then the payday lenders, had raised its profile to the point where people were expecting them to act like a national advocacy organization. "Basically, we realized we [at Self-Help] were spending all this time on these requests anyway, so why not get some help?" Mark Pearce said. One key turning point, Mike Calhoun said, occurred while he was reading through a predatory lending bill that activists were championing in Alabama. "It copied verbatim our bill, down to the references to North Carolina statutes," Calhoun said.

Still, Herb Sandler needed to phone several times before Eakes finally decided to get serious about launching a national organization. "He's been calling and calling," Calhoun said, "until finally he has to say to Martin, 'I really mean it, I'll provide you some money. So would you goddamn send us a proposal?'" Sandler had looked at others but, to him, "Martin was the only one up to the enormity of the challenge," he said. "He was the only one with the capability and the passion and the strategic ability and the leadership quality to get his arms around a challenge of this size."

Inside Self-Help, they huddled to figure out how much money they might need to start such a group. It was Eakes, Pearce said, who suggested asking for a number large enough to provide an endowment sufficient to remain independent and not constantly fret over raising money and uncertainty about next year. "Are you fucking crazy?"

Sandler cried out over the phone, or something to that effect, when Eakes told him of the tens of millions of dollars he thought he needed to start a national Center for Responsible Lending. Sandler remembered Eakes telling him he wanted an endowment big enough to generate $8 or $9 million per year: a sum well over $100 million. In time, however, it would become clear that money would not be a problem for Herb and Marion Sandler.

Nine

"No Experience Necessary"

DAYTON, 1993–2008

Allan Jones had inherited his father's debt collection business; Jared and David Davis had a wealthy father who served as the chief executive and president of Cincinnati's second-largest bank, a publicly traded corporation. And there were all those executives from Citigroup, First Union, and other financial behemoths who had stooped down to see the riches that could be made operating on the fringes of the economy. They had near-limitless access to whatever capital they might need to move aggressively into a new business.

By contrast, Fesum Ogbazion, who would also find his fortune in the poverty industry, began with nothing. His parents had been born in a tiny farming village in Eritrea, a small country on the northeast tip of Africa sandwiched between the Sudan and Ethiopia. His father had been taught to read and write by Christian missionaries who opened a school in his town in the 1950s. His mother attended school there as well. Back then, Eritrea was under the rule of Ethiopia, a communist-ruled country that didn't have much tolerance for people preaching the gospel. His parents were jailed several times, Ogbazion said, and nearly killed "for being Protestant, for speaking out, for not being happy with Ethiopian rule." Ogbazion was nine years old when the family moved to Florida to join their father, who had gone ahead to study at Hobe Sound Bible College, and then to Ohio, where the senior Ogbazion earned a master's degree at Cincinnati Christian College. His father found work as a pastor at an area church while his mother settled into the role of pastor's wife. They no doubt had a great deal to contribute to their eldest son's moral and spiritual development but they could offer little in the way of working capital.

Allan Jones describes himself as a born entrepreneur. So eager was he to learn the collections business while he was still a teenager that, after his freshman year, he secured a summer job at another collection agency—and sat in his car for three hours on his first day of work, waiting for the office to open. Jones, however, had nothing on Ogbazion, who held two or three jobs through high school. He hawked snacks as a vendor at Riverfront Stadium, where the Reds and Bengals played, and at different times worked the mailroom at two of Cincinnati's larger corporations, CIGNA Insurance and Procter & Gamble. When he was nineteen and still a freshman in college, he wrote in his diary that he felt depressed because he still hadn't started his own business.

"I didn't drink a single beer in college," Ogbazion told me when we met in Dayton. "I was that focused."

I met Ogbazion, whom everyone calls Fez, shortly after the check cashers' convention in Las Vegas. The roster of attendees at the convention—we all received copies in our goodie bags—included a woman representing a Dayton-based company called Instant Tax Service. That sounded promising. H&R Block, Jackson Hewitt, and Liberty Tax Service were the Big Three in next-day tax refunds, a product that generates more than $1 billion in annual revenues, but I thought it might be interesting to talk with a smaller player seeking to strike it rich in this corner of the poverty economy. I wrote her a note proposing that we meet the next time I was in Dayton and she suggested I talk with Ogbazion, whom she described as the company's founder and chief executive. Their offices, she said, were downtown, at the corner of Third and Main.

That made sense. Third and Main is a major transfer point on the Dayton city bus system—an ideal locale for a business catering to the working poor. Spotting the Instant Tax Service sign, I peeked inside. It was a run-down storefront with walls pleading for a new coat of paint. Founder and CEO—the dual titles seemed a bit much. I imagined myself sitting in a banged-up folding chair while Ogbazion sat behind a battered metal desk like one you might find in a county welfare department or a homicide detectives bullpen while outside a large plate-glass window half of Dayton milled about waiting for the 41 crosstown bus.

I began to suspect I was wrong when I found a human-interest article in the *Dayton Daily News* about this émigré from East Africa who had founded one of the city's more successful new businesses. By the time the article appeared in 2004, Ogbazion was running more than one hundred Instant Tax Service storefronts in ten states and crowing about opening a thousand more. The woman from my initial email exchange hadn't flown to Las Vegas to learn more about the business. She was there to woo potential partners interested in opening a franchise. Their come-on seemed particularly effective: "Work just seventeen weeks a year! No prior tax experience necessary! Low start-up costs! Franchise fee deferment!"

It wasn't until the day I was scheduled to meet with Ogbazion, though, that I looked more closely at the address. It was located across the street from the Instant Tax Service storefront I had perused a few days earlier, in one of the town's marquee buildings, a brown granite structure grandly dubbed One Dayton Centre. I took an elevator to the fourteenth floor. The waiting room was richly appointed, with blond wood paneling and handsome wingback chairs. When I was ushered in to see Ogbazion, he gave me a choice between a leather couch or the seat opposite him at the handsome wood desk where he worked.

Instant Tax Service's archetypal customer, Ogbazion said, is the assistant manager at a McDonald's earning $19,000 a year. Yet clearly business was booming. There are well-regarded law firms in town that can't afford the rents at One Dayton Centre but Ogbazion leased the entire fourteenth floor and much of the fifteenth. At thirty-five, he was running a business with 1,200 stores and kiosks scattered across thirty-nine states, ranking it just behind the Big Three in a listing of the largest tax preparation firms in the country. It was an enterprise he built using another element of the fringe economy: the subprime credit card.

I n Silicon Valley, young upstarts generally innovate and the big boys play catch-up. The same can't be said of Ogbazion's business: H&R Block first started offering its customers the "refund anticipation loan" (RAL), more commonly (and not quite accurately) known as the "instant tax refund."

A taxpayer opting for an instant tax refund is not receiving his or her refund any faster than anyone else. What they're receiving is actually a loan arranged by a tax preparer. The collateral is the refund that the IRS typically mails out in two or three weeks after an electronic return is filed. That loan generally comes at a stiff price. Unlike a payday advance, there's little risk that the IRS won't pay a tax refund. Yet, like the payday lenders, the rates vendors charge for RALs, when expressed as an annual percentage rate, are typically in the triple digits, commonly in the 100 to 200 percent range.

The roots of the refund anticipation loan can be traced to the Nixon administration and a welfare reform measure called the earned income tax credit. The idea as conceived was a sound one. Rather than give cash payments to a mother with two children, provide her with a tax credit. It's simpler and cheaper to administer and the incentive is tied to the amount of income that a low-wage parent is able to generate. In 2009, a mother with two children receives a cash refund equal to 40 percent of the first $12,000 or so she earns each year (that figure is closer to $14,000 for a couple); the credits start declining once she starts earning more than $16,420 in a year. A home-care nurse with two kids making $15,000 a year would receive an earned income credit of more than $5,000. An LPN with those same two kids and earning

$22,000 would receive a refund closer to $3,000. This provision of the tax code put an additional $43 billion in the pockets of the poor and working poor in 2008, according to federal data.

"There would be a depression in this country every year if the earned income tax credit wasn't there," Ogbazion said. "It means billions of dollars each year that goes to buy cars, to pay the landlord, to pay the Christmas bills, to buy furniture." And of course that same $42 billion has served as the honey pot allowing Ogbazion and a host of others to grow very wealthy despite the most modest clientele.

"It's a beautiful, beautiful thing that Richard Nixon gave the country," he said.

"We focused on the low-hanging fruit." That's how John Hewitt, one of the early champions of the refund anticipation loan, explained the idea in a newspaper interview. They targeted, he said, "the less affluent people who wanted their money quick." Hewitt, who founded Jackson Hewitt and Liberty, two of the Big Three, recognized a simple truth: People who earn $15,000 or $20,000 a year live in a perpetual state of financial turmoil. They're constantly behind in their bills, put off all but the most essential of purchases, learn to do without. And then once a year they receive a check from the IRS that can be equal to several months' pay. Are they willing to pay one hundred dollars or more on top of tax preparation fees to receive the money tomorrow rather than anxiously watching the mail for two or three weeks? Financial planners might scoff but instant gratification is one of our defining national traits.

Beneficial Finance, one of the giant consumer finance companies, invented the concept of these specialized, tax-time, short-term loans but H&R Block jumped when Beneficial pitched the idea. Starting in the late 1980s, the tax giant became the first tax preparer to offer its customers a "rapid refund" arranged by Beneficial. By 1993, when Ogbazion entered the business, Bank One, based in Chicago and then the country's sixth-largest bank, was also offering these instant gratification loans. It was Bank One, in fact, that agreed to partner with a twenty-year-old sophomore at the University of Cincinnati who wanted into the business.

The entrepreneurial bug bit when Ogbazion was around sixteen years old and working in the Procter & Gamble mailroom. His inspiration was the articles he was reading in *Fortune* and *Forbes* profiling the young titans of technology making mountains of money at an improbably young age. He read about Michael Dell, who had started his computer company in his dorm room, and Bill Gates, who was still at Harvard when he founded Microsoft. "I became obsessed with this idea that I needed to start my business by nineteen or it'd be too late," he said. He was the president of his class in high school and graduated as valedictorian. But unlike Dell or Gates, Ogbazion didn't have a passion for computers or for anything really beyond a desire to become rich. "I knew I wanted to start a business," he said. "I just didn't know what kind of business."

Ogbazion was a senior in high school when he received a letter from H&R Block inviting him to have his taxes done at no charge. He drove to an office in a strip mall near his parents' home, where he was shocked to discover he needed to wait to see a tax preparer. He was still thinking about the packed waiting area days later when a friend mentioned that he too had gone to Block, where he used a nifty new product called the rapid refund. "He tells me, 'You pay a couple of hundred bucks but you get your money in a few days,'" Ogbazion said. "That's when the lightbulb went on. I understood why H&R Block was so packed." H&R Block's offer of free tax services, he realized, was nothing but a clever marketing ploy to sell RALs to people his age. Thinking back, he realized that the woman who had prepared his taxes had tried to sell him one but Ogbazion was that rare high-schooler who actually owed money to the U.S. Treasury. That fall he would enter the freshman class at the University of Cincinnati, living at home and commuting to school each day. He decided to also find an office in a central location large enough to house a tax preparation business.

Ogbazion still has the fax from 1992 that Bank One sent to a Mail Boxes, Etc. near his parents' home, laying out the steps he would need to take to offer customers a refund anticipation loan underwritten by the bank. But he got cold feet that first year and almost postponed his plunge the next year as well. That's when he wrote in his diary that he was depressed. "Bill Gates and Michael Dell had started a company at nineteen and I hadn't," he explained. It never seemed to dawn on him to do any research into the pros and cons of the business, as if starting a business required nothing more than nerve. He was probably right.

Ogbazion tells the story of finding his courage, in a hushed voice, as if sharing a moment of divine fortune. "I can still picture it," he said. "I'm driving along and just happened to look to my left. I think about that sometimes. What if I hadn't happened to look to the left at that moment?" He was driving to school and he noticed a FOR RENT sign in the window of the very office where he had gone to have his taxes done in high school. The landlord told him H&R Block had moved to a larger office a few miles away and it would cost $3,000 to rent the office for six months.

At that point Ogbazion had saved around $10,000. He had a Sears card and a Discover card that combined carried a cash limit of $5,000. He secured another $5,000 through a low-interest student loan. He re-contacted Bank One, where somebody told him he needed to select a software maker from the vendor list the bank provided. He randomly chose a Columbia, South Carolina, company and spoke to someone there. "They tell me, 'You don't need to know anything about the tax business; the software will walk you through everything; you hook up with Bank One and, congratulations, you're in the RAL business,'" Ogbazion said. But he was also risking everything on this one idea. They offered a two-day tax preparation workshop and Ogbazion elected to pay for a trip to South Carolina.

Ogbazion gets dreamy as he describes those first few months he was in the tax refund business. He was carrying a full load at school and overseeing a staff of five or six he was paying $8 an hour apiece. He was a twenty-year-old African-American running his own business, but the only weirdness he felt was the age gap between him and his employees, one of whom was a retiree in his sixties. "The age thing was something

I was much more self-conscious of than race," he said. He named his new business Instant Refund Tax Service.

Ogbazion doubts he would have survived that first year if he hadn't had the good fortune to take the place of an established giant like H&R Block. He stretched a cheap sign inside the store's plate-glass window and distributed some door hangers around the neighborhood but other than that he did nothing to advertise. "I was blessed that six hundred people came back to that spot looking for H&R Block," he said. "If I had located anywhere else I would have been out of business my first year." He was fortunate as well that the great majority of his customers also opted for a quick payout that put extra money in his pocket.

Making it through that first year seems to have emboldened Ogbazion. He knew he would have to advertise and recognized that telling people about his one store would cost nearly as much as telling people about four stores. Ogbazion didn't bother approaching any banks. He knew that he would need to find an alternative funding source.

Once again Ogbazion was fortunate. The credit card industry was also undergoing sweeping changes in the second half of the 1980s, among them the spreading popularity of the subprime credit card. There was no single creator of the subprime credit card (which could be said to have been invented the first time a bank decided to charge some of its customers 19 percent interest instead of 12 percent) but one early innovator and its most avid early champion was Andrew Kahr. An eccentric man with long, stringy hair and a generally antisocial personality, Kahr had earned his Ph.D. from the Massachusetts Institute of Technology when he was twenty years old and spent the next several decades striving to strike it rich. Earlier in his career he had even done some work for Associates, where he created a credit card product aimed at those with a taste for debt. This was in the late 1970s, when around half the people holding a credit card typically carried a debt. That figure was closer to 90 percent for those using Kahr's Associates card.

Most of Kahr's biggest breakthroughs, though, came once he ventured off on his own and started a company called First Deposit (later renamed Providian Financial). Making big money in the credit card business, he understood, meant attracting a customer who was at once comfortable owing a lot of money yet loath to default on that debt. Providian was the first to send out mailers with teaser rates so low that a large portion of those already deep in debt were likely to transfer that debt to them. These customers, Kahr's research showed, weren't price sensitive but instead preoccupied by the minimum payment they needed to make each month. Providian could get away with charging an APR of 23 percent rather than 18 percent because the company more than halved its minimum payment, from 5 percent of the total owed to 2 percent. Under the Providian model, the credit card was little more than a small loan device—and if Kahr's ideal targets weren't the world's safest customers, they were certainly lucrative. In time, others would follow Providian into these treacherous but financially rewarding waters, including now well-known brands such as Capital One and Advanta (bought by JPMorgan Chase in 2001). Ultimately many of the big banks would brave these same frontiers. It was no wonder. Publications such as *American Banker* reported that subprime credit card lenders were posting profit rates two or three times greater than those booked by more risk-averse lenders.

Inside his office, Ogbazion bent down to remove a box from one of his desk drawers. He has a round, pleasant face, thinning hair, and a small mustache. He was wearing jeans, running shoes, and a yellow fleece West Point pullover from his younger brother's alma mater. He repressed a small smile as he removed the box's top and leaned it forward. Inside he had more than one hundred now-defunct credit cards. "I look at this and I wonder what I was thinking," he said. But of course he knew exactly what he was thinking. He wanted four stores and, once he had four, he wanted eight. He would max out one card and then another but there were always more companies eager to extend him another. So he would transfer as much as he could to these new cards, thereby freeing up the old ones for further cash advances. He knew he was playing a dangerous game. "I was paying rates as high as twenty-five, twenty-six, twenty-eight percent," Ogbazion said. A store would typically break even its first year and, if it was in a good locale, start generating profits approaching 50 percent in its second. But Ogbazion was too impatient to continue opening a few at a time. So in 1998, he opened another eighteen locations. "I hit three hundred grand, four hundred grand in credit card debt several times," he confessed.

Ogbazion's company was in its sixth year in 1999 when Jackson Hewitt, the number-two player in the field, contacted Ogbazion about buying the chain. They were offering $2 million. At that point, he was twenty-five years old and operating twenty-six stores around the greater Cincinnati area, a part-time business generating $2.2 million in annual revenues. He had 150 or so tax preparers working for him, and of the 26,000 returns they had prepared that tax season, 20,000—three in every four—included a rapid refund arranged through Bank One. His business had grown bigger faster than he ever imagined and he was reluctant to sell. "It was almost like Bill Gates before Microsoft trying to imagine the computer business being as big as it would be," he said. Sure, Ogbazion was hundreds of thousands of dollars in debt, but could you imagine Bill Gates selling Microsoft only six or seven years after he started it?

In the early days, the challenge was convincing the skeptics that there was a market for a fast tax return. "People often ask why anyone would pay extra money to borrow against a refund," Jeanie Lauer, an H&R Block marketing director, conceded in a newspaper interview appearing shortly after the company started offering this novel new product. "Some people have a certain mindset in which they just want the money now and they don't care if they have to pay an additional fee." But then H&R Block faced something like the opposite problem: the intrusion of countless imitators craving the kind of profits H&R was earning from its RAL customers. None proved more aggressive or more ambitious than John Hewitt.

There's an increasing sameness to working-class neighborhoods in America today, in no small part because of Hewitt. Just as there are commercial signifiers that indicate a person has entered a relatively affluent neighborhood—a Banana Republic, a Pottery Barn, a Barnes & Noble, a Williams-Sonoma, a corner Starbucks—there is a similar geography of poverty that tells visitors they have crossed to the other side of the tracks. The region of the country or the race of a community's inhabitants do not matter so much as its economics. Whether in a rural town, an aging first-ring suburb, or the urban neighborhoods that house a city's low-wage workers, you'll find the same small coterie of big-name poverty businesses. There'll be a check-cashing outlet near a pawnshop near a Rent-A-Center or Aaron's rent-to-own. And invariably one will also find a Jackson Hewitt, the company John Hewitt founded in 1982, or a Liberty Tax Service, the chain Hewitt created after Jackson Hewitt was sold out from under him for nearly $500 million. At the start of 2009, there were 6,600 Jackson Hewitt outposts scattered in working-class communities across the country—a number that dwarfs the combined number of the country's Gap and Banana Republic stores. Liberty Tax Service is only about half as large as Jackson Hewitt yet there are more than twice as many Liberty branches in North America as Barnes & Noble, Williams-Sonoma, and Pottery Barn stores put together.

John Hewitt has always been a man in a hurry. A self-described math whiz ("I was the best I'd ever met," he told one interviewer), he dropped out of college at nineteen to take a job doing taxes at an H&R Block. Less than two years later he was promoted to assistant district manager. He had recently turned thirty and was working as an H&R regional manager when Hewitt, his father, and a small group of other investors bought a six-office company, called Mel Jackson Tax Service, based in Virginia Beach, Virginia, for him to run. His budding chain, which he bought for $375,000 and renamed Jackson Hewitt, was still a pipsqueak when Hewitt boasted about the day he would surpass his old employer, a company then more than one hundred times as big as his own. If anything, Hewitt pushed the rapid refund even more aggressively than Block. Like its rival, Jackson Hewitt partnered with Beneficial and then started pushing its product on television. You can almost see company president Esther Gulyas's head shaking in wonder over the hundreds of people who descended on Jackson Hewitt's Boston offices. "The fee for the refund anticipation loan is high," she conceded in an interview with *American Banker,* "[but] customers always take that option."

Block had introduced the anticipation loan to the tax world but Jackson Hewitt used the product to build a small empire. For Hewitt and his cohorts, the RAL wasn't just a way to boost revenues, it was also the linchpin of its growth strategy. Where the venerable Block operated offices in a mix of neighborhoods, Jackson Hewitt focused almost exclusively on less affluent areas. In 1989, the company cut a deal with Montgomery Ward to open mini-offices inside its department stores; a few years later, it signed a similar deal with Walmart. It even experimented with tax desks inside a pair of national mailbox chains. When in 1997 the company turned to Wall Street for additional capital to speed its expansion, it released a prospectus documenting the details of its operations. Four in every five Jackson Hewitt customers, the company reported, earned under $30,000 and well over half of its customers chose its "instant refund" program. Those participating, the prospectus revealed, paid a $24 application fee, a $25 "document processing fee," a $2 electronic filing fee, plus 4 percent of the refund. Someone who wanted her $2,000 in one or two or three days rather than waiting two or three weeks would pay $131 for the privilege. When Jackson Hewitt started peddling the refund loans, the company was operating fifty offices in just three states. Five years later, John Hewitt was boasting of nine hundred offices in thirty-seven states.

Still, the refund anticipation loan has never been Jackson Hewitt's main source of revenue. Nor has it ever been Ogbazion's. Jackson Hewitt's prospectus showed that its RALs accounted for around 30 percent of the $31 million in revenues it collected in 1997. But the RAL is also the primary reason these stores exist, if not the only reason. "Obviously that's why people come to us: because we can get them their money quickly, usually within twenty-four hours," Ogbazion said. The RAL brings people in the door but it's the $300 or so the chains typically charge a customer to prepare their taxes that account for the lion's share of revenues. Still, the fees harvested from these short-term, tax-time loans are pure profit. The good news for Instant Tax Service,

Ogbazion says, is that 80 percent of the people who have their taxes done at one of his stores end up taking out a tax loan. Competitors like Jackson Hewitt and Liberty, he said, post similar numbers in the 70 to 80 percent range. "The instant refund is the key to our business model," Ogbazion said. "Just like it's been the key to the success of Jackson Hewitt and Liberty." Avoid neighborhoods with a large concentration of higher-income individuals, the company's 2008 franchise manual counsels, because those people tend either to hire professional tax preparers or use a software program to do it themselves. "We recommend that you locate your office where the household income is $30,000 or less," the manual advises.

Instant Tax was John Hewitt's kind of company and he met with Ogbazion when his young counterpart neared fifteen stores. But Hewitt would be pushed out of his eponymous company in 1996, several years before Jackson Hewitt would again approach Ogbazion. Hewitt wasn't ready to sell but his investors were and so he was pushed out. (The Cendant Corporation, a conglomerate that already owned Avis, Century 21, and several hotel chains, including Ramada and Days Inn, paid $483 million for Jackson Hewitt at the start of 1998. That translated into a return of $400,000 for every $1,000 invested, Hewitt said.) Hewitt thought about a business that specialized in cleaning carpets; he talked wistfully with a reporter about his desire to spend time feeding the hungry. But a year after leaving Jackson Hewitt, he founded Liberty, which Hewitt is always sure to describe as the "fastest growing retail tax preparation company in the industry's history."

Our goal, he told me, "is nothing short of being the biggest tax service in the universe." Hewitt's successors at Jackson Hewitt seemed no less intent on growth than he was—maybe more so given the steep price Cendant had paid. Jackson Hewitt needed to "find ways of attacking entire metropolitan areas," Keith Alessi, the company's CEO, said shortly after its sale to Cendant. In 1999, that meant knocking on the door of a twenty-five-year-old who owned more than two dozen stores in working-class communities scattered around the great Cincinnati metro area. Ogbazion declined $2 million but couldn't resist when

Jackson Hewitt upped its offer to $3 million. Saying yes meant wiping out several hundred thousand dollars in credit card debt and still walking away with nearly $2 million in the bank after taxes.

After the sale, Ogbazion applied to Harvard Business School and was surprised to be denied admission, despite his success and his grades. He hadn't applied to any other schools and, not knowing what else to do with himself, he decided to get back into the tax game. The terms of his contract prohibited him from opening new stores within ten miles of Cincinnati, so he moved to Dayton, which allowed him to avoid any legal troubles but remain close enough so that he was only an hour's drive from his family. He thought about buying a house but concluded that any money committed to a down payment was cash he wouldn't have to open stores. He opened the first Instant Tax Service office in 2001.

It was much harder this time than it had been in Cincinnati seven years earlier. All the best spots in Dayton had been taken and so Ogbazion needed to focus on the less obvious ones. He opened the downtown store but otherwise focused on white working-class neighborhoods and the area's less prosperous suburbs. Instant Tax Service was up to seven hundred storefronts by the time of my visit but Ogbazion had opened only seven in the Dayton area. With the exception of the downtown locale, all are in white working-class neighborhoods; several are located fifteen or more miles from downtown. "I moved to where opportunities were still available," Ogbazion said with a shrug. He owned some stores himself, and he co-owned stores with friends and relatives he set up in the business (a cousin in D.C., a buddy who moved to Chicago, a friend living in Indianapolis eager to get in on the business), but mainly he has grown through franchise agreements.

"These are people who have less than $50,000 in the bank and they want to get into business," Ogbazion says of his franchisees. "They know a Subway franchise costs a quarter of a million dollars. They know a McDonald's costs $1 million." He requires a $14,000 down payment on the $34,000 he charges as a franchise fee; leasing and outfitting an office and hiring a part-time staff requires roughly another $10,000. All told, he has sold Instant Tax Service franchises to three hundred people. The average age of a new franchisee is thirty-six and more than a quarter are from Ethiopia or Eritrea. "What would you do with a nine-month vacation?" the company asks in an ad campaign it ran in *Franchise Times*, among other publications. In theory his is a business where you work your tail off for three or four months and then have most of the rest of the year off. But Ogbazion admits that plenty of people within his franchise family still work second jobs to make ends meet. "The money isn't as great as sometimes our critics make out," he says. Unless, of course, you're collecting a 20 percent share of the gross revenues every year from hundreds of Instant Tax stores around the country.

Tax preparers who cater to the professional classes typically don't start feeling around-the-clock stressed-out until late February or March. In Ogbazion's world, the tax season starts in mid-January. By mid-February, when many in the middle and upper classes are only starting to think about their taxes, Ogbazion has filled out more than 80 percent of his client's tax returns. "People basically start bombarding us with calls at the end of December," Ogbazion said. "Can I do my taxes with my pay stubs? Do I have to wait for the W-2? It's nuts. Basically come the first of the year, people want their money."

Or sooner. In 2006, Jackson Hewitt started offering something it called the pay-stub loan. These are loans made in December based on the promise of next year's refunds after an examination of a person's pay stubs. "It was a bad idea," John Hewitt said, but the paystub loans were proving popular with Jackson Hewitt's customers and he felt he has no choice but to follow suit. "Jackson Hewitt had a one-year monopoly on paystub loans but the next year the banks let us and Block and the mom and pops do it." The consumer advocates were apoplectic about this new product costing the working poor even more money, but it was a moot point. "The banks lost tens of millions of dollars doing these things," Hewitt said. "They all basically said, 'Never again.'"

There have been other controversies. Mainly the authorities have been concerned with nomenclature rather than the nature of these loans. Over the years the attorneys general in several states, including California and New York, have rebuked the tax preparers over the language they use to advertise the service. "You can't say you'll get your refund back in a day or two," Ogbazion said. "They're very big on that: 'It's not a refund; it's a loan.'" These cases have cost the Big Three millions in fines as they've stretched the boundaries of what's permissible but Ogbazion finds the whole thing ridiculous. "Our customers know exactly what's going on," he said. "They know it's a loan." To him the authorities fine them over wording because they can't do anything about what really troubles them, which is that his customers choose to use his product. Over the years, Ogbazion watches H&R Block and learns from them. "We basically follow their lead," he says.

Ogbazion also has little use for critics of the refund anticipation loan. In their study of the 2006 tax season, the product's two most prominent critics, Chi Chi Wu at the National Consumer Law Center and Jean Ann Fox at the Consumer Federation of America, found that more than 12 million Americans spent a collective $1.24 billion in interest and fees because they were either too desperate or too impatient to wait a few weeks for their refunds. The study went on to advocate a "RAL Reform Agenda" that called for greater regulation of commercial tax preparers, better funding for free tax preparation programs—and a ban on tax loans made against the earned income tax credit.

Ogbazion didn't know the names of either woman but he thinks he knows the type. "They look at our customers and say, 'Why don't they just borrow the money from an uncle?' 'Why don't they just wait two or three weeks?'" he said. "But they don't get it. These are people who can't wait. Gas and electric is off at home. They're facing an eviction notice. They've been putting off all these bills."

Another thing they don't appreciate, Ogbazion said: He's more than just an emergency banker to the working poor. As he views it, he's a positive force for economic development in communities desperate for commerce. Instant Tax provides part-time jobs for six thousand people. He occupies storefronts that would otherwise be dark. "Look at where our stores are," he said. "There's no Gap. There's no Nordstroms. We employ people from the neighborhood. We're paying rents in those neighborhoods.

"People want to close us down," he continued, "but that would mean more boarded-up businesses and more boarded-up homes." When I mentioned that I had peeked into his store across the street, Ogbazion flinched. The place, he said, was in dire need of an overhaul. He tapped on his keyboard and then swiveled around his computer screen. He wanted me to see pictures of stores that had recently had a makeover. There were shops with wood floors and ficus trees and handsome hardwood desks and stylish couches—the sort of environment you'd happily visit again next year if necessary.

"Basically our deal is we tell our customers we know a bank that is willing to loan them money on their refund when no one else will do it," he said. "And if we can make them feel a little better about the experience, then I think that's a good thing." Ogbazion said he hoped to add one hundred new locations during 2009. Hard economic times would make it more difficult for potential franchisees to raise the start-up capital but low-cost storefronts, especially in the hard-pressed communities in which his industry flourishes, would no doubt be plentiful, and people desperate for money only increases the demand for rapid refunds.

Ogbazion initially deflected questions about the interest rates the banks that underwrite his refund anticipation loans charge his customers. "What's the fair rate to charge?" he asked me. "We don't really care what that is. We get our tax preparation fees and we get a little more if they want an instant refund." When pressed, he defended his partners. "They've burned the banks," he said of his customers. "They've bounced too many checks. They've mismanaged their finances. Their credit is poor." Still, the rates the banks charged seemed excessive given the risks. People owe money for back taxes or for child support but the banks tell Ogbazion that they default on maybe one in every one hundred customers. Yet Wu and Fox found that banks charge an APR between 83 percent and 194 percent for a RAL. JPMorgan Chase would boast that it had lowered its RAL rate, but, including fees, the APR on a RAL still worked out to more than 60 percent on the average sized return.

Ogbazion didn't know the names Wu and Fox before I sat down in his office, but he wants to argue with them. "Sometimes when I hear people like that putting the industry down, it really bugs me," he said. "It's not like me or any of these franchisees would be the people who would climb through the ladder at a Big Four firm even if we were to become CPAs. You go with the hand that you're dealt and you make the best of it." Looking out the window of his fourteenth-floor office, he asked, "What else was I supposed to do?"

Ten

Same Old Faces

MANSFIELD, OHIO, 1997–2007

An agitated Jared Davis paced the top floor of the prosperous looking offices he and his brother built for themselves a few years back
on a glitzy edge of Cincinnati. The 1,300 or so Check 'n Go payday
loan stores they operated then, at the end of 2008, may share strip mall
space with low-rent cousins such as Rent-A-Center and Jackson Hewitt
but the bosses work down the street from a Nordstrom, a Restoration
Hardware, and other establishments that suggest that the poverty industry is far away. With slate floors and the sleek modern furniture in
the conference room where we met, the Davis brothers seemed to have
spared little expense in the building of what rival Allan Jones described
as a "fancy monument."

Jared Davis is a large man standing around six feet, five inches tall
with a pear-shaped body and a big lump of flesh under his chin. The
day I visited he was wearing a salmon-colored dress shirt open at least
one button beyond modesty. His hair was unkempt and his face was
covered with stubble. A "big old goofy-looking dude who always needs a
shave" is the way Allan Jones described him. Jones then blinked one of

his eyes rapidly as if sending a Morse code message. By that time I had
met Davis and knew Jones was doing a crass imitation of his competitor.
During our time together Davis was a bundle of movement. He pulled
on the leaves of a nearby plant; he kept jumping out of his seat as if the
point he was making got him so worked up that he physically needed to
move. But mainly what one couldn't help notice was the uncontrollable
tic that caused one of his eyes to blink spastically. Davis later referred
to it as his Tourette's. The more voluble he grew, the more vigorously
he blinked.

I was in Cincinnati primarily to talk about the early days of payday
lending and a specific store that Check 'n Go has operated in Mansfield,
Ohio, since 1997. Davis, however, was spoiling for an argument with all
those who question the way he and his brother make their money. In
the old days, Davis said, the town druggist or Walt over at the general
store would let you run a tab when money was tight. "What used to
happen, if you needed eggs or milk, the basics, the local grocers let you
buy it on credit," Davis said, pacing back and forth. Try that today at
your local Kroger, he said, throwing his hands into the air, "and they'll
throw you out of the store." That's where the payday lenders come in.
But try explaining this to a media hopelessly biased against you and
with frauds like Martin Eakes donning a cape as if Supermen. "Anyone
with half a brain," he said, "can see that the reason Self-Help and Eakes
are against us is because they're our direct competitor."

Eventually Davis began talking about the early days of payday when
the country seemed one giant opportunity to explore and conquer. He
lost his share of races, like the time he thought he had found a choice
storefront in the center of one modest-sized town in Kentucky and then
learned from the real estate agent on the property that Check Into
Cash had gotten there a few hours before him. But he lucked out in
Mansfield, a small city of fifty thousand in an otherwise rural stretch of
Ohio that had no doubt been a happier place before its largest employer,
Westinghouse, shut its plant, as did Tappan and a depressingly long list
of other manufacturers.

"You wanted to be the first or second chain to discover some new town because once those two or three good spaces were taken, the game was over," Davis told me. Billy Webster had beaten them to Mansfield but the Davis brothers were second and they leased the perfect spot, a storefront just off the main highway into town. There, next to a Mr. Hero sandwich shop, they installed a woman named Chris Browning to open and manage their fifth store in Ohio and around the seventieth overall. Browning, who had spent the previous fourteen years working collections for various car dealers around town, was a minor payday miracle. The turnover rate among store managers at the big chains exceeds 50 percent a year yet Browning lasted for more than ten years before being fired in the middle of 2007.

Chris Browning knows she can be difficult. But what are you going to do when you're surrounded by idiots and fools? "To me what's right is right, what's wrong is wrong, and why mince words?" she told me in a voice just a little too loud. "I'm pretty straightforward, bold, and vocal. I tell it like it is."

Inside Check 'n Go, Browning's direct supervisors didn't always appreciate her brassy demeanor. "Chris has a management style that is extremely hard to supervise," the regional manager assigned her area wrote of her early in her tenure. "She constantly berates her direct superiors and shows little confidence in corporate personnel. Chris has a tendency to feel everyone is against her." But there was no denying she was very good at what she did. A well-run store in a choice location back then might bring in $150,000 or $170,000 in fees each year; a strong store maybe $200,000. Browning, managing a store in a remote outpost two hours from the nearest big city, generated $247,000 in fees her first full year on the job and $251,000 in her second. "I wish I had eight of Chris," the same manager wrote, running the eight stores under his control.

"As long as she continues to put up the numbers," he added, "I will continue to work towards a better understanding between us."

Browning is a short, stout woman who lives in a small ranch house surrounded by soybean and wheat fields. She and her husband chose a home in so remote a location thirty miles from Mansfield, she said in a scratchy smoker's voice, because they wanted to insulate the kids from "a town gone to hell in a hand basket." She was a few months shy of her sixty-second birthday when we met in the fall of 2008. She greeted me at the door wearing a red Ohio State Buckeyes sweatshirt and jeans. She wore her hair in a short gray bob and when she smiled I noticed she was missing a front tooth. Within minutes of my entering her home, she was practically yelling. It was more than a year since she had been pushed out but she was still smarting from the way she had been treated.

"They fired me because eventually their policy became, if a body walks in the door, you loan 'em money, and I wouldn't do that," Browning said. That's no doubt too facile an explanation, but sitting behind her counter every day, staring out a plate-glass window onto a street populated by the Big Lots, Subways, and Wendy's that litter the edges of any city, Browning had a perfect perch for watching the rapid rise of a new industry and its impact on the people of the community. Increasingly she found she didn't like what she was seeing. And as her attitude toward payday soured and the competition grew more heated, Check 'n Go decided it had little use for a store manager with the fighting spirit of a longshoreman posting only average numbers.

The Ohio legislature said no the first time they were asked to legalize payday lending within the state's borders. But then the Ohio House of Representatives switched from Democratic to Republican control in 1994 and the enabling legislation, championed by the state's check cashers' association, passed at the end of 1995, without anyone really noticing. "It really flew below the radar," said Bob Lambert, who was a lobbyist for the state's pawnbrokers, a group already in the small-denomination loan business. As Lambert remembered it, he was the only person to testify against the measure.

Around one year later Chris Browning spotted the classified ad

Check 'n Go ran in the local paper for a branch manager of the new store they would be opening in town. Branch manager: She liked the sound of that title. The starting salary was lousy, only $21,000 a year, and the benefits mediocre (three vacation days that first year), but they also told her she could earn as much as $6,000 more a year in bonuses. She didn't know what a payday loan might be when she first saw the ad but once it was explained to her it made immediate sense. Her husband had worked as a welder who more than once had been laid off. In time, Browning confessed, they would use a payday loan to help make ends meet.

"There was a need for something like this for working people around here," Browning said. "The credit unions weren't licensed to make small, short-term loans. The smaller finance companies were closing up and getting out of Dodge."

Browning straightened her back proudly and peacocked a bit while talking about her early days with Check 'n Go, when she was something of a star inside the company. A typical store could take six or more months to break even but hers was profitable after just two. She told me about the calls from David Davis to tell her what a good job she was doing and to ask her for ideas. She helped develop some of the early training materials the company used and they were always imposing on her to help them train a new manager for some other store. She kept her bad debt low and her numbers continued to grow; her employee reviews show that her hard work was paying off in a robust bonus every quarter.

She was the dutiful employee in those first years she worked for Check 'n Go. She left flyers for the store at all the local Laundromats and car repair shops and though she hated doing it, she also tried dropping them off at medical offices around town as well. "Doctors were real touchy about brochures," she said, but at least a few succumbed. "You'd get a new kid on the block," Browning said. "His receivables are up; he wants his money for treating John Doe's son"—and soon that doctor's office starts sending patients and their families to her store. "If somebody couldn't pay the deductible or the co-pay or whatever, the clerk says, 'Here's a brochure, these people might be willing to help you out.'"

More payday outlets opened up in Mansfield. Where there had been five stores in town in 1999, there would be twelve by 2001. The battle was no longer a race to see who could secure a prime location but a war of dueling rewards programs and rival marketing campaigns. By 2000, she was no longer clearing $250,000 in fees per year, but revenue was in the $210,000 to $220,000 range through 2003, and it edged back up to $235,000 in 2004, by which time there were twenty payday loan stores in town. Maybe that was the truly shocking thing about payday and also the tragedy: Rivals could keep opening new stores but revenues at the existing establishments would remain fairly steady.

Ultimately, this modest-sized working class enclave would become home to twenty-seven shops offering payday advances. It fell on people like Browning to keep people coming in the door. And as the pressures increased to collect more revenues from loyal clients and as corporate hounded her and the other managers to find new customers to replace the old ones whom they would invariably lose, so did Browning's cynicism about the service she was supposedly offering. It didn't help that whereas once hers had been the only store in her stretch of Mansfield, by 2006 three competitors had opened outlets only steps from her own.

There was something claustrophobic about those hours I spent in a home overstuffed with Beanie Babies and other collectables. There were so many lighthouses scattered about Browning's home—lighthouses of wood, lighthouses carved out of stone, lighthouse clocks, lighthouse paintings, a lighthouse thermometer—that I couldn't imagine a safer place to navigate a ship at night. The breakfast nook where we sat was piled high with bills, magazines, and other daily detritus; a shelf stuffed with assorted dolls loomed. But the good news was that this same tendency to save spilled over to her job. She had detailed records showing how her store performed month by month for her entire tenure at Check 'n Go, including a running tally of the proportion of her loans falling into default each month and the number of customers she was serving. She kept copies of her employee reviews and copies of emails and other missives from corporate. I might have suspected hyperbole if she didn't have a copy of the actual Check 'n Go directive informing store managers that they were to loan "to anyone getting social security who had at least one dime to their name."

Check 'n Go printed cards offering regulars a $20 discount for every new customer they brought in. The other big chains did the same. "Now, remember," Browning said in a deep voice, in imitation of one of her manager's, "give two referral cards every time you make a loan." She reverted to her own voice: "The idea was that we could get you to convince your mother, your cousin, your next-door neighbor, your best friend to come to our place." To extend their reach, the home office instructed that they leave brochures in factory break rooms and in the mailrooms of apartment complexes around town. The company had brochures printed in Spanish. "Grow your fan base by using the Hispanic marketing materials," read one missive from corporate. Another encouraged store managers to treat even phone calls from people asking for an address or the store's hours as an opportunity to sell. "Don't simply answer these questions," a memo advised. "Find a way to make them your customer!"

But of course new customers wouldn't do the company much good unless they were converted into semi-regulars. So Check 'n Go programmed its computers to spit out lists of customers who had gone sixty days without taking out a new loan. "We got one of those reports every single morning," Browning said. "We were supposed to call every person on that list and then also send them a letter. And that person kept showing up on your reports until they came back in." Management taught her little tricks. "You were supposed to say, 'I notice you haven't been here in two months; why don't you stop by later, we'll update your information. I'm sure you can use some extra money right now.'" And to keep Browning and her cohorts motivated, corporate offered both a carrot and a stick. Store managers would receive an extra bonus if enough of their sixty-day borrowers returned each quarter—or would get grief if their "customer reactivation rate" was too low. Mainly Browning got grief.

"As far as I was personally concerned, we were being told to harass these people until they walked back in the door," she said.

Another order that she found even more noxious was the practice of up-selling a loan. Check 'n Go, like most payday lenders, allows people to borrow up to one week's salary. Up-selling was aimed at a customer who earned enough to borrow $500 at a time but borrowed less than that. "I was to repeat, no less than three times, 'Now, are you sure you don't want to borrow $500 before I print this contract?'" Browning said. While she was printing the contract, she might say, "You know I can void this out; are you sure you don't want that extra money?" Reviewing the contract offered one more opportunity to make her pitch. On the final page of the agreement it laid it out in black and white: We have offered you $500 but you are taking a lesser amount. And Browning would say, "Now you see, you qualify for $500; are you sure this $200 is going to be enough money?"

Collections was its own torture. "If a customer was late paying us back, we were to contact that customer a minimum of three times a day," Browning said. People give three references when taking out a loan and she was instructed to phone them as well. If they were still late in paying off the loan, she was to phone their place of work. "It was no holds barred," she said. "You were supposed to do whatever you need to do to get the company's money back."

At least the home office didn't force her to make what some of her rivals referred to as "field calls"—visiting people at home. "If they weren't there," Browning said, "they'd have to put on a door hanger that says, 'You owe us $575, you need to contact our office immediately,' or whatever, and then it's there for everybody who comes to the door to see. I had customers tell me they even had people knock on their next-door neighbor's door to ask what time they'd be home. The idea was to embarrass them into paying any way they could."

Through her large plate-glass window, Browning could see the Advance America outpost that had opened directly across the street in

2006. Cashland had leased a storefront a few doors down from her own in 2003 and a fourth store called Quik Cash opened in 2005. And so Browning would amuse herself during idle moments watching people play a kind of human pinball between shops.

Her store could boast the biggest parking lot so generally people made her shop their first stop. "They'd borrow money from me and walk straight from my door across the street to the Advance America," she said. "I don't know what they did in there, whether they were paying back or borrowing more, but then I'd watch them walk to the next store and then finish up by walking across the street to Cashland. Then they'd walk back up to my place to get their car." The whole sequence usually played itself out in forty-five minutes or less.

Browning would see the occasional new face inside her store, but she spent most of each day loaning money to the same core of customers. Browning is a talker and inevitably many of these people became friends. They would bring her leftover slices of birthday cake; they would surprise her with cupcakes they had baked. One couple popped in one day for no other reason than to drop off a few apples from the bushel they had bought at a roadside stand out on the highway. Is it any wonder, Browning asked, that with time she saw her job as less about earning quarterly bonuses and more about getting a good night's sleep so she could survive another day?

"The whole thing came to be about money and greed," she said.

Maybe a bartender has the same feeling when the glum-faced man who every once in a while used to sneak in for a mid-afternoon snort starts showing up at 11 A.M. for his first nip and eventually is stopping by every day before work. After a time Browning took to applying a kind of shock therapy to her regulars. She would lecture them about the high cost of a payday loan. Stop buying that six-pack of beer, she would order them. Stop going out to eat. And then to punctuate her point she would swivel her computer monitor around. On the screen there was a tally of all the fees they had paid the company over the years.

Browning tried the gambit on a woman named Susan and it worked exactly as she had hoped it would. Susan, an administrator at the local hospital, had been borrowing the same $500 every two or three weeks for almost two years. That $500 was costing around $1,500 a year in fees. "I thought I was going to have to pick her up off the floor," Browning said. Worse, the woman was borrowing money from other stores. At Browning's suggestion she borrowed $450 instead of the usual $500, and tried to borrow $50 less each successive time. The last time Browning ever saw her was when she came in to pay back the $150 she owed plus the $22.50 fee.

But far more common were customers like David, a GM pensioner who was as reliable as the morning mail. Each month began the same way, Browning said, with David standing outside her door, two cups of coffee in hand. "If it was the first of the month," Browning said, "I knew I could count on a McDonald's coffee." David, she said, received a monthly pension of around $2,600 plus another $1,800 or so from Social Security—more than $50,000 a year. His house was paid for. But he was an inveterate gambler and always broke. Every month he would borrow the $500 maximum—and then $800 starting in 2005, after the legislature increased the ceiling on a payday loan. It had been costing him $900 a year in fees to borrow $500 a month and then $1,400 a year once he was able to borrow $800.

Browning would plead with him to borrow less. "We really need to get you out of this," she would tell him. It was too late, though. He owed money to stores all around town. When Browning ran into him at the local Walmart in the fall of 2007, a few months after she was fired, he confessed to her that he was juggling loans at seven stores. She figured that in the ten years and three months she served as a manager with Check 'n Go, David had paid $9,150 in fees on 115 loans. That, of course, didn't count the tens of thousands of dollars he was paying to other stores. And he was hardly alone. Browning said she did the math. In the final two years she ran her store, six in every ten people she would see in a given week were customers she saw at least once a month.

She fantasized about quitting. The job was affecting her sleep and making her irritable. "No one in my family was happy with me," Browning said. "I was tense. I was upset. I was depressed. I had fifty thousand different kinds of emotions I did not like." It seemed so tempting when the managers at rival stores were always quitting. "I know of a few who just got up and walked out the door," she said. "They'd wait for their supervisor to make a visit and then literally say, 'That's it, I'm done.'"

But Browning was pushing sixty and by that time was earning a base salary of around $30,000 a year. Neither she nor her husband had saved enough for either of them to stop working, and no one was dangling jobs that would pay her that much money. The plan was to put in a few more years and retire.

Still, she was hardly acting like an employee eager to stick around. When a manager from the next region over, a guy named Maurice, began a conversation by saying, "Here's what I need you to do for me, Chris," she couldn't help herself. "I said—and this is word for word—'What I need you to do, Maurice,' I says, 'I need you to go downtown in front of the courthouse. I'll meet you there so I can shove my foot up your ass.'" When I asked her why she would have spoken to a boss like that, she looked at me incredulously. The words practically exploded out of her mouth: "Because he was an idiot!" Only later did she explain to me her real reason for getting angry. Maurice, she said, was phoning to tell her she needed to do a better job recruiting back old customers. "Every morning I'd get a printout listing out all the people who hadn't been in the store in at least twenty-four months," she said. "These are ones who managed to get out of the cycle. And I'm supposed to sit there late every night on the phone, bothering them at home? They know where to find me if they need me."

One day, she spotted three young black men lurking outside her store (roughly 20 percent of Mansfield's population is African-American). Fearing she was about to be robbed, she hid a couple of thousand dollars in cash in a filing cabinet. It turned out to be a false alarm, but, unfortunately, her immediate supervisor chose that hour or two when she was feeling paranoid to make a surprise visit. Finding that she had socked away around $2,000 in a filing cabinet, she was fired. She is now suing Check 'n Go for wrongful termination.

Jared Davis went off when I mentioned Browning's name. How good a manager could she really have been if she was lending out money to people owing money to all these other stores? That made a person a greater credit risk—and you weren't doing that person any favors in the long run. "If we abuse a customer, is that customer coming back?" he asked in a pleading tone. "Come on." He shook his head as if to ask how anyone could believe such nonsense as Browning put forward.

Davis denied that it was Check 'n Go policy to up-sell customers ("If you're asking me did it ever happen—I'm not saying there's not some employees out there who've never done something wrong") but he readily admitted to its practice of contacting those who have not visited one of their stores in sixty days. "Payday lending isn't like it used to be where you just open a store and make money," he said. "You have to keep your brand out there in front of people." With increased competition, he said, "we all do what we can to find an edge."

The company's public relations director, Jeff Kursman, sat in our meeting and he piped up. "We work very hard here at being a good corporate citizen," Kursman said. He pointed his chin at the shiny green press packet in front of me. Inside were a series of slick brochures offering parents advice on protecting their kids ("Halloween Safety Checks for Children," "Summer Safety Checks for Children") that Check 'n Go, working in partnership with the National Center for Missing and Exploited Children, distributes at all its stores. The packet also included a copy of *CheckPoints*, a short pamphlet Check 'n Go put together with tips for its customers on saving money. The "$10 tip" is to return DVDs on time; the "$40 tip" is to pay your credit card bills before the due date.

"I think we're doing right by people," Davis said. But people like

Browning gave the industry a bad name. "It's irresponsible the way she was acting," he said. "The part she never learned is that we're in this for the long haul. If we're abusing people, do you think they're coming back?"

Perhaps—but perhaps people just don't feel like they have any other choice. A few days after my visit, Browning responded to a follow-up email I had sent to her suggesting that I might phone her daughter. "She can speak with you," Browning wrote, "from a former customer perspective about how they kept chiding her to borrow more money." In the end, even after Browning's warnings, her own daughter succumbed. She had fallen so deep into debt, Browning said, that she and her husband needed to bail her out.

Eleven

The Great What-If

GEORGIA, 2002–2003

Over barbecue in a town that might as well be a suburban Mayberry, Roy Barnes, self-described good ol' boy, was telling me how close Georgians came to saving the world from itself in 2002. He still thinks about the bill he had signed into law during his final months as Georgia's governor, convinced that had it been allowed to stand, Lehman Brothers and Bear Stearns and the whole lot of them on Wall Street might not have been so quick to buy whatever junk a subprime mortgage lender was peddling. "I was just trying to put my momma's rule into law: You have to live with your choices," Barnes said in a drawl that calls to mind Andy confiding in Aunt Bee. "There had to be accountability. These banks; think about what would have happened if they knew they would have to pay a price for all those loans that were no good."

Vincent Fort, a black state senator who jokingly describes his politics as "neo-confrontational," told me more or less the same story in a conference room across the street from the state capitol. "I'll tell you what, man," he said in a deep bass voice. "You just had to see the way they came after us to know that we were on to something." Like the 1999 North Carolina law, the bill that Fort drafted and Barnes refined was aimed at clamping down on predatory subprime loans but went one critical step further. It dictated that any entity taking possession of a "high cost" subprime loan—including a big investment bank on Wall Street that held it only long enough to sell it off in small tranches to municipalities, pension funds, college endowments, and anyone else in the market for a mortgage-backed security—was legally liable for the integrity of that loan. The law defined high cost as a loan carrying more than five percentage points in up-front costs or an interest rate more than eight percentage points higher than the rates on a comparable Treasury bill. Perhaps if they knew they might get sued, the banks might have taken at least a cursory look at a loan's terms before snapping it up on a secondary market and selling it off in small slices to investors as far away as Reykjavík and Berlin.

Eventually other states, including New York, would follow Georgia's lead and pass similar laws. And those states would then learn that there was another impediment in their way as they tried to crack down on the most reckless subprime lenders. But in Georgia, in 2002, a half-dozen years before the world would be lamenting America's subprime mortgage mess, lawmakers had devised if not the perfect prophylactic against financial disaster, then at least the beginnings of a solution. "In Georgia," Fort says, "of all places."

"I twisted arms," Roy Barnes said. "I called in favors. I had legislators out to the mansion every morning. I threatened everyone. It was the hardest bill I ever passed—and I changed the Georgia flag." And then, when the state's white majority denied Roy Barnes a second term that November because he sided with the blacks and the liberals and others seeking to erase the Confederate stars and bars from the Georgia state flag, Fort said, the real fight began.

Vincent Fort was teaching at Morehouse and other local colleges in the early 1990s when Bank of America announced it was shutting down branches in black neighborhoods around town, including one not far from his home in south Atlanta. Fort, whose specialty was black studies and the civil rights movement, had always stressed the centrality of economic institutions to the health of the black community. Fort began speaking out at community meetings around town and working with others to organize demonstrations. "We beat up on them pretty good," Fort recalled with a laugh. When the dust settled, black Atlanta still had several fewer bank branches but it also had a new leader, then in his late thirties. "I said then a day will come when we'll engage these folks again," Fort said.

That day came a half-dozen years later when he was nearing the end of his first term in the state senate. Andrew Cuomo, the HUD secretary, was coming to Atlanta for the first of five hearings he was holding around the country to investigate predatory lending. A friend of Fort who was helping to organize the event suggested he attend. Cuomo was already on record calling the issue of high-interest mortgages and excessive fees a "national crisis . . . with a troubling racial factor." Fort decided to sit in.

Bill Brennan testified that day, as did one elderly African-American widow facing foreclosure and another seemingly on the verge of disaster. Fort had spent most of his first term championing an anti-hate law in Georgia but sitting in the audience that day he wondered how he could be on the sidelines when abusive lenders were targeting the city's black neighborhoods. A HUD study released shortly before Cuomo's visit found that a borrower living in a predominantly black community in 1998 was five times more likely to end up in a subprime loan as someone living in a community that was predominantly white. Even an upper-income African-American, the study found, was twice as likely to hold a subprime mortgage as a lower-income white homeowner. Worse, Fannie Mae had analyzed its portfolio of mortgages for that same year and discovered that half of all those paying the higher rates and fees on subprime mortgages qualified for conventional loans. Fort was so incensed by what he was learning that he stood up and audaciously declared that he would see to it that Georgia passed the country's strongest anti–predatory lending law.

"That would be my first mistake," Fort said with a deep rumbling laugh. A lobbyist with the Georgia Association of Mortgage Brokers sidled up to Fort and offered him his card. "He tells me how much he's looking forward to helping me with my legislation," Fort said. "And then from that point on, he and his folk would work tooth and nail against me."

Fort is on the short side, a portly man in oversized tortoiseshell glasses. He is bald and sports a graying beard. He can be an easy political foe to underestimate. The day we met he was wearing a white dress shirt marred by two large coffee splotches, a wide-lapel pinstripe suit he described as "very off the rack," and Rockport-style walking shoes. Even the cultured, refined way he speaks is more professor or preacher than state senator. "I think it really bothered a lot of these good ol' boys I was taking on that I wasn't a real politician," he said. "I didn't go out of my way to be aggressive but at no time was I going to stoop or bow."

Those first months would be an education. Fort had assumed Bank of America's decision to shut down branches around town was a cost-saving measure. Only once he dove headfirst into the anti–predatory lending fight and started hanging around with the likes of Bill Brennan ("he would become a good friend," Fort said) did he learn that at the same time they were shutting down full-service branches, the big banks were purchasing subprime lenders. Bank of America, for instance, bought the subprime lender SP Financial Services during the 1990s. "It's not like these brand-name banks really fled our neighborhoods like we originally thought. They just replaced their branches in working-class neighborhoods with these off-brands making subprime loans to people and making enormous amounts of money," Fort said. "Citigroup, Bank of America, Wachovia, First Union—they all did it." Was it any wonder, then, that the Federal Reserve showed that while the volume of conventional mortgages remained flat between 1993 and 2000, subprime loans grew sevenfold? Unsurprisingly, foreclosures spiked 68 percent through the second half of the decade despite a robust economy. In Atlanta, the numbers were even more shocking. The foreclosure rate between 1996 and 1999 fell by 7 percent for those holding a conventional home loan but it soared by 232 percent among those holding subprime loans.

Fort introduced his bill at the start of the 2001 legislative session. He might have chided himself for telegraphing his intentions but it probably wouldn't have made any difference. North Carolina had caught the industry by surprise but by 2001 the big banks and other lenders were ready. A few in the press had a good time with a Dallas-based conference that served as a kind of predator's ball, where what the *New York Times* described as a "swat team" of lobbyists formed, ready to parachute into any state wherever they might be needed. To beef up its political connections, Household Finance hired Thomas McLarty, Clinton's former chief of staff, and Connie Mack, the former Republican senator from Florida, to serve on a board of advisers and the big banks like Citigroup had their own teams of staff lobbyists at the ready.

The industry didn't try to beat back Fort's legislation so much as they tried to co-opt it. The Georgia Senate's Banking and Financial Institutions Committee passed a predatory lending bill carrying Fort's name but by that time it had been so thoroughly eviscerated it bore no resemblance to the legislation he had written. The Georgia House never even bothered voting on the measure. It was time for a Plan B.

By instinct, Fort was more community activist than politician. The day after the end of the 2001 legislative session, he headed to a CitiFinancial office in Clayton, one hundred miles away. There he stood next to an older black woman he said CitiFinancial "had put into one of the worst predatory loans I've ever seen." That would be the start of an unusual media campaign designed to sway an audience of one: Governor Barnes. "I knew I didn't stand a chance if I didn't bring Roy Barnes on board," Fort said. "I was doing anything I could think of to make sure he made this part of his legislative package in 2002."

The first thing he would stipulate for the record, Roy Barnes told me as I slipped into a booth across from him for our lunch interview, was that people with poor credit should pay more for a loan than people with good credit. "I'm a capitalist through and through," he told me. He and his brother have started two banks together and they've bought a third. As governor he angered environmentalists by pursuing an aggressive growth agenda and he worked hard to abolish teacher tenure. He's been a Democrat all his life, but he is not what anyone might call a classic liberal.

Perhaps because at heart he was an old-style banker he took the changes he witnessed in the finance industry more personally than most. Interest rates nationally were strikingly low through the first half of the 2000s but people of modest means were paying more than ever for their money. "When I was a young prosecutor," Barnes said, "we prosecuted people who charged more than twenty-five percent a year as loan sharks. Now Wall Street welcomes them as respectable businesses." For years Barnes had fought what in Georgia they call the industrial lender—homegrown consumer finance shops that make small-denomination loans at annual interest rates of 60 percent. Now the payday lenders and title loan shops (called title pawn lenders in Georgia) charged closer to 400 percent.

"Under normal circumstances, I'd say sixty percent is usurious," Barnes said. "But compared to what the title pawn and payday lenders are charging, they're low-cost." When he was younger Barnes backed a law that would have capped the fees tax preparers could charge for an instant refund and he worked with the consumer groups to rein in rent-to-own. But now, Barnes said, "in the rank ordering of things, these things don't seem so bad. We've become immune." The biggest shock—and the most distressing to him personally—has been all those old-line institutions that succumbed to temptation. "Some of the most recognizable names are the biggest predatory lenders," he said. He mentions Wells Fargo, a bank with roots dating back to 1852 and a bank he had long respected. "Wells Fargo! Wells Fargo funds these predatory lenders," Barnes said. "Wells Fargo made all these predatory loans. Banks have a responsibility to serve the community. It's outrageous."

Barnes is a bulky man with blue eyes, a thick mane of gray hair, and the breezy, aw-shucks style of a country lawyer. A successful legal practice and those banks he owns with his brother gave him a net worth estimated at more than $10 million but the day we met he dressed like an English Lit professor in a brown corduroy sport coat and seemed to greet every person we passed on the street with a "Hi, how y'all doin'?" He was twenty-six years old when he was first elected to the Georgia Senate and practically grew up there, cutting deals and learning the nuances of cloakroom politics. It was no wonder that Fort, the former black studies professor, saw Roy Barnes as the perfect partner. The case against Fleet Finance had been one of the biggest of Barnes's legal career, and Barnes wasn't just the sitting governor but also a master at twisting arms and counting noses.

Another elected official would have sought a meeting with Barnes or at least one of his top people. Instead Fort took to the airways. If nothing else, Roy Barnes was a politician who read the polls, especially then as he geared up for a tough reelection. Getting Barnes to embrace predatory lending as a priority, Fort figured, required him to move the public opinion dial. And so Fort was all over the local media as 2001 turned into 2002, doing what he could to call attention to the problem of predatory lending in Atlanta.

Mainly that meant borrowing from the Bill Brennan playbook and offering the media the stories of elderly Georgians facing the street because of a deal they had done with a subprime lender—people like Ralph and Ethel Ivey. They had been making do since Ralph, eighty, a retired construction worker, had been incapacitated by a series of strokes, but then they needed a few thousand dollars' worth of home repairs on the small turquoise-colored bungalow they had paid off years earlier. So they turned to Household Finance for help. "Atlanta is under siege by predatory lenders," a consumer reporter told listeners on the town's ABC affiliate. "These lenders were your friend so long as you owned equity in your home," said Fort in an interview with *Creative Loafing*, the local alternative weekly. "They'd get as much out of you as they could and then . . . they took your house." Where once the polls had shown only nominal interest in the problem of abusive mortgage lending, by 2002 between 70 and 80 percent of the electorate was in favor of predatory lending legislation.

"I'd hear the stories and get mad," Barnes said. "They were loaning money to people who couldn't afford it. They were churning people through loans to collect more fees. They were not using any underwriting criteria because they were just going to sell the thing on Wall Street through securitization. So I had my administration take over Senator Fort's bill."

The governor's people fiddled with the language but otherwise left the key provisions in place. As in previous legislative efforts, the bill created a special category for "high cost" loans. The bill defined that as any home loan carrying fees exceeding 5 percent of the loan amount (versus 8 percent under the federal HOEPA law) or an annual interest rate more than eight percentage points higher than the corresponding Treasury bill (Fort had initially proposed six percentage points). The proposed law would ban balloon payments and prepayment penalties on any high-cost loan and required a borrower to receive counseling from a nonprofit organization before a deal could be consummated. The bill also capped the financial reward a lender could give a mortgage broker for putting a borrower into a more expensive loan (in the trade, a "yield spread premium") and stipulated that there must be a clear tangible financial benefit to a refinancing on a loan less than five years old. And, as Fort's original bill had done, the proposed legislation also gave any borrower burdened by a high-cost home loan the right to sue not only the original lender but anyone taking possession of that loan.

"I saw that as the key," Barnes said. "Wall Street had legitimized subprime lending and predatory lending by allowing for the securitizing of mortgages. We had to get at that if we were gonna get a handle on all the abuses."

The bills might have been virtually the same but the result wasn't. Again the legislation came before the Senate Banking and Financial Institutions Committee but this time it passed unanimously and cleared the full Senate by a vote of 52–2. It was in the Georgia House that the lenders would make their stand.

Wright Andrews, Jr., ran the National Home Equity Mortgage Association out of his offices in Washington, D.C. From those same offices he ran a group he called the Coalition for Fair and Affordable Lending and also a third that went by the name of the Responsible Mortgage Lending Coalition. Andrews was a top lobbyist for the subprime mortgage industry so Bill Brennan was understandably surprised to hear Andrews inviting him to a conference in Palm Beach, Florida. They were having a panel discussion on regulation and would Brennan participate? Seeing this as a perfect chance for some choice reconnaissance work, Brennan readily said yes.

The trip wouldn't disappoint, but only because Brennan, being Brennan, stayed through to the end for some final remarks from Andrews. "He tells everyone that the next battlefield is Georgia," Brennan recalled. "He tells the group, 'We're going to Georgia to stop Roy Barnes from passing this anti-lending ordinance.'"

Barnes took to calling his bill the Lobbyist Relief Act of 2002. Between the mortgage brokers, the local banks, the out-of-state banks, and nonbank lenders such as Countrywide and Ameriquest, Barnes said, "they hired every lobbyist in town." And then there were troops who had been flown in from out of the state. Fort remembers in particular a pair of female lobbyists for Ameriquest ubiquitous in those weeks when the two sides were vying for support in the House. "One was black and one was white and they're both in their mid-twenties," Fort said. "And I'll tell you what, they were both really attractive." In a series of articles that ran at the end of 2007, once the subprime market was already showing deep cracks, the *Wall Street Journal* reported that one of Wright Andrews's groups, the Coalition for Fair and Affordable Lending, spent $6.3 million to blunt state laws like Georgia's, and that Ameriquest, then the country's seventh-largest subprime lender, by itself made more than $20 million in political contributions.

Andrews offered something of a mea culpa in the *Journal* series: "I certainly was not aware of the degree to which many in the industry clearly failed to follow proper underwriting standards—the standards which they represented they were following to us who were lobbying." But in 2002 Andrews was describing the proposed Georgia law as "so bad" it might even prove a good thing. Georgia should "wake up and truly unite" the mortgage industry, Andrews told *American Banker*, to the need for federal legislation that would "pre-empt" those state and municipal governments trying to impose limits on subprime lenders and in the process creating a balkanized and confusing regulatory system.

The other side, of course, was offering much the same complaint: A fractured system meant fighting the same battle in town after town and in state after state. At the end of 2001, the Federal Reserve, which Congress had deputized to monitor the field, modified its definition of a "high cost" loan to include any loan carrying an interest rate eight percentage points higher than a Treasury bill, putting it in line with the North Carolina law and Georgia's proposal, and declared that any lender making a "high cost" loan needed to take into account a borrower's ability to repay the loan. Yet both sides had their powerful stalwarts in Congress, and neither could muster enough support to change the system. So despite the wishes of either side, the fight played out in states and cities around the country, creating a complex and multilevel battlefield (if not also a lucrative one) for Andrews and other lobbyists.

Martin Eakes had proven that a lender could make loans to subprime borrowers at rates around one percentage point above the going rate for prime borrowers and at least break even. Self-Help was a nonprofit, but even if charging only two or three percentage points above the conventional rate, a lender could still make double-digit profits. Georgia's proposed law only applied to mortgages that charged rates eight percentage points above conventional rates, yet Andrews and his colleagues deemed the proposed new rules unduly excessive. It will hurt first-time homebuyers. It will chase away the legitimate lenders, not just the crooked ones. "I had one bank CEO in my office telling me that Georgia is going to become an island; no one is going to make a loan here," Barnes scoffed. "We were the third or fourth fastest-growing state in the nation, at least at the time. I just couldn't believe no one was going to loan us money when we were growing that fast." In one meeting, a contingent of out-of-town lenders argued that if Georgia insisted on imposing its own rules on mortgages, then it would be difficult to sell them in the secondary market. Mortgages are the latest commodity sold on the global market, they explained, but Barnes was thinking these guys weren't thinking beyond next quarter's bonuses.

"I'm telling 'em, 'You're in for a crash here, this isn't going to end well,'" Barnes said. "But they're looking at me like I'm the one who doesn't understand."

Barnes was confident he could outmaneuver the out-of-town lenders. He knew he could best the mortgage brokers, but the state's biggest banks, even those not making high-cost loans, were also aligned against him and that had him worried. So he called them into his office to threaten them en masse. "I have this vacancy on the banking commission," Barnes recalled telling them, "and if y'all don't back off this bill, I'm going to do a nationwide search to find me the most sandal-wearing, long-haired, liberal consumer activist I can find to regulate every last one of you.'" Whether that was a bluff was not something they were willing to find out. "I finally backed them off," Barnes said.

Even many of his fellow Democrats were opposing him. "You'd've thought I was proposing the repeal of the Plan of Salvation, that's how much they were fightin' me on this," Barnes said. Some told him that they were worried his measure would make them appear antibusiness. "This ain't about business," he'd tell them, "this is about taking advantage of folks." And when reason wouldn't work, he reminded them that he was governor and could make life miserable for them if he set his mind to it. "They were mostly mad because they were enjoying those thick steaks and the cold liquor they were getting from the lobbyists," he said.

Fort confessed to experiencing a few pinch-me moments during those weeks of arm-twisting and uncertainty. He would be sitting in a hearing room overstuffed with lobbyists and activists and feel something like shock. "The whole focus nationally was on stopping us in Georgia so it wouldn't spread to other places," he said. "It was almost surreal to think what we had started in 2000 had gotten to this level." Fort had staked out the conference room next to his legislative office, where every Friday a small coterie of strategists would gather. He had Bill Brennan on hand to help him monitor small changes in the bill, along with Self-Help's Mike Calhoun, who had helped Fort write the original bill. Another regular, Kathy Floyd, a lobbyist for AARP, arranged for tens of thousands of its members to phone legislators in support of the Barnes-Fort bill.

"As this process moved along, my job was to make a lot of noise," Fort said. "It was to our benefit for them to think I was militant or racial or whatever. The crazier they saw me, the more dealing with Roy didn't seem so bad."

Despite everything they were doing, Fort thought they were a goner when Fannie Mae waded into their fight. In a letter addressed to Barnes, the government-backed mortgage giant warned that the measure "could unintentionally shrink the availability of responsible credit for the most vulnerable consumers." Fannie Mae asked to be exempted from the bill. But rather than respond directly to Fannie Mae, one of the governor's people enlisted Fort. "So I blast Fannie Mae and hint at the crowds we'll mobilize to protest their actions," Fort said. And the next thing he knew, Fannie Mae had rescinded its statement and issued one in support of the bill. The agency blamed the whole thing on a low-ranking staffer.

Barnes probably compromised more than Fort would have had he been the chief negotiator. The biggest concession was giving up on judicial foreclosures. In many states, foreclosures are overseen by the courts but not in Georgia. There are strict rules governing the procedure, but a lender can auction off a property without ever going before a judge. The Barnes-Fort bill sought to change that but Barnes dropped that proposal to win the support of the Speaker of the House, a Democrat. But the bill passed mainly intact, including the provision that would allow a borrower to sue anyone who takes possession of his or her mortgage. "There's a compassion issue here," state senator Bill Stephens, a Republican, told the *Atlanta Journal-Constitution*, explaining why he and so many other members of the GOP voted for Barnes's bill. "You can't hear the stories without having it tug at your heart."

Barnes signed the bill into law in April 2002. He held a signing ceremony in Atlanta and similar events in Savannah, Augusta, and Macon. Before the week was out, he would hold no less than seven public ceremonies to sign a bill that advocates and critics alike were describing as the toughest anti–abusive lending law in the land.

Barnes had generously singled out Bill Brennan and his staff during that first signing in Atlanta. This would never have happened, the governor said, without them. What passage of this bill meant to Brennan nearly a dozen years after he first came across that first flurry of Fleet cases became clear to Fort a few weeks later, at a celebration sponsored by Atlanta Legal Aid. No one expected them to win, Fort said from the podium. Not the good ol' boys who were still stunned that they had lost—and not even those pushing for the bill. While he was speaking, Fort recalled, he spotted Brennan standing off to the side, overcome with emotion. "Bill doesn't know that I noticed," he said, "but I saw tears coming down his cheeks."

On election night, Roy Barnes saw the early returns from the rural white counties and knew he was in trouble. He might have won a John F. Kennedy Profile in Courage award for changing the Georgia state flag but apparently not everyone was so impressed with his convictions. In the end, the 2002 race wasn't even close; GOP challenger Sonny Perdue beat Barnes by five percentage points and, for the first time in 130 years, a Republican was seated as the governor of Georgia. "Bill, you know it's over," Fort said when he called Bill Brennan the next day. And even Brennan, ever the optimist, had to confess that his friend was probably right.

Lenders had threatened to stop making loans in North Carolina but studies showed that those were empty threats. A Morgan Stanley survey concluded that rather than reduce the availability of subprime loans there, the law had saved consumers in North Carolina at least $100 million in fees. But Georgia, of course, had implemented a more restrictive law. Countrywide and Option One announced they were greatly curtailing their activity in the state and Ameriquest announced it was pulling out of Georgia altogether. In time it would become clear that this should have been cause for celebration but at the time it had the intended effect of spooking more than a few legislators. Freddie Mac compounded the fear by announcing it would no longer buy any "high-cost" loans from Georgia lenders. One might have asked why a government-sponsored mortgage finance company like Freddie Mac was trafficking in these high-priced loans but the news further softened legislators to the industry's argument that there were unintended consequences to the Barnes-Fort bill.

Still, the original legislation might have survived largely intact if it were not for the unexpected intervention of the nation's largest credit rating agencies. Less than two weeks after Sonny Perdue took over as governor, Standard & Poor's announced that it would no longer rate the creditworthiness of any mortgage-backed security that included even a single loan out of Georgia—even conventional mortgages. Since any party purchasing a predatory loan was potentially subject to a lawsuit in Georgia, the New York–based rating agency reasoned, and since the Georgia law placed no cap on potential damages, the legal exposure was incalculable. Moody's Investors Service and Fitch Ratings soon followed suit.

If one were assembling a list of actors whose reputations were badly tarnished by the 2008 subprime meltdown, the big three credit rating agencies would likely be near the top. Far from being reliable third parties offering impartial financial judgments, together they were "a central culprit of the financial crisis," Eric Dash of the *New York Times* would write in mid-2009. They stamped their highest ratings on junk. The problem was that the very people asking them to rate the integrity of these mortgage-backed securities were also the same people paying their fees. Dash likened the system to one in which Hollywood studios paid movie critics to judge their films. In 2003, however, the announcement caused panic inside the Georgia Capitol. The legislature was suddenly in a great rush to undo the damage.

Those who had authored the law had not done themselves any favors: It turned out that the law needed fixing as soon it had been passed. Fort described it as a matter of a few minor "tweaks," but that meant opening the bill to reconsideration during the next legislative session, which played into the hands of the opposition. Fort and his colleagues proposed a cap on the financial liability of any single investor, but the legislature was intent on going much further. The amendment that Sonny Perdue signed into law in early March 2003, just five months after the original law had taken effect, limited liability to the original issuer of a loan while watering down a number of provisions in the Barnes-Fort bill. "It's as bad as not having a bill at all," a dispirited Fort told the Associated Press.

Not that their efforts were for naught. Like North Carolina, Georgia helped to inspire activists and legislators living in other locales. Soon after Georgia, New York State passed a tough anti–predatory lending law that also gave borrowers the right to sue whatever institution held their mortgage, even if it was owned, by a third party. But that right was granted only if someone could prove that the third party had been complicit in committing fraud (or, in the event of foreclosure, a borrower could get out of his or her financial liabilities to a third party if the loan is deemed predatory under state law). The New York law went into effect in April 2003. Other states followed. Every state after Georgia was certain to put in place a cap on a mortgage holder's potential liability. "That way the rating agencies like Standard & Poor's could at least calculate the potential for damages," said Patricia McCoy, a professor at the University of Connecticut School of Law, who has studied the issue.

But victories in New York and elsewhere would do little to help those communities in Georgia devastated by the subprime meltdown. By 2006 the state would rank third in the nation in foreclosures.

Predictably the problem was felt much more acutely in the state's black precincts. Nearly half of all blacks buying a house in Atlanta in 2005 or 2006 ended up with a subprime mortgage, according to a 2007 analysis by the *Atlanta Journal-Constitution*, compared to 13 percent of white homebuyers. The difference was even more pronounced among those earning more than $100,000. Four in ten black homeowners earning in the six figures ended up in a high-interest subprime mortgage compared to less than one in ten whites in that income group. The rate of foreclosure among those blacks would be disproportionately high.

Bill Brennan continued to do what he could, one client at a time. If there was an upside to the 2002 fight, it was that now Brennan had an ally in Fort who could frighten banks into doing the right thing. In recent years, Fort has phoned top bank executives ranging from Countrywide's Angelo Mozilo to Bank of America's Ken Lewis to scare them into fixing the most egregious of Brennan's cases. Fort depicted for me what happens after he leaves a message with one of their assistants. "They'll google my name, they'll figure out who I am, and then my phone rings an hour later," he says. "They figure it's better to work things out than face a picket line."

"That's how we settle a lot of cases nowadays," Brennan told me. "Not all but well over half."

A man named John D. Hawke, Jr., played only a peripheral role in the legislative fight over predatory lending in Georgia. As head of the U.S. Office of the Comptroller of the Currency (OCC), Hawke regulated the country's national banks. He blanched every time a state encroached on his turf, and even before the Barnes-Fort bill took effect, he had already granted a blanket exemption to the banks under his supervision. That didn't help giant mortgage lenders like Countrywide or Ameriquest but it provided relief to big banks like Wells Fargo and Washington Mutual. But it was another judgment Hawke made in 2003, one month after Sonny Perdue broke the hearts of Fort, Brennan, and others in Georgia, that stands out as the other great what-if of the early

2000s. Bill Clinton had nominated Hawke to a five-year term as OCC chairman that began in 1999 and from the start he seemed intent on standing in the way of those trying to crack down on predatory lending.

It was more than just legislators in states like North Carolina, Georgia, and New York who were eager to do something about the more egregious forms of subprime mortgage lending. A number of state attorneys general were also intent on taking action, so much so that within their national association they had formed a predatory lending committee. Iowa Attorney General Tom Miller, whose investigation of Ameriquest led to that company paying a $325 million fine, served as co-chair of the committee. So too did North Carolina's Roy Cooper, who had been displeased with Hawke ever since the latter exempted (as he would do in Georgia) national banks from the state law Cooper had championed while he was president of the North Carolina Senate. In April 2003, a small contingent of attorneys general converged on Washington hoping they could convince Hawke to work with them instead of against them.

Hawke agreed to a meeting but then asked himself why he had even bothered. He was annoyed with the lot of them even before they showed up at his offices. The day before they were scheduled to arrive, Eliot Spitzer, then the New York attorney general, had held a press conference blasting Hawke as a pinheaded bureaucrat for standing in the way of his efforts to crack down on unfair lending practices, especially in black and Latino neighborhoods. Spitzer wasn't at the meeting with Hawke but his presence was felt just the same. "Are we here for a press event," Hawke began when he took his seat, "or do you want to talk issues?" The attorneys general were no happier with their publicity-hungry colleague from New York but there was also nothing they could do. "We couldn't control Spitzer but that didn't change the fundamental issue that we were there to talk about," Cooper said.

Their meeting lasted only an hour. It was decorous despite its contentious start but hardly satisfying for either side. The attorneys general asked for more latitude in cracking down on predatory lending; Hawke held forth on the doctrine of preemption and why it was critical that the federal government not relinquish any regulatory power. We're not trying to intrude on the business of ensuring the safety and soundness of the nation's banks, the attorneys general countered, but we have the right to protect our citizenry from the oppressive loans that some lenders under your charge are making. States have also always had the right to regulate real estate transactions within their borders, Cooper argued when it was his turn to speak, and they have the power to enforce consumer rights laws even if that abuse is at the hands of a nationally chartered bank (or a bank's subprime subsidiary, for that matter). There were more practical considerations as well: The states were closer to the problem and could react more quickly than the federal government. Hawke, however, would not budge.

"He took fifty sheriffs off the job when the lending industry was becoming the Wild West," Cooper, who was still angry with Hawke when I visited him in North Carolina, told me at the end of 2008. "What was going on was unrestrained and uncontrolled. You had these no-doc [no documentation] loans. You had lenders that weren't even looking at the borrower's ability to pay because they knew they would just be selling these loans on the secondary market." If the federal government had chosen to remain neutral, Cooper said, "I believe the fight against these lenders would have spread like wildfire across the country because of just the basic unfairness." Instead, Hawke and the OCC threatened lawsuits at every turn.

"I blame him for the meltdown," Bill Brennan said of Hawke. "He knew exactly what was going on and didn't do a thing about it."

Hawke was fed up with that kind of statement by the time I reached him at the end of 2008. "Everyone's looking around for a scapegoat," he said. "So people point a finger at me." It's not as if he did nothing, he said. He asked the attorneys general to give his staff any evidence they had of reckless lending "but they just completely dropped the ball on that." He suspected that's because their main interest was in generating headlines. He pointed out that shortly after meeting with Cooper and his colleagues, he sent out rules clarifying the OCC's position: Loans should be based not solely on the worth of a borrower's collateral but also on his or her ability to pay. To him, if people are looking for someone to blame, look at the investment banks and their "unquenchable thirst" for more subprime loans they could package and sell.

Hawke is a heavyset man with thinning gray hair and dressed in suspenders and a bright blue-and-white striped dress shirt. After his term expired in 2004, he returned to Arnold & Porter, the Washington, D.C., powerhouse law firm where he had worked prior to his appointment. There he represents some of the same banks he had supervised as the chairman of the OCC, but to his mind there is no conflict of interest because his fight with the states had been over jurisdiction and never the behavior of the banks under his domain. "One of the benefits of being a national bank is you can operate under a single set of rules," Hawke said. As he had done in his meeting with the attorneys general, Hawke gave me a short lecture about the Constitution and the primacy of delegated federal authority over states' rights. "Preemption is not something for us to give up on because it might be convenient," he said.

If ever he doubted himself, Hawke had the courts to provide him solace. The OCC filed suit against Spitzer after he opened an investigation of possible discrimination by banks under his charge. The federal district court ruled in favor of Hawke's agency and the U.S. Court of Appeals upheld the lower court's decision. "He challenged us," Hawke said of Spitzer, "and we beat 'im every time." Six months after my visit, though, Hawke was no doubt feeling less smug. The U.S. Supreme Court concluded that the OCC had been wrong and had had no right to block a state trying to enforce its own law. An unusual coalition had formed behind this ruling, with Antonin Scalia writing for the majority in an opinion that also had the consent of the Court's four more liberal justices.

The alarms, meanwhile, continued to ring, even as most people in power chose to ignore them.

Twelve

Public Enemy Number One

DURHAM, NORTH CAROLINA, AND WASHINGTON, D.C.,

2002–2006

The first thing Steven Schlein wants you to know about the ongoing, epic struggle between his clients—the payday lenders—and their critics is that it's not a fair fight. Payday's foes, and especially Martin Eakes, have too much money and too much power. "They've got more lobbyists than we do," he complained when we sat down together in mid-2008. "They have more money. We're completely outgunned!" I raised a skeptical eyebrow and Schlein, payday's main spokesman, slowly shook his head in disappointment. He has a strained, Brooklyn-tinged voice that he raises an octave. He sounded as if he were pleading rather than making a rhetorical point. "Go take a look at the $25 million monument Eakes bought for himself," he said. He pointed his chin toward the window and the multistory building the Center for Responsible Lending (CRL) bought a few years earlier to serve as its Washington, D.C., office. "Go there right now and then tell me they're just this scrappy, underfunded public interest group up against this big, bad industry."

We're sitting two blocks from the CRL building in the offices of

Dezenhall Resources. That's how bad it had gotten for Allan Jones, Billy Webster, the Davis brothers, and the others. In 2004, they started paying for the high-priced services of a crisis management firm that specializes in the representation of unpopular industries such as the chemical manufacturers, pharmaceutical companies, and Big Oil. The firm's founder and chief executive, Eric Dezenhall, laid out his approach to helping beleaguered industries in his 1999 book, *Nail 'Em! Confronting High-Profile Attacks on Celebrities and Businesses*. "Damage control used to be about soft, fuzzy concepts like image," Dezenhall wrote. "Now it's about survival, and this had made the battle bloodier." THE PIT BULL OF PUBLIC RELATIONS—that was the headline *BusinessWeek* used above a 2006 profile of Dezenhall. The actual job of defending the payday lenders, however, fell mainly on Schlein and a younger woman named Lyndsey Medsker.

"They have people in Washington," Schlein says of Eakes and the Center for Responsible Lending. "They have people in North Carolina. They have an office in Oakland. Here it's just me and Lyndsey." Schlein complains about the disparity in the size of their respective ground forces when the payday lenders gather for meetings of their trade organization. The opposition, he'll tell them, is meeting with newspaper editorial boards; they're organizing in this state or that. But invariably his calls for more help go unanswered. Perhaps the pooh-bahs know that each big chain has its own team of government affairs people and its own public relations staff on the payroll.

Schlein wonders if it would even make a difference if he had more people. Dezenhall has represented the likes of Exxon Mobil and a former Enron executive but payday lending seems to occupy a category all its own. "I've been in this business twenty-five years," he said, "and I've never seen such closed-mindedness about an issue." He hears the same from the lobbyists they hire whenever the Center for Responsible Lending or some similar-minded group is pushing a bill that would shut down the industry in some far-flung state. "They'll all say it," Schlein said. "Working for the gun lobby, or working for tobacco, is like working for Goodwill compared to the hostility they face working for the payday lenders." Schlein tells of the time he phoned the *Washington Post* about meeting the newspaper's editorial board. The District of Columbia City Council was considering a bill that would cap the rate payday lenders could charge (the bill passed by an eight-to-one margin, with only Marion Barry voting against it) and he thought the paper might be curious about what the industry might have to say. "This woman I spoke with at the *Post*, she basically ranted at me, 'I'm not giving you slime-balls a minute of my time,'" he said. He shook his head and looked momentarily hurt. "She used terms you wouldn't believe."

Schlein is a trim man, around fifty years old, with close-shorn gray hair. Those in the public relations trade tend toward the bubbly, or at least upbeat, but Schlein by disposition is far more dour, more life-weary and rough-hewn. He's also more than a little obsessed with money. Over breakfast he told me about his grandfather, who had moved to this country from an Eastern European *shtetl* with next to nothing. He left a pair of successful jewelry stores to his heirs but Schlein wishes his grandfather had been a pawnbroker. "It was totally random, him getting into the jewelry business," Schlein explained. And pawn sales, he went on to point out, are "going gangbusters right now." At that same breakfast, he asked me to explain how a person could work as a business reporter at a place like the *New York Times* or *Wall Street Journal*. Some barely earn six-figure salaries. He can't imagine working that hard, he told me, for so little money.

Schlein clearly is well paid. He wears expensive suits and a pair of fashionable rectangular steel glasses. Dezenhall's offices are sleek, modern, prosperous looking. Yet one might ask Schlein why he does what he does for a living. His job hasn't been much fun, he confessed, at least since taking over the payday account. He'll work on a friendly reporter he knows, hoping to persuade him or her to see beyond the 391 percent APR, but then *60 Minutes Wednesday* runs a segment on payday that begins, "It may sound like loan-sharking, but in most of America, it's perfectly legal." That particular story was set in North Carolina, of course. Look behind every effort to ban payday lending, Schlein said, and you'll find "Martin Eakes and his little empire."

It galls Schlein that people, especially reporters, hold up Eakes as some kind of white knight. To him, Eakes is a competitor who first opposed payday lending in North Carolina "because he runs a credit union and he had an economic stake in seeing us gone." With no payday loans to help bail people out, the credit unions, like banks, earn a lot more in bounced-check fees and overdraft protection products. And once Eakes defeated them in North Carolina, he said, "he became enthralled with his power."

"Just listen to the guy speak," Schlein said. "He oozes elitism out of every pore. He's the only one who knows what's best for everyone else. He really thinks he's the last honest man."

Martin being Martin. That's how Mark Pearce, the Self-Help executive Eakes chose to serve as the first president of the Center for Responsible Lending, described the decision to spend $23 million to buy the eleven-story office building that has pretty much destroyed Steven Schlein's peace of mind. The building is located in Farragut Square, three blocks from the White House. "It was Martin's way of saying we're here and we're not going anywhere," Pearce said. It was also an aggressive business decision by an advocacy group that feels entirely at home playing the real estate game. The CRL, founded in 2002, occupies one floor and leases out the other ten, providing the organization with a steady income that more than covers the mortgage. Plus, Eakes said, the building is already worth more than $30 million.

Mike Calhoun admitted he was shocked to discover how rich and big the CRL was relative to other advocacy outfits. "We looked at groups like the Consumer Federation, PIRG, and the Consumer Law Center and we realized we were huge, relatively speaking, compared to these other groups," said Calhoun, who took over as president of the CRL in 2006, when Pearce took a top regulatory posting with the state of North Carolina. "And these were organizations which had much wider mandates than us, with utilities and health care on top of consumer finance and mortgages." To CRL's great relief, these other groups were "gracious and welcoming," Calhoun said, to this new giant in their midst (the group has a staff of sixty spread across three offices) and invited them to take the lead on predatory lending issues. The challenge, then, was figuring out what they would do in their newfound roles at the vanguard of the consumer rights movement.

The CRL would focus mainly on businesses that catered to the poor and working poor, but even then that left them with an impossibly broad terrain to cover. Subprime credit cards, rent-to-own, used car finance, refund anticipation loans, even the humble corner pawnbroker: There seemed no shortage of ways entrepreneurs had devised for getting rich working the easy-credit landscape. There was even a fledgling industry devoted to helping hospitals and doctors collect the money owed to them by the uninsured and underinsured. These companies, part of what *BusinessWeek* would dub the "medical debt revolution," normally don't charge the hospital or physician anything for its services but instead earn their profits from the fees and interest rates (typically between 14 and 25 percent) they tack onto the bills they have been assigned.

The CRL would naturally focus on exploitative subprime mortgages. The problem had grown only more acute since they had sided with Freddie Rogers in his fight with Associates and there was no doubting their authority in this realm. Kathleen Day remembered when she was covering the banking industry for the *Washington Post* and for the first time saw Eakes testify before Congress. Most striking, said Day, who now runs the CRL's public information office, was how differently Eakes came across compared to the other consumer advocates speaking that day. "He starts off telling people he's been in this business for twenty-five years," Day remembered. "And he tells the committee, 'You can't tell me it can't be done because I'm doing it, and I'm doing it right without screwing people.'" The banking lobbyists Day happened to share a cab with after the hearing were all in a huff about Eakes, she said. They didn't say he was wrong: They didn't say he didn't know what he was talking about. "All they could say," Day recalled, "is that they thought he was sanctimonious."

The payday lending industry would be CRL's second priority. Martin

Eakes and Self-Help were too invested in that fight to consider dropping it, especially once they had the money to build a national organization. Their third and final priority would be the more predatory side of the credit card industry, including practices the consumer activists called "fee harvesting." The insidious part of fee harvesting is that the consumer, her credit damaged and her funds tight, starts off feeling grateful that a lender is willing to trust her with a credit card. But then she receives the first bill. There are card activation fees and origination fees (commonly $100 or more) billed as a cash advance and also an "account maintenance fee" (maybe $10 a month). The fees eat up a goodly share of the available credit, typically between $300 and $500, and therein lies another huge moneymaking opportunity for the card issuer: the fine for going over your available limit. In time, the CRL would also add banks to their list of targets and specifically the overdraft fees they charged. "These fees are becoming the main profit center for these banks," Eakes said, "which means they're making the bulk of their profits off their poorest customers." Still, the CRL would devote a lot more time to fighting the mortgage lenders and the payday advance industry than to battling the banks that were issuing subprime credit cards.

The payday lenders lost in North Carolina in 2001 and then again a few years later in Georgia and Arkansas. Even so, they were slow to recognize that they were in an existential fight for their livelihood. "These were three very different situations," Billy Webster said. North Carolina was Martin Eakes, Georgia boiled down to the political clout of the industrial loan stores that Roy Barnes had battled, and Arkansas was a quirk: A legal battle they lost because Arkansas is the only state in the union with a usury cap (17 percent) written into the state constitution. Still, the same year that they lost in Georgia, the big chains hired Dezenhall. We need to be more aggressive, Webster explained in an *American Banker* article about the payday lenders "going on the offensive." We need to explain to people that a payday advance is cheaper than missing a credit card payment or a series of bounced checks.

Steven Schlein had just been hired but he was not wasting time. The Center for Responsible Lending might sound as if it has the best interest of consumers at heart, Schlein said, but he shared with *American Banker* a report he had put together dismissing the CRL as nothing but a front group for a Durham-based credit union.

But payday hardly seemed an industry in need of outside help. As rapidly as payday had grown in its first seven years, it grew more rapidly still over the next few years; where there were 10,000 payday stores in 2000, that number exceeded 21,000 by 2004. Success inspired more success. As industry trailblazers such as Check Into Cash, Check 'n Go, and Advance America continued to thrive, large companies that had grown rich feasting in other corners of the poverty universe started offering payday loans. That included chains in the check cashing, pawn, and rent-to-own businesses. Regional powerhouses such as the Money-Tree in the Northwest helped to fuel the expansion, as did people like Mike Hodges. Hodges was twenty-four when he opened his first payday store in Nashville, in 1996. By 2008, Advance Financial was operating twenty stores within thirty miles of Tennessee's state capital.

And there were those late to the poverty business who were no less eager to make their fortune. Just as Mike Hodges was poring over maps in search of gaps in the Nashville metro area, so too were people like Erich Simpson, a former DuPont factory worker who opened his first of three payday shops in a rural stretch of South Carolina in 2004. The industry would add two thousand more stores in 2005.

The big payday chains even started to spawn their own competition. Jones would grumble about the mid-level managers who gave notice "thinking that making it was as easy as figuring out what kind of plane they was gonna buy." Billy Webster voiced the same complaint. Greg Fay served in the army for seven years right after high school, then went to work first in the rent-to-own business and then in payday finance. When Fay came into a little money, he opened his first payday store just outside Dayton in 2003 and was soon eyeing locales in and around Toledo, 150 miles up the highway. Ultimately he, his partner, and an outside pair of investors would open a half-dozen stores in western Ohio.

The issue of whether Wall Street could fully embrace payday lending was put to rest in 2004 when Advance America announced that it was going public and that Morgan Stanley, a top-tier investment bank, led the offering. The investment banking arms of Wells Fargo and Bank of America were among those lending their names and sales teams to the effort. If there was a taint to payday, the 23 percent profit margin Advance America was reporting in its prospectus made it all okay. Usually only the most successful technology companies consistently posted numbers that good.

The bankers had priced Advance America stock at between $13 and $15 a share. It opened at $15 and then soared above $21 before closing at $20.50—a 37 percent jump in one day of trading. Billy Webster had cashed out around $9 million worth of stock but still owned shares valued at more than $100 million. His partner and financier, George Johnson, cashed out $22 million in stock that day but still owned a $260 million stake in the company.

The numbers Advance America was posting naturally attracted even more wannabe moguls to the business. Every year at the annual meeting of the payday lenders, Steven Schlein rubs shoulders with some of the new arrivals, who give him hope for the industry. "You walk around and you think you're seeing all of America in one room," Schlein said. The crowd skews white, he acknowledged, but otherwise they strike him as a perfect cross-section of America, with people old and young and from all regions of the country. Schlein told me of a kid he had recently met who had gotten into payday lending while he was still in college but already owned five stores. "Think how rich he's going to be when he already has five stores at twenty-two," Schlein said.

But if Schlein was brightened by the native entrepreneurialism of a can-do country, Billy Webster was worried that he was witnessing his own doom. "One of the things I never dreamed would happen is we would have so many people in this business," he told me when I visited him in Spartanburg. As a reference point, he harked back to his decade in the fried chicken business. "You'd never have seen a Popeyes and a KFC on the same corner as a Bojangles," he said, "but that's what you have now [with payday lending stores]. So you end up not just with saturation problems from a business perspective but also multiple loan problems."

Inside the CRL they dubbed themselves the "road warriors." These were the staffers so committed to defeating the payday lenders or their counterparts in the mortgage industry that they proved willing to turn their lives upside down and live in another state for weeks, if not months at a time. Martin Eakes described one of the warriors, Uriah King, as a "human vacuum cleaner sucking up everything he could about payday." King, who read Clausewitz on war to gird himself for battle, could drive him batty, Eakes said, but what King lacked in experience he more than made up for in energy, enthusiasm, and native savvy. It fell to people like King and his colleague, Susan Lupton, to help fill in the narrative and demonstrate that the payday advance was, to borrow a vivid metaphor from Robert H. Frank, an economics professor at Cornell University, like "handing a suicidal person a noose."

It helped that Advance America and a second payday company, QC Holdings, a chain of three hundred stores based in Kansas City, went public in 2004. The documents both companies are required by law to regularly file with the Securities and Exchange Commission have provided a treasure trove of information. So too have the quarterly conference calls that most publicly traded companies routinely record and post on the Internet as well as the detailed reports written by financial analysts who earn money selling stock advice to wealthy clients.

From the start, the payday lenders have said theirs is an occasional emergency product used by the rational consumer facing the prospect of a bounced check. Yet those in the business of following the industry seemed to come to precisely the opposite conclusion. "A note about rollovers," an analyst named Elizabeth Pierce with Roth Capital Partners wrote in a research report about First Cash, a pawnshop chain that had gotten into payday. "We are convinced the business just doesn't work without them." That view was echoed by the accounting firm Ernst &

Young: "The survival of payday loan operators depends on establishing and maintaining a substantial repeat customer business because that's really where the profitability is." Even Dan Feehan, the chief executive of Cash America, the country's largest pawnshop chain and another major player in the payday industry, said much the same when explaining the business to potential shareholders at an investor's conference. "The theory in the business," Feehan said, "is you've got to get that customer, work to turn him into a repetitive customer, long-term customer, because that's really where the profitability is."

The CRL was convinced the payday cash advance was an inherently defective product, trapping people as if by design. The single mother with two kids might be avoiding a costly bounced-check fee that first time she borrows $400 but how is she ever going to cover that $460 check two weeks later when she brings home $1,100 a month? "They sucker you in with that first loan," Eakes said, "and then they gotcha." It became essential, then, to collect the tales of customers like Sandra Harris, an accounting technician in Wilmington, North Carolina, who borrowed $200 from a payday lender to pay her car insurance after her husband lost his job as a cook. Eight thousand dollars in fees later, the couple ended up losing the car and avoided eviction only because of a sympathetic landlord. John Kucan, a former Connecticut state trooper, had a less tragic story but one offering no less flattering a view of payday. He retired to North Carolina after being shot in the line of duty but then needed to borrow $850 from a payday lender because the state had overpaid some benefits and wanted its money back. Living on a fixed income, however, Kucan would need to renew the loan fifteen times, racking up $2,000 in fees before he was able to pay it off. When you're desperate for quick cash, he told one interviewer, "what's flashing in front of you is the dollars you're looking for. The percentage rate isn't something you're even considering."

The CRL's first big media triumph came in the spring of 2005, when CBS correspondent Scott Pelley traveled to North Carolina to report on the state's efforts to evict the payday lenders from within its borders. Sandra Harris told her story, as did John Kucan. Listeners also heard from a woman named Ginny McCauley, who ran an Advance America store in Illinois for six years. McCauley estimated that 60 to 70 percent of her customers were rollovers during that time. Pelley asked Jim Blaine, the CEO of the State Employees' Credit Union of North Carolina, what he would tell someone who was planning on taking out a payday loan. "I'd say go get a loan shark," Blaine said. "They're cheaper." A typical loan shark, he explained, only charges an APR of around 150 percent.

The only payday lender willing to talk on camera was Willie Green, a former NFL wide receiver who opened his first payday store as his playing days were ending in the mid-1990s; he ultimately opened ten stores. Pelley asked Green, who was from a poor background, what he would say to a Sandra Harris, who had lost a car and almost a home. "How about, 'Thank You, Mr. Green or Mr. Check Casher or Mr. Payday Advance Store for helping me out when I was in a time of need?'" Later in the segment, when Pelley brought up the prospect of Green's wife taking out a payday advance, he essentially confessed that she was too smart for that. "She has a master's degree in accounting," he said.

The next year brought another body blow to the industry. This time it wasn't the CRL leading the charge (though Eakes's group would provide critical behind-the-scenes lobbying help) but the commanding officers at military bases around the country, unhappy that the payday operators had opened so many shops outside their gates—"like bears on a trout stream," a pair of academics concluded in a 2005 study of the geography of payday lending. Was it any wonder, given that the country's military bases were thick with young, financially inexperienced people getting by on modest salaries? In the mid-2000s, the typical army private first class started at an annual salary of $17,000 a year and nearly three-quarters of active-duty military personnel never made more than $30,000 a year. There were reports of soldiers discharged because they defaulted on a loan and many others were stuck stateside because of a military rule that stated that anyone owing more than 30 percent of his or her salary could not be dispatched overseas. "I have guys guarding my gate here when they should be deployed in Iraq," the commanding officer at a naval base in San Diego told the Associated Press. The CRL waded into the fight with a study concluding that one in five active-duty military personnel had taken out a payday loan in the previous year versus one in every sixteen adult Americans. At Fort Bragg, North Carolina, credit counselors said they were seeing an average of two to three soldiers a week who owed money to a payday lender, according to a report cited by *Bloomberg Markets*.

To the extent that the payday industry has clout on Capitol Hill, it's in the Senate Financial Services Committee, but this fight was waged instead in the Armed Services Committee. In the summer of 2006, Senator Jim Talent, a Missouri Republican, and Senator Bill Nelson, a Florida Democrat, added an amendment to the annual defense authorization bill that capped the rate military families would have to pay for a payday loan at 36 percent. It passed, and when the defense authorization bill became law that fall, payday lenders could charge active-duty personnel no more than $1.38 on every $100 they borrowed. With a stroke of the pen, the country's payday lenders were essentially banned from doing business with the military. It didn't elude the industry that it wouldn't take much of a logical leap for a legislative body to conclude that if payday loans were so destructive to the emotional and financial well-being of America's fighting men and women, they might also be harmful to some of their other constituents.

At the start of 2006, people inside Self-Help and the CRL started to notice a spike in the number of subprime home loans. Even as late as 2003, subprime accounted for only 8 percent of the overall residential mortgage market, but by 2006, subprime loans accounted for more than one in every four home loans written—28.7 percent of the mortgage market, according to the Fed. Worried that this would spell doom for the home ownership dreams of a great many low- and moderate-income people, a research team was created inside the CRL to predict what might happen. Ellen Schloemer, the CRL's research director, told me that their conclusion, that this trend would lead to 2 million subprime foreclosures, was so incredible that they rewrote a report they called "Losing Ground" six times before releasing it at the end of 2006. The Mortgage Bankers Association denounced the study as wildly pessimistic but in time it would become clear this was one of the few early warnings of the economic carnage to come. "That study really put us on the map in Washington," Mike Calhoun said. At the start of 2008, the publication *Politico* declared that the CRL was "the main intellectual engine driving the Democratic response to the housing crisis" in no small part because "the Center has been more right than wrong." That same year the Federal Reserve Board would single out the CRL for its research when appointing Mike Calhoun to a three-year term on its Consumer Advisory Council.

Steven Schlein, though, has not been nearly as impressed with CRL's research capabilities. "They do not do scholarship," Schlein said. "It's a joke what they call a study. They're done by a bunch of twenty-four-year-old kids sitting in some office in North Carolina, plucking numbers from out of the air."

In fact, some of CRL's payday reports have tended to overreach. Its first big industry study, for instance, released in 2006 and called "Financial Quicksand," asserted that 90 percent of the revenues payday lenders collect in any given year are "stripped from trapped borrowers." Under the CRL's definition, though, a trapped borrower was anyone taking out as few as five payday loans a year. The study also alleged that the "typical" payday borrower ended up spending nearly $800 to repay a single $325 loan, or more than $450 of accumulated fees. That's because the average payday customer, the CRL found after examining data from eight states, took out nine loans per year. Inside the CRL, they assumed that meant a person took out a single loan and then flipped it eight times before paying it back, but it seemed just as reasonable to conclude that the typical borrower took out a new loan every few months but needed an extra couple of payments to wipe out the debt.

But one could also ask what difference it made. Maybe five loans a year didn't call to mind a "trapped" borrower but it also didn't conjure up the customer needing a bailout because (as Willie Green had told Scott

Pelley) "God forbid, an emergency comes up where the refrigerator goes out or the child needs to go to the doctor." And did it make much difference whether a person flipped a single loan eight consecutive times or took out multiple loans in a given year? The bottom line was the same: nearly $500 in payments to a payday lender rather than money that might otherwise go into a savings account.

The industry would again find fault in some of the more sweeping assertions made within the CRL's next big study, "Springing the Debt Trap," released in 2007. But the power of that report wasn't in its conclusions; it was in the data the CRL collected from states that tracked and published customer usage statistics. In Colorado, for instance, one in seven payday borrowers in 2005 remained in debt for at least six months before paying back a loan. Regulators there also found that customers taking out twelve or more loans in a year generated 65 percent of the industry's revenues in the state. Other states reported similar findings when singling out those taking out twelve or more loans in a year: Oklahoma (64 percent of their revenues from this group), Florida (58 percent), Washington state (56 percent). At least one in five borrowers in each of those four states had taken out twenty-one or more loans in a year. In this regard, the APR no longer seemed an imprecise measurement of what was in fact a fee but a close approximation of the interest a good portion of the industry's customer base was paying for its short-term cash needs.

The number of loans the average payday consumer took out in a year was another point of contention. Industry sources tended to say seven or eight loans per year while payday's critics claimed those numbers lowballed the problem. The Woodstock Institute, an advocacy group based in Chicago, concluded that the average payday user in Illinois took out thirteen loans in a year. Policy Matters, a liberal research group based in Cleveland, would reach the same conclusion about borrowers in Ohio. John Caskey, a sociology professor at Swarthmore College and the author of *Fringe Banking*, studied payday lending in Wisconsin in 2000. He found that 49 percent of the state's payday borrowers had taken out eleven or more loans over a twelve-month period and that nearly one in five borrowers had taken out twenty or more loans during that time. There was no dispute over the size of the average payday loan, however: $325.

The industry tended to cite one of two studies. One was by Donald Morgan, a researcher at the New York branch of the Federal Reserve who sought to test the thesis put forward by CRL and others that a payday advance was a "predatory debt trap." According to his research, people in North Carolina and Georgia, two states that had recently banned payday loans, bounced more checks and filed for Chapter 7 bankruptcy at a higher rate than people in states where payday loans were available. Studies by researchers inside academia, though, have shown precisely the opposite, at least on the issue of bankruptcies; relying on payday loans, several studies have found, accelerates the chances that a person will declare bankruptcy. The CRL also cast doubts on the bounced-check claim by noting that Morgan used data from large stretches of the South as a proxy for Georgia and North Carolina.

The other study that advocates of payday lending quote was written by an economics professor at Indiana Wesleyan University named Thomas Lehman. "You cannot read Dr. Lehman's work without walking away thinking payday lending is absolutely necessary and, if used responsibly, an absolute Godsend," said Larry Meyers, a former screenwriter turned pro-payday blogger ever since he and a partner started investing in budding payday chains. Yet while journalists regularly quote the CRL in articles about payday, Meyers complained, they never quote Lehman. While testing that hypothesis I came across Lehman's name in *BusinessWeek*. He wasn't mentioned in an article about payday, however; it was about seemingly independent voices who are in fact "quietly financed by powerful interests." Lehman served as *BusinessWeek*'s poster boy for the practice after he confessed to the magazine that in fact the industry had paid him to do his study.

Martin Eakes figured he must be doing something right. He had enough critics throwing mud at him to convince him the CRL was having an impact. One of the sillier attacks came from a group that called themselves the Consumers Rights League, a name chosen presumably so they could appropriate the CRL acronym. They dubbed the original CRL a "predatory charity" that contributed to the world's economic woes in 2008 by promoting "public panic" about the subprime meltdown.

One of the nastier assaults has come at the hands of a group called the Capital Research Center, a D.C.-based think tank that keeps tabs on liberal advocacy groups. Eakes's longtime friend Tony Snow, a conservative stalwart, compared his old running buddy to Jack Kemp, an active combatant in the war on poverty while serving as a Republican representing the Buffalo area in Congress. Eakes even uses the same term to describe his politics—he calls himself a "bleeding-heart conservative"—as did Kemp, a former vice presidential candidate and the director of HUD under the first President Bush. Yet Eakes was more liberal and therefore a foe. "A Leftist Crusader Wants to Dictate Financial Options to Consumers" was the headline over the first of several unflattering pieces about Eakes that the Capital Research Center published. Among Eakes's various crimes: He uses Self-Help to "form political coalitions with radical left-wing groups whose purpose is to bully banks into changing their lending practices"; despite Self-Help's stated mission of helping the disadvantaged, it has loaned millions to its own executives and officers over the years; and its borrowers have delinquency rates seven to ten times higher than their credit union peers. A second article made fewer personal charges but instead criticized Eakes, among others, for "demonizing" the practices of some of the country's leading subprime lenders. In that article, Capital Research lauded Countrywide, New Century, and other subprime lenders for increasing "home ownership opportunities for minorities and low-income borrowers" while ripping "left-wing advocacy groups" like Self-Help that "oppose consumer choice."

In Durham, people didn't know whether to laugh or cry. Capital Research was accusing Eakes of enriching himself at the hands of the poor yet Self-Help's salary cap meant their boss and the other top staff were getting paid no more than $69,000 a year. Still, they earned too much to join the credit union they ran and therefore were ineligible for loans. For his part, Eakes was relieved that the *Raleigh News & Observer* had recently named him its 2005 "Tar Heel of the Year." To ensure they hadn't chosen wrong, the paper had a reporter check Capital Research's charges. "It was bad luck for them that the *News & Observer* had already picked me for this thing," Eakes said. "They had to get to the bottom of this and investigate." Making insider loans and reckless lending "would be worrisome," the *News & Observer* wrote in an editorial appearing shortly after Capital Research's first attack, "if there was a word of truth to them."

At least one of Capital Research's charges was true: More of Self-Help's borrowers were thirty or sixty days late in their mortgage payments when compared to the typical credit union. But that was to be expected given Self-Help's role as a self-styled bank of last resort. "Our customers don't have the same cushion that middle-class borrowers have," Eakes said. "So if they lose a job or someone gets sick, they're more likely to fall behind a month or two. But then they catch up because keeping a home means that much." Through the economic turmoil of 2008, Self-Help, despite its low-income clientele, had consistently maintained a loan default rate of less than 1 percent.

Bonnie Wright, Eakes's wife, believes the attacks on her husband help to sustain him. Longtime Self-Help colleagues say the same, but on some level the assault on his character seems to bother Eakes. He cracked jokes about some of the more personal charges foes have leveled at him but back at his office, he wanted to read me a quote from Eric Dezenhall, Steven Schlein's boss. It took him less than thirty seconds to find it: "Modern communication isn't about truth, it's about a resonant narrative. The myth about PR is that you will educate and inform people. No. The public wants to be told in a story who to like and who to hate."

"They don't understand idealism," Eakes said of the payday lenders and other businesses aligned against him. "They can't believe idealism exists. So they think, 'You have to be doing this because you want our business.' They have the most cynical motives so they conclude everyone else has cynical motives."

Eakes, Ralph Nader–like in his asceticism, hardly offered a fat target for those looking to tarnish the CRL. The same could not be said of all of its donors, though, starting with its top two funders, Marion and Herb Sandler, former owners of the World Savings Bank in Oakland, California. It was Herb Sandler who had first approached Eakes about starting a group like the Center for Responsible Lending, and the Sandlers proved generous benefactors. Mike Calhoun told me the couple had given the CRL roughly $20 million in its first half dozen years but Herb Sandler said the actual dollar figure was "well over" that amount.

Eakes had never heard of World Savings or the Sandlers when Herb Sandler first phoned him proposing a meeting, but he asked around and liked what he had heard about the couple and their bank. They were stand-up lenders, he was told, who concentrated on writing mortgages for middle-class borrowers. They had testified before Congress about sound lending practices and feature articles generally heralded them as humane and socially conscious—old-fashioned bankers succeeding in a modern world. World Savings held on to its loans rather than selling them off on Wall Street. The Sandlers gave generously to the American Civil Liberties Union and Human Rights Watch.

The Sandlers still enjoyed a solid reputation when Wachovia bought Golden West Financial, the parent company of World Savings, for $26 billion in 2006. Their share of the purchase price was a reported $2.3 billion. But then the housing bubble began to deflate and with it the Sandlers' reputation. Wachovia's stock plummeted by nearly 80 percent as reports spread of heavy losses in its mortgage holdings. Wachovia had made its share of irresponsible loans long before merging with World Savings but it was the World Savings portfolio that was blamed, at least initially, for the implosion of this bank that had been founded in 1879. At the peak of the credit crisis, in the fall of 2008, federal regulators pressed Wachovia to sell itself to a more secure partner. Wells Fargo bought Wachovia in October of that year, for $15 billion.

World Savings had specialized in a product called an option ARM. These were adjustable rate mortgages—loans that would see interest rates fluctuate over time—that allowed borrowers to choose how much they would pay each month. The Sandlers dubbed World's product Pick-A-Pay: A customer could make a full monthly payment or they could pay an amount that wouldn't even cover the interest for that month. To the Sandlers, theirs was a more humane product that insulated borrowers from payment shock should there be a spike in interest rates and also gave them the flexibility to ride out financial bumps in the road, whether a lost job, a divorce, or a health-care crisis. The problem with the loan was what bankers call negative amortization: Choose to pay the lower rate and the amount of money you owe rises over time rather than shrinks. Critics dubbed the option ARM and Pick-A-Pay in particular a fundamentally dishonest loan product—essentially an expensive way for people of modest means to rent a home because those always choosing the lesser payment were unlikely to ever have the money to buy the property. The product might make sense when housing prices were soaring—it's a very good deal if you can sell for $400,000 the home you bought for $250,000, even if you paid down little if any of the principal—but a lousy deal when prices fell. Then it only seemed a way of lending to people with little or no regard for their ability to pay. Inside the CRL, they don't seem to have anything good to say about the option ARM. But that wasn't something people internally would talk about on the record. "Our stance," Kathleen Day, CRL's main spokeswoman told me, "is that the Sandlers are perfectly capable of defending themselves." She then added, "We are grateful they have been so generous in their funding of our efforts," and noted that their contributions have never come with any strings attached.

By the time I caught up with Herb Sandler to hear his side of things, he was so fed up with the media that he sputtered more than explained. *Time* magazine put the Sandlers on its list of "25 People to Blame for the Financial Crisis." The *New York Times* named them in a front-page article as two of the chief villains behind the economy's collapse. CBS's *60 Minutes* devoted an entire segment to a former World Savings employee who claimed he had repeatedly tried to warn higher-ups about the destructive nature of the loans they were peddling. The Sandlers were even parodied in a mock C-SPAN press conference aired by *Saturday Night Live*. When their turn came to stand at the podium, they were identified on screen as "Herb and Marion Sandler: People who should be shot."

Herb Sandler seemed most angry about the article in the *New York Times*, which ran on Christmas Day 2008. It wasn't hard to see why. World Savings was an odd choice for anyone looking to single out some of the worst villains of the subprime meltdown. It had not gotten caught up in the securitization frenzy at the heart of the credit collapse. Loans made through World Savings were held on to rather than sold on Wall Street. The Sandlers were pushing adjustable rate mortgages, sure, and they would play a role in the great global recession, but they were not ensnaring people with teaser rates as low as 1 percent annually and then hitting borrowers, two years later, with rates that reset at 6 or 7 or 8 percent. They didn't target minorities or the working poor like many other lenders. World Savings stood as a perfect laboratory for examining how the housing frenzy overtook even seemingly well-meaning businesspeople but instead World—and the Sandlers in particular—was lumped in to listings of the country's more reckless, covetous lenders. Among those delighting in the misfortune of the Sandlers was Steven Schlein, who never seemed to tire of pointing out that the "founders of the Center for Responsible Lending" had been exposed as the "toxic mortgage king and queen."

As if all the negative reports about the Sandlers weren't bad enough for the CRL, another major donor, John Paulson, wore a similarly large target on his back. Paulson was a hedge fund manager who so firmly believed that loose lending standards would cause deep troubles in the broader economy that he bet against the real estate market. Paulson & Co. made $15 billion in profits in 2007, $3.7 billion of which Paulson himself pocketed. That is believed to be the largest one-year payday in Wall Street history. In 2008, his firm collected another $5 billion in profits. In different circumstances, Allan Jones might have been impressed, but Paulson had donated millions to the CRL, so Jones was disgusted.

"It was un-American what he did," Jones said. "He made his money betting against our country. This is who's funding the CRL." Jones then brought up the Sandlers, who he claimed "started the credit meltdown" when they sold Golden West to Wachovia. "You look at how dirty the CRL is," he said. "And after knowing that, you'd even listen to a word they have to say about us?"

Thirteen

Past Due

COLUMBUS, OHIO, 2002–2008

Bill Faith didn't mince words when his fellow activists in Dayton asked him at the start of the 2000s about Dean Lovelace's plan to introduce a local law to restrict the city's predatory home lenders. "I told them, 'No offense, but you don't have the capacity, you don't know what you're doing,'" Faith said. The states and the federal governments have agencies in place to monitor lenders, he told them; cities don't. But Faith was also the state's most prominent housing advocate, so when his allies in Dayton moved ahead anyway, he did what he could to help. Faith shrugged when we met in his offices a few blocks from the state capitol in Columbus in the fall of 2008. "I figured if it got attention for the issue, that'd be a good thing," Faith said. The city councils in Cleveland and Toledo would pass bills similar to Dayton's.

In theory, Ohio was a strong home-rule state that granted municipalities broad powers over the regulations inside their borders. In reality, though, the mortgage industry had the cash and the clout to convince the Ohio state legislature, one year after Dayton's legislation, to pass a law stripping Dayton, Cleveland, and Toledo of the authority to regulate the mortgage lenders operating within their city limits. The boilerplate anti-predatory language its sponsors added to the bill was largely lifted from the 1994 HOEPA statute, and therefore already law, but that didn't prevent Governor Bob Taft, a Republican, from patting himself on the back. This bill, Taft declared when signing the measure into law, proves that in Ohio "we will not tolerate predatory lenders, or loan sharks, who take advantage of senior citizens, people with limited incomes, or people with bad credit histories." More revealing, though, were the reactions of partisans to its passage. "We certainly think it's a good bill," said Dayna Baird, the head of the Ohio Consumer Finance Association and the chief lobbyist for large lenders such as Household and CitiFinancial. In contrast, Jim McCarthy in Dayton dismissed the new law as a "canard" and Bill Faith dubbed it "the most arrogant bill I've seen in all my years in Columbus.

"There's this subprime problem going on all over the state and what do our legislatures do?" Faith asked. "They pass a bill that says to the cities, 'We're going to preempt you from doing anything about preda-tory lending, that's the state's job, but, oh, by the way, we're not going to do anything about the problem." If there was the occasional tale of a borrower harmed by a particularly noxious subprime loan, legislators were told, that was the work of a rogue agent whose misdeeds had been exaggerated by a press corps on the hunt for the sensational. Politi-cians on both sides of the aisle, it seemed, were inclined to extend the benefit of the doubt to any lender willing to work with borrowers of modest means.

The bill, passed during the 2002 legislative session, did create a sixteen-person Predatory Lending Study Committee that would travel the state to assess the problem. When they hit Dayton, so many people wanted a turn at the microphone that, despite a strict five-minute limit on speeches, the meeting lasted three hours. The committee chairman Chuck Blasdel, a Republican state legislator who had been the primary sponsor of the preemption bill, told the *Dayton Daily News* that he was very moved by some of what he had heard that evening, but he warned against any new laws. Tighten regulations, he said, and watch credit dry up in those communities most in need. A year later, Blasdel's task force made its recommendations but they quietly died in committee.

Among his fellow activists, Bill Faith, the executive director of the Columbus-based Coalition on Homelessness and Housing in Ohio, or COHHIO, is celebrated for his ability to get along with legislators on both sides of the aisle. Around the state capital, you're as likely to spot Faith out with a Republican legislator as a Democrat, and over the years he would describe any number of conservative legislators as his friends. Ron Bridges, a lobbyist for AARP, only wishes he could be more like Faith. The AARP was a key ally in the fight against predatory lending and more than once Bridges joined Faith as he tried to work on Blasdel. "I was always two seconds away from wringing the guy's neck because I see all the people getting hurt," Bridges said. "But Bill sees the same thing, which is why he makes sure to get along with guys like Blasdel. He sees the bigger picture." Apparently, though, that means sometimes missing the smaller details. A few years later, Faith and Bridges were on the verge of finally besting the mortgage industry and Bridges looked down to discover that his friend had just spent an hour meeting with the Ohio Senate leadership while wearing two mismatched shoes.

Bill is different than most activists," Mike Toman, a partner in the lobbying firm The Success Group, is explaining to me at his office a block from the state capitol in Columbus. "He knows the inside game." To Toman and his partner, Dan McCarthy, lobbying is best left to the professionals—but Faith is one of those rare social justice crusaders who not only understands how to sell a story to a member of the legislature but also has an innate sense of who to approach and when.

"Most activists want to be right," McCarthy said. "But Bill wants to get things accomplished."

"He's still an activist," Toman said. "He has that passion."

"But he understands how to make a deal," McCarthy said.

And then both more or less said in unison: Bill Faith likes to win.

Faith is a beefy man with a bearish physique and white gray hair that seems perpetually unkempt, as if he is suffering from an incurable case of bed-head. He wears a goatee and has a husky, heavy person's voice that can sometimes makes him sound a bit like John Madden. He's a talker, so much so that his friends joke that they don't dare call him unless they know they will be in the car for at least an hour. He smokes, he swears, and he obviously drinks; when we met at the bar at Mitchell's, a stylish steak house one block from the capitol, a Ketel One and cranberry cocktail appeared in front of him without him needing to ask for it. He wore a sport coat and tie that night, a common occurrence for someone who runs a statewide nonprofit with a multimillion-dollar budget, yet somehow the outfit seemed wrong on him. It might have been the quizzical, boyish way he examined the toast points and goat cheese that accompanied his beet salad (he may be a regular at the bar but he runs a housing advocacy group, and if he eats at Mitchell's, it's a rare treat because someone else is picking up the tab); it might have been the informal "How ya doin'?" greeting he gave most everyone, from the retired Senate president having a drink in the bar area to the hostess showing us to our seats.

His mother would drag him to civil rights protests as a kid. His father, a Presbyterian Republican raised in rural Indiana, was unhappy she was bringing their son to places where they were often the only whites in the room aside from the media. His mother was devastated when Martin Luther King, Jr., was assassinated. His father considered the civil rights leader a communist who had brought tragedy upon himself. Faith grew up in the People's Republic of Youngstown, a staunchly pro-union town and firmly Democratic, but that's only because his father was a farm implement salesman dispatched to eastern Ohio to grow the market there. "A lot of my relatives still live in rural Indiana and rural Illinois," Faith said. "So I know those people. I can talk to them."

Faith was never much of a student. He dropped out of college at the end of his freshman year, but a year back in Youngstown was all he needed to get serious about his studies. "I didn't want to work in the mills," he said, "but that's exactly where my life was headed." He was accepted into Ohio State in the mid-1970s, where his future started to take shape. He read about the Catholic Worker movement and imagined himself as a social worker. He liked the fit and even converted to Catholicism. "I was looking at this small sliver of the Catholic Church and ignoring the other ninety percent," he said. "The first nun I met wore jeans."

Faith's first job after college was at an institution for the mentally ill called Orient, located about thirty miles from Columbus. Orient was a shock to his system. One resident there spent his days chewing his shirt; another, he said, the staff simply tied to a chair. The entire facility reeked from urine. "It's a lot better than it used to be," the facility's superintendent assured him. After Faith discovered that his immediate boss was stealing money from patients, he began surreptitiously removing incriminating documents from work, and eventually a complaint he filed with the state attorney general's office led to the man's removal. Faith left Orient after two years to help open an alternative community for the mentally disabled that he and his fellow idealists called The Ark. Among the residents there was a man with Down syndrome named Richard Wilson, who had lived at Orient for four decades. "He lives in this godforsaken place for forty years but he loves life," Faith said. "He had no reason to but he had this great attitude. He was a kind of life guru for me."

Faith lived the life of a committed leftist coming of age during the first half of the 1980s. He got involved in the peace and sanctuary movements; he joined the Committee in Solidarity with the People of El Salvador (CISPES). Now on the other side of fifty, he sometimes wonders what his younger self might have been thinking. One time he traveled to Washington to join a group of Catholic workers who had chained themselves to the Pentagon to protest U.S. policy in Central America. It might have felt cathartic to speak truth to power, Faith said, but they had no real strategy other than voicing their collective outrage. On the other hand, he had good things to say about the two weeks he spent in the D.C. city jail on trespassing charges. "When does a guy like me ever get to see the inside of a place like that?" he asked.

Back in Columbus, Faith got involved with a group trying to feed and house the homeless. While he was working behind the steam table at one of the soup kitchens, a man pulled out a shiv and slashed Faith's face from ear to lip. What most amazed the people who worked with Faith is that, despite the hundred-plus stitches it required to close the wound, he took his regular turn serving just days later. Faith said he was fine with it ("Maybe he just wasn't on his medications that day," Faith had told the *Cleveland Plain Dealer* when that paper profiled him as its man of the year in 2003) until the guy tracked him down years later to offer an apology. "I kinda had a fantasy vision of shooting him between the eyes," Faith said.

When Greg Haas thinks of his friend back then, he imagines him wearing denim—a denim jacket, a denim shirt, and of course jeans. Faith favored sandals and wore his hair in a fierce bush of curls. The two met when Faith was helping to organize a series of protests at city hall aimed at establishing shelters for the homeless around Columbus and Haas was running the mayoral campaign of an old-school social services Democrat. Faith might have looked like every other protester, Haas said, but even then he stood out from the crowd. "Rather than humiliate people, or just hit them in the face with an issue, Bill seemed to be someone searching for a solution," he said. It was Faith, Haas said, who hammered out a compromise with the city's social services director—find a community willing to take a shelter, the agency head said, and we'll provide the funding—and Faith, after calling what seemed like every landlord and bureaucrat in town, made it happen.

That fight was winding down when Faith was offered a job running the Coalition on Homelessness and Housing in Ohio. He moved out of the Ark and started wearing a tie to meetings, and eventually added a sport coat to his wardrobe. He focused on affordable housing and the homeless through most of the 1990s but by the end of the decade he started talking about predatory lending as well. He thought he had a simple and elegant solution to the problem: Simply apply the state's existing consumer protection laws to the mortgage business. How could it be, he asked, that Ohio protects its citizens from getting ripped off when they plunk down $25 for a toaster but not when they sign papers committing themselves to an $80,000 loan?

Faith shifted strategy after the 2002 legislative session. If the legislature refused to intervene, Faith said, he would "pound the issue in the court of public opinion" until elected officials relented. He began contacting reporters he knew, hoping to get them interested in the issue. He offered the same message to each: The poverty industry is far more pervasive than you think. "I kept telling them, 'Don't talk about black folks,'" Faith said. "There are these loan sharks in the suburbs. There are loan sharks in the town squares of rural areas."

While he was working the phone, he learned that two reporters at the *Columbus Dispatch*, Jill Riepenhoff and Geoff Dutton, were already starting to look at the dramatic spike in foreclosures in the Columbus area. He might have made a pest of himself during the nine months he worked with the pair on their series but it seemed well worth it. The resulting series, "Brokered Dreams," published in September 2005, seemed to have exactly the kind of impact Faith was hoping for. "All of Columbus read it," AARP lobbyist Ron Bridges said of the *Dispatch* series. "Or at least all of political Columbus read it." Bridges, who is black, grumbled that it wasn't until a series of articles showed that the problem had spread to the white suburbs and rural areas that the legislature felt it needed to act, but when I visited him in his office several years later he still had a small stack of reprints right behind his desk.

The two reporters didn't completely ignore the center of town, of course. Dutton's "Flipping Frenzy" piece revealed how wealthy investors with money in a New York–based hedge fund called Stillwater Capital Partners profited from subprime in Columbus, and that kept him running around some of Columbus's poorer neighborhoods in search of vacant properties and the "straw buyers" whose names and signatures were needed to bid up the prices of these boarded-up messes. But the shock in the series was its finding that foreclosure filings had risen faster in the state's suburban and rural counties than in urban ones.

"Foreclosures were predictably concentrated in poor, inner-city neighborhoods," Dutton wrote. "But, surprisingly, clusters of dots circled the outskirts of the city, in the newest subdivisions of suburbia." Even a small Amish community in the northeastern corner of the state felt so under siege that the county posted public service billboards on the more popular horse-and-buggy routes. "You can be robbed when you are away from home," the signs read, "or you can be robbed over pie and coffee. Be skeptical of door-to-door mortgage salesmen."

In her reporting, Riepenhoff focused on a single subdivision on the city's far western suburbs, called Galloway Ridge. It had been developed by Dominion Homes, a publicly traded real estate development company that built subdivisions in central Ohio and Kentucky. Galloway Ridge was a relatively new development but one in six homes were already in foreclosure or part of a bankruptcy proceeding. When Riepenhoff asked the executives at Dominion for an explanation, they blamed it on the irresponsibility of their buyers. "These people are not of the same credit quality, the same earnings level, the same understanding of credit as people in other parts of town," company CEO Douglas G. Borror told the *Dispatch*.

However, the credit counselors, bankers, appraisers, and others in the real estate industry appearing in Riepenhoff's article offered an alternative explanation for the high rate of foreclosures: a lack of checks and balances in the company's sales transactions. Five years earlier, Dominion had created a new division, Dominion Homes Financial Services, to act as a mortgage broker for those looking to buy any of the properties they built. That meant a single company was constructing the homes, setting the prices, and playing a large role in establishing the loan terms. Dominion even went one step further by helping those without any money raise a down payment—or, as Riepenhoff wrote, the home builder "found a way around a federal law barring sellers from giving money directly to buyers for a down payment."

A California-based nonprofit called the Nehemiah Corporation of America was the key. Dominion would send a prospective buyer to Nehemiah, which would send Dominion borrowers the 3 percent down payment required to qualify for a loan through the Federal Housing Administration (FHA). Then, within a few days, Dominion would donate that amount of money to Nehemiah, plus a service fee. (For years HUD, which oversees the FHA, has tried to block this practice but the agency had never prevailed in the courts.)

What was the harm if a sizable corporation wanted to devote a portion of its profits to helping people of modest means raise a down payment for a house? For one thing, it wasn't a gift; Dominion officials admitted to Riepenhoff that they simply passed along the cost of the down payment to the buyer, just as it would the cost of a specially ordered stove. Moreover, there were risk-management studies that led the government to impose the 3 percent requirement in the first place. A 2002 HUD study of Nehemiah-assisted loans in four cities found default rates higher than 19 percent. At 11.5 percent, the Dominion default rate was much lower but it was still twice as high as the Ohio average and more than two and a half times the national average.

The paper found that Ohio's mortgage default rate had reached nearly 6 percent—tops in the country in 2005. The surge had started in 1999, shortly before Faith and the people in Dayton began clamoring for someone in power to act. That year there had been 31,000 new foreclosure filings in Ohio but by 2005 there would be more than twice that number: 64,000. The list of culprits the *Dispatch* series singled out was long and included mortgage brokers who put borrowers in loans they could not afford and unscrupulous appraisers inflating the worth of a property. The series also included a chart of Ohio's ten largest subprime lenders, a roster that included Countrywide, H&R Block, Citigroup, and Wells Fargo. "I think a lot of Columbus was in shock while that series was running," Ron Bridges said.

People inside the *Dispatch* weren't the only ones to notice this creeping menace, of course. Almost as soon as she took office in 2004, Joy Padgett, a state senator representing a predominantly rural district in central Ohio, began to hear from residents worried they were going to lose their home after refinancing with an unscrupulous lender. "At first, I thought they might just be isolated incidents," Padgett said, but the consistency of the calls and the volume convinced her otherwise. Researching the law, she discovered the same loopholes that others had spotted years earlier. At the start of 2006, she introduced the Homebuyers Protection Act, which would broaden the state's consumer protections laws so that they covered mortgage brokers, loan officers, and nonbank lending institutions. The bill also empowered the attorney general's office to prosecute appraisal inflation and other practices that are often part of mortgage fraud. Padgett was a Republican representing a conservative district, but Faith, the left-leaning homeless advocate, finally had his champion. "She ended up becoming a good friend," Faith said.

As 2005 was turning into 2006, Bill Faith was missing a key component in the narrative he was trying to construct. Martin Eakes and his allies had Freddie Rogers, the widower and single parent who drove a bus for the Durham public schools. Bill Brennan and Howard Rothbloom put forward several older women whose plight came to serve as the public face of predatory lending in Atlanta at the start of the 1990s. Bill Faith had a raft of sobering statistics on his side and an ominous sense of a pending crisis, but it wasn't until a lawyer named Rachel Robinson at the Equal Justice Foundation told him about Martha and Larry Clay that he found those Faith dubbed "predatory lending's poster couple."

The Clays, who lived in a white working-class neighborhood in Columbus that locals call the Bottoms, were both blind. Their home had cost $15,000 when they purchased it in the mid-1980s. Larry Clay had worked as an X-ray technician at a nearby hospital for thirty-nine years but that facility closed its doors in 2002 when he was in his mid-sixties. After that the couple lived on a monthly $1,700 disability check. They attended services at a nearby church, where Larry Clay sang several times a week and volunteered at its soup kitchen. Martha Clay had recently survived ovarian cancer. By the time Bill Faith learned these and other facts about the Clays, they had been talked into so many refinancings that the couple owed $80,000 on a home the county assessor claimed was worth only $37,000, and they were facing eviction. The closing costs and broker's fees on the last four refinancings alone added up to $20,000. As Martha Clay described it, they had been paying 7 percent interest on a $72,000 home loan but then the same mortgage broker who had put them in that loan only eight months earlier told them he could get them a better rate. But then the Clays ended up signing papers on an $80,000 loan carrying a 10 percent interest rate. So whereas the couple had been paying $480 a month on their home prior to that final refinancing, their new monthly bill was $702. For his troubles, the mortgage broker paid himself a $3,200 fee.

"Both blind, from a poor white neighborhood in Columbus, scammed into mortgages six different times," Faith said. "Good religious people. He sings in the choir. I mean, she's got cancer and they're doing this to her." Faith couldn't suppress the sly grin tugging at the corner of his lips. Despite the great sympathy he felt for the Clays, he's a political pragmatist who recognizes an opportunity when it is presented to him. "A legislator can argue with me," he said. "But what are they going to say to the Clays? 'You should have known better?' 'You should've read the documents closer?'" The *Dispatch* told the Clays' story in a page-one article that appeared on a Sunday in February 2005, and Faith arranged it so the couple testified in both the Ohio House and Senate when it came time for the appropriate committees to debate Joy Padgett's bill.

The Republican leadership proved critical to its passage. It helped that Faith had a good working relationship with both Bill Harris, the president of the senate, and his top lieutenant, Jeff Jacobson. Both Harris and Jacobson had sided with the industry in 2002 (the Ohio Association of Mortgage Bankers gave Harris its "Legislator of the Year" award that year) yet both joined the reform side in 2006. "I think they recognized that what they were hearing from all these mortgage guys was a bunch of crock," Faith said. Perhaps, but Ron Bridges was inclined to give Faith some credit for helping to nudge them along. Bridges joined Faith when he visited Jacobson, who represented the Dayton suburbs, to talk about Padgett's bill. "Do you want your mother, because she walks into the wrong door on High Street, you want her to lose her home?" Faith asked him. Not for a moment did Bridges think this powerful senator's mom might find herself in that predicament, but it didn't matter. "He got that this was about protecting people's mothers from falling prey to these people," he said of Jacobson. So strongly did Harris and Jacobson back Faith on this bill that when their Republican counterparts in the House tried to water it down, the pair bullied them into backing off.

At Faith's suggestion, the signing ceremony, held in June 2006, took place in the Clays' backyard. "That was a great day in our lives," Martha Clay said. For the occasion she wore a turquoise pantsuit with a green top and a gold heart necklace and Larry Clay donned a sport jacket and tie. Several of the Clay grandchildren also attended. During the signing itself, Governor Taft, as he had done in 2002, congratulated himself for a job well done. With Faith standing behind him, the governor said, "It shouldn't take a miracle to allow our homeowners to stay in their homes and enjoy the American dream."

The bill, which took effect on January 1, 2007, would do some good as the problems in Ohio and elsewhere got worse. The law would give prosecutors additional tools to go after those who had abused borrowers. By the start of 2009, Faith said, the Ohio attorney general had filed multiple suits under the new law.

Still, the victory felt hollow and it would come to feel more so in the coming months. "We knew at the time we were too late," Faith said. No one on his side of things was particularly surprised, he said, when "six months later the wheels fell off" and Ohio's problems transmogrified into a worldwide calamity.

Not long after the signing ceremony, Bill Faith made the three-hour drive to Youngstown to visit his mother. He hoped to do a little boasting, he admitted, or at least get some rest, but instead she started lobbying him. She told him about people she knew from church who had gotten themselves into a deep financial hole using the services of payday stores, and she mentioned people they both knew from the neighborhood who had gotten themselves in trouble the same way.

"I have this big win and my own mother, she's on me about dealing with this other thing," Faith says. "I'm all excited, 'We did it,' and she's like, 'That's nice but what about payday lending?'" he said. He hacked out a throaty smoker's laugh, shot me a glance, and asked, "Ya know?" With time, the payday lenders would grow to despise Faith with nearly the same intensity they normally reserved for Martin Eakes.

There's something monomaniacal about Bill Faith. He burrows so deeply into an issue or a project that it's as if the rest of the world ceases to exist. His wife of more than twenty years, Barb Poppe, describes it as "the zone." It doesn't make a difference if her husband is working at the computer or deep into a document or just playing cards. "When he gets in the zone, that's what he totally focuses on," Poppe said. But that also means Faith can miss a lot while he's concentrating on something else. For the longest time this advocate for the poor was oblivious to all the payday stores opening in and around Columbus. To the extent he even understood what a payday loan was, he figured it was something people took out once in a blue moon. "I'm embarrassed to say that the cycle of debt and people getting sucked in was something that never even occurred to me," Faith said.

Before his mother brought up the problem, Dan McCarthy, his lobbyist friend, and Tom Allio, a political ally running the social action arm of the Catholic Diocese of Cleveland, did. McCarthy had never taken out a payday loan, but he knew his sister had because she put him down as a reference and lenders started calling *him* at work whenever she was late on a payment. It got so bad, McCarthy told Faith, that he had written a big check just to make the phone calls stop. McCarthy, who had worked with Faith on the predatory lending bill, had even half joked with his friend on the night they finally won, "Now we go after the payday lenders."

For Allio, payday had become his issue a couple of years earlier when he first learned about a woman named Peggy Daugherty. Daugherty, traveling back and forth from central Ohio to Cleveland to get medical attention for her daughter, had borrowed $300 to pay for work on her car. By the time a friend intervened, Daugherty, a middle-aged woman living on a monthly disability check of about $900 a month, owed money to five different stores and had already spent more than $1,000 in fees. To Allio, payday was nothing but an extension of the predatory subprime mortgage lending problem, and in fact he had irritated Faith no end by suggesting they add a payday rate cap to the predatory lending bill.

"We already were up against the entire mortgage industry," Faith said. "At that point we didn't need a whole new set of enemies lining up against us."

Faith had promised Allio he would turn his attention to payday finance as soon as the mortgage fight was over, but months passed without Faith making any commitments. "I was still dragging my feet," Faith said. "So now Tom is getting even more pissed." It was no longer a question of what he thought of payday loans. A woman on his staff was getting calls at work because of a sibling who was past due on some loans and he heard from another friend whose sister had also gotten herself into a deep hole using them. "Once you start looking into this thing, you see it's a really ugly world," Faith said. But Faith, ever the pragmatist, wanted to see if they stood a chance before jumping into the fight. He checked in with a few friendly legislators and he set up a meeting with the governor-elect, a Democrat named Ted Strickland. Strickland, who would take office at the start of 2007, asked him to wait, but he also made it clear he would sign something if it reached his desk. Faith had similarly encouraging signs from the others, so he informed Allio he was on board.

The group called themselves the Ohio Coalition for Responsible Lending—a self-conscious nod to the Center for Responsible Lending. Jim McCarthy and Dean Lovelace were members, as were a long list of labor leaders, housing activists, community organizers, legal aid attorneys, and those representing faith-based organizations around the state. "To many of us this wasn't just an economic issue but a moral one,"

Allio said. "The high interest rates they charge is a modern-day form of usury. I don't care what the text, whether it be Jewish or Catholic or mainline Protestant, there's clear statements in each against usury and the need to offer fair interest rates." The group decided that its aim would be to cap the interest rates that payday lenders could charge and limit the number of loans a person could take in a given year. "We had people calling the office every day who are like, 'I've got five, six, ten payday loans, I'm trapped,'" said Nick DiNardo, a legal aid attorney in Cincinnati. "And there was nothing we could really do short of helping them if the collections got too aggressive." It fell to Faith to find a lead sponsor for their bill.

The new governor was a Democrat but the Republicans still controlled both the Ohio House and Senate. So instead of starting with a good liberal, Faith surprised his allies by first approaching a conservative legislator named Bill Batchelder. With Leonid Brezhnev eyebrows, oversized Mars Blackmon glasses, and a tendency to quote Adam Smith, Batchelder hardly seemed to fit the bill of consumer champion. But if they could first muster Republican support, Faith reasoned, some of the bipartisanship good feeling they had nourished during the mortgage fight might carry over to payday. Besides, the two got along famously. Unlike most every other lobbyist traipsing through his office, Batchelder told me, he always found Faith a man of conviction "who was actually looking to engage you in a serious policy debate." If some of Faith's allies were inclined to describe Batchelder as one of the legislature's "cavemen conservatives," that was all right with Batchelder, who reacted to the characterization with a burst of delighted laughter.

Batchelder and Faith might disagree about most everything but he was an easy sell on payday lending. Batchelder told him he was happy to sponsor the Coalition for Responsible Lending's bill, not despite Adam Smith, the first apostle of laissez-faire, but because of him. "The rates lenders charged were a moral question for Smith," Batchelder said. "Smith pointed out that if you charge too much, you damage a society. And he's right. You can't charge people these kinds of interest rates without hurting their situation and society." In October 2007,

Batchelder and Robert Hagan, a liberal Democrat from Youngstown, introduced a bill that would impose a 36 percent rate cap on the interest rates payday lenders could charge.

In Washington, D.C., Steven Schlein reacted to the news with an indifferent shrug. After four years with the payday lenders, he had learned not to get too worked up over every dispatch from the hinterlands. "Every year a bunch of states put payday into play," Schlein said. "But then in the end you have few actual fights." They had lost legislative battles in Oregon and New Hampshire over the previous few years but mainly they ended up with a compromise that the big chains could live with. "Ohio didn't seem one of the places we should worry about it," Schlein said.

In Spartanburg, Billy Webster was similarly unconcerned. The market was too important and the industry too strong in Ohio to lose. Check 'n Go was based in Cincinnati and the Davis brothers several years earlier had had the foresight to spend the money necessary to lure away a top Ohio Senate staffer to run its governmental affairs office. There was also CheckSmart, based in Columbus, a chain of 175 payday and check-cashing stores that had just been sold to a large New York–based private equity fund for $268 million. After writing a check that big and with half of its stores in-state, CheckSmart's investors weren't going to sit idly by. "We were told time and time again," Webster said. "With Check 'n Go and CheckSmart there, there was no way Ohio would be in play."

The Coalition for Responsible Lending held forums across the state and organized small delegations to meet with individual legislators and with the editorial boards of all the big daily newspapers. A local research group, Policy Matters Ohio, released a report demonstrating that payday had become widespread even in the state's suburban and rural areas. When, in the autumn of 2007, Marc Dann, the state's Democratic attorney general, announced he would be holding hearings investigating the lending practices of the state's 1,600 payday stores, the search was on for customers and employees, or at least former employees, willing to talk about their experiences.

The first of three hearings was held in a large Baptist church on Cleveland's east side. The industry might have been confident about a victory but they were hardly complacent. Its supporters showed up in full force, wearing yellow "I Support Payday Lending" buttons and made sure their perspective was voiced. They pointed to the list of "best practices" their trade association had developed, including a twenty-four-hour rescission policy and a once-a-year extended payment plan for customers who get themselves into financial trouble with a payday loan. Payday's critics, many of whom sported buttons showing a shark's snout biting into a large stash of cash, dismissed these voluntary policies as not worth the paper they were printed on. One of the more moving speakers in Cleveland was a man named Charles Mormino, who told the crowd about a family member with psychiatric problems (he was no more specific than that) who had gotten into trouble with a trio of payday stores. He settled up her debts at all three and then sent a certified letter to each alerting them to the family member's problem. But all three—Advance America, CheckSmart, and ACE Cash Express—continued to do business with her.

A former payday manager named Tom Kirk spoke at the attorney general's hearing in Columbus. On paper, Kirk said, the payday lenders were generally responsible citizens. There were in fact rules at the company where he worked against lending to a customer carrying loans at multiple stores, and there were policies to protect borrowers from overzealous collections. The rub was that employee bonuses were based largely on volume. "The policy manual of the company I worked for was good," Kirk said. "The problem is that the district manager and the store managers and the store personnel don't always follow it."

Those who supported the Batchelder bill might have felt encouraged by their organizing efforts if not for one failing: They seemed to be getting nowhere in their hunt for legislators willing to join their crusade. Particularly baffling was the reluctance of House Democrats to commit to their cause. "Several of the legislators were not friendly, verging on hostile," said Jeff Modzelewski, an organizer for BREAD, a church-based group in the Columbus area, who met with all twelve legislators representing the capital and its suburbs in the statehouse. Even Joyce Beatty, the House minority leader, a black woman representing central Columbus, proved frosty. "We figured she would be strongly enthusiastic," Modzelewski said. "She represents a black, poor urban district with inner-city problems. But meeting with her—she was among the worst. I'm there with twenty church members and she's talking to us like we don't know what we're talking about."

There are people in the black community, of course, with a favorable view of the poverty industry. In South Carolina, I spent an evening with Willie Green, the former pro football player who had proven brave or foolish enough to appear on *60 Minutes Wednesday*. Green, who by this time had gone to work for Advance America, spoke rhapsodically about the critical role these fringe financial institutions played in the life of the black community. "Check-cashing stores and pawnshops and payday lending stores, those are the poor man's institutions," Green said. "You go to any poor black person, and I guarantee you, they've borrowed money from a payday person, a title loan person, or a pawnshop. That's what you do if you don't have the luxury of going into a bank and borrowing money." Green's father, a janitor at a movie theater in Athens, Georgia, had raised nine kids on $85 a week. "He used to play golf on Saturdays and Sundays and then go to the pawnshop," Green said. "He'd pawn his clubs and he'd pay for my school, or whatever I needed to succeed in life. And then he'd go get his clubs at the end of the week when he got paid.

"He made that sacrifice for us. If my dad had not had the ability to use a pawnshop, I wouldn't be where I am. I wouldn't have been able to go to college. I wouldn't have been able to play professional sports."

But Joyce Beatty was another story. The *Cleveland Plain Dealer* revealed that CheckSmart, the company that had just been sold for more than a quarter of a billion dollars, put Beatty's husband, himself a former legislator (she had taken his seat in the legislature), on the CheckSmart payroll. Even the whiff of controversy was all the motivation many in Beatty's caucus needed to make up their minds about the evils of payday lending. "A lot of wavering Democrats suddenly had very strong opinions," said Jim Siegel, who covers the state legislature for the *Dispatch*. Even Beatty came out in support of meaningful payday reform, as if to show that she was not in bed (so to speak) with the industry. Now all they had to do was convince enough Republicans that there was a compelling reason to add to the state's job loss and shutter an industry that employed several thousand people across Ohio.

In the eight years he served in the Ohio House of Representatives, Chris Widener remembers a gavel being used during a committee hearing only a few times—and all of them were in the winter and spring of 2008, when his committee, Financial Institutions, was debating payday lending. Widener is an architect by profession, thorough and precise, a thin man with blue eyes, metal-framed glasses, and a receding hairline. He believed that any person wanting a chance to speak should be given one and so he held four hearings on the issue, one of which lasted nearly seven hours.

The crowds were large and often raucous. What Chris Browning remembers about her time in front of Widener's committee was the hissing and the jeering that accompanied her testimony. She told the committee about the GM pensioner who had borrowed money from her store for 115 consecutive months—and people wearing yellow "I Support Payday Lending" buttons and yellow shirts booed and yelled out things like "liar" and "bullshit." She declared that "repeat borrowers are the payday loan institution's bread and butter," which prompted more catcalls and cries. "Widener's banging that gavel of his and telling people they'll be quiet or he'll remove them but it's not making much difference," Browning recalled.

An unhappy Allan Jones took his turn at the witness table. He had better things to do than try to explain his business to people who didn't understand it, yet suddenly he had been told that he needed to worry about shutting down all his stores in one of his best markets. "It's like overnight we're hearing we might lose Ohio," he recalled. With foreclosures starting to spike across the country and the economy starting to teeter, he was worried that payday would end up collateral damage. "Payday didn't cause any of this but I realized we were being used as an easy scapegoat," he said. You might not like how I make my money, he told the committee, but the people you'd be hurting if you imposed this cap "were the ones who without us couldn't pay the electric company or the repair shop if their car breaks down."

Bill Faith listened in amazement to this heavyset man from Cleveland, Tennessee, who had flown to Columbus in his private jet to lecture the Ohio state legislature about the plight of the working man. "We provide them an essential service to help them when they're most in need," Jones said earnestly. Who *is* this guy, Faith asked himself—and then quickly realized it was his best friend. "I just wanted him to talk and talk and talk," Faith said. "Because the more he talked, the more he offended everybody." Faith had the opposite reaction when Lynn DeVault, a Jones underling serving as the president of the payday trade group, took her turn at the microphone. Rather than dismissing the critics as pointy-headed elitists, she acknowledged the payday horror stories but then blamed them on mom-and-pop shops refusing to adopt the industry's best-practices pledge. Our customers like us, she said, and if that wasn't quite true, they certainly didn't dislike them so much that they did something about it. Only about a dozen people a year typically filed a complaint about a payday lender with the state—a small number when compared to those filed against check cashers and others in the poverty business. "Customers are intelligent people who choose the lowest-cost alternative for themselves at a particular point in time," DeVault told the committee. They can pay us $15 to borrow $100—or they can pay the bank $35 every time they bounce a check or blow $50 paying a utility company a restore-service fee because they were two payments late on their electricity bill.

Terrence Jent, who had worked as a regional director for Check 'n Go, offered a very different perspective than Jones or DeVault. Jent had started as a store manager in his last semester of college and quickly worked his way up from district manager to regional manager. What bothered him about his four years in the industry, it seemed, was the aggressiveness with which they pursued someone who was late in paying them back. "You will receive harassing phone calls three to four times a day," he told the committee. "All of your personal references will receive phone calls each day. You will be visited at work in an attempt to embarrass you into paying your loan. You will be visited at your home so that you understand that the payday lender knows where you live."

Yet the hearings, while raucous and often dramatic, weren't swaying opinions. Widener regularly polled committee members, as did Jim Siegel over at the *Dispatch*. Both were hearing the same thing. Republican members might be willing to do something about payday but nothing so radical as a rate cap. "They were telling me, 'We might have to do a bit of tinkering, we might need to put on some kind of limit, but we don't want to shut an industry down,'" Siegel said. Widener was searching for a compromise that set aside the rates the payday lenders charged but limited people to two loans at any given time or perhaps eight loans a year. "At that point, it didn't look like anyone was passing anything," Siegel said.

Steven Schlein might want to claim the role of underdog but in Ohio the payday lenders were anything but outmanned. Schlein's group, the Community Financial Services Association, had six lobbyists on the payroll during those months they were debating a payday cap (including Chuck Blasdel, the former state representative who had done the bidding of the subprime mortgage lenders in 2002 and 2006). A group calling itself the Ohio Association of Financial Service Centers had its advocates, as did the individual chains. Cash America, with 139 stores in the state, hired two lobbyists. Rent-A-Center, with fifty-three stores in Ohio offering payday loans, hired four. "You could see it just sitting there," Faith said. "It's like each little delegation sitting in the crowd had their own lobbyist."

In the end, though, the rival lobbying seem to carry less weight than the gathering economic cataclysm that was threatening to engulf the state. The Republicans had already lost the governorship and they were scrambling to maintain their majorities in the Ohio House and Senate. The Speaker of the House, Jon Husted, wanted the party to be on the side of reform. So one day in early April, with the hearings over, Husted held an impromptu press conference with a small gaggle of Columbus reporters.

"I sense growing support for a rate cap in our caucus," Husted announced. That of course wasn't what they were hearing or what Widener had been telling them, but the Speaker was sending a message. He wanted to see a rate cap passed and he wanted it to happen quickly.

Strickland, the new governor, also turned up the heat after Bill Faith ran into him in the hallways of the capitol. The two had known each other for years, and when Strickland asked Faith how it was going, Faith told him he could use his help on the payday lending bill. That day Strickland's staff penned a letter with Faith's help. "It is my hope," the governor wrote, that the legislature would approve a 36 percent rate cap and that "I would have the opportunity to sign this policy change into law in the near future."

That weekend Husted called Widener. He was not about to be out-flanked by a popular new Democratic governor on an issue he had already staked out. Perhaps the simplest solution, Widener suggested, was to take away what the legislature had granted the industry back in 1995, when it exempted these short-term loans from the state's 28 percent usury cap. That was a cap even lower than the one Strickland had endorsed, which sounded fine to Husted. Twenty-nine Republicans joined forty Democrats to pass the bill by a 69–26 margin. The bill also limited people to four payday loans in a year.

The industry made a last-ditch stand in the senate. They hired more local lobbyists, flew in more troops from out of state, and held a giant rally in front of the statehouse. About two thousand people, most of them payday employees, gathered to listen to speakers and chant, "Save our jobs!"

But it was too late. The day after the rally, the state attorney general released his report on Ohio's payday lenders. There was "compelling evidence of an industry that uses deceptive practices to target some of the state's most vulnerable citizens," Marc Dann wrote. He dismissed payday loans as "a deceptively attractive choice for those in need of quick cash." Widener's bill flew through the senate with only minor changes and Governor Strickland signed the bill into law in early June.

The payday lenders, though, would have the last laugh. "It's a sad day when the opinions of editorial writers and so-called consumer groups count for more than the opinions of the people," Lynn DeVault said in a statement released on the day Strickland signed the cap into law. The next day, DeVault and her allies did something about this grave injustice when they filed paperwork with the secretary of state's office indicating their intention to repeal the new rate cap through a statewide referendum. The foes of payday lending would have to win twice, though this time in an expensive statewide ballot fight that seemed well beyond their budget.

"I was," Bill Faith said, "more surprised than I want to admit." At a press conference, he told the assembled reporters, "You ain't seen nothing yet," but in truth he was nervous. "I had pulled every rabbit out of a hat I could think of," he said, and his reservoir of clever ideas seemed dry.

Fourteen

Maximizing Share
of Wallet

LAS VEGAS, OCTOBER 2008

Tim Thomas, the owner of Daddy's Money Pawn Shop in Wichita, could not really say why he flew from Kansas to Las Vegas for the twentieth annual check cashers' meeting. Around us the ambitious scurried about, dreaming of new markets to conquer, but Thomas was content with the way things were. "I've got a good manager so basically my time is mine," he said. Thomas typically shows up at his shop mid-morning. He inspects the previous day's receipts, does a quick scan of the books, and makes up the day's lunch schedule. Except for tax season, that's his workday, pretty much over just two hours after it starts. Sometimes he goes to the health club to work out but mainly, Thomas said, "I play a lot of golf."

Thomas, who was fifty-four when we met in the fall of 2008, didn't choose the poverty business as his path to Easy Street so much as it chose him. He was in his mid-thirties and working a route for a vending machine supplier when a childhood friend asked him to help him open a pawnshop in Wichita. That didn't quite work out as either had hoped but a new world had been opened to Thomas, and in short order he was managing a rival pawnshop doing a robust business cashing people's checks and making payday loans. In 1999, after eight years of working for someone else, he opened Daddy's Money. It too would be a full-service financial center making pawn loans but also handling a range of low-denomination financial interactions. What started out as a modest-sized, 1,500-square-foot shop is today an 8,000-square-foot superstore employing a staff of ten.

Daddy's Money faces stiff competition. A partial list of rivals within the Wichita city limits includes A-OK Pawn, the Pawn Shop, King's Pawn, Cash Inn, Money Town, A Loan at Last, Aces' Pawn, Air Capital Pawn Shop, Cash Inn Pawn, C&C Pawn Shop, Country Pawn, Easy Money Pawn Shop, Mr. Pawn, and Sheldon's Pawnshop. But apparently even in the country's fifty-first most populous city, with 350,000 residents, there's more than enough business to go around. Daddy's Money, Thomas acknowledged, turns a handsome profit.

"I'm making a lot of money," he said shaking his head, as if he were as astonished as the next guy over his good fortune.

For months I had talked with poverty industry pioneers who had portrayed what they did for a living as noble. To hear them tell it, it was never about the money but instead about helping people and providing a valuable service. But Thomas didn't reach for the high moral plane when describing how he made a living. That became immediately clear once he started talking about his various businesses, starting with check cashing. Check cashing generates only a few thousand dollars in fees per month, accounting for a small sliver of Daddy's Money's revenues, but it's also a lucrative piece.

Kansas is one of seventeen or so states where there's no cap on the fees a check-cashing establishment can charge. Thomas takes a relatively small portion (2 percent) when a customer presents a payroll check but a high one (10 percent) if it's a handwritten personal check. On the surface that makes sense. Cashing a handwritten check seems far riskier than cashing one issued by an established business. But

Thomas has removed almost all the risk inherent in the transaction before a clerk slides over any money. By that point, an employee has spoken to both the person who has written the check, to verify that it's good, and to the bank, to make sure the funds are available.

Why, then, does he still take one-tenth of the face value of a check given the improbability that it will bounce?

"Because I can," Thomas said with an amiable smile. "Other states have their rules but in Kansas I can charge as much as I want. It's part of the game you play."

Playing the game means taking whatever nips Thomas can from every check cashed inside his store. People who don't have a bank account must pay their gas and electric and cable bills in person, using cash, or they must pay someone like Thomas to pay the bills for them—at $2 per bill. He has also partnered with Western Union for those customers, immigrants especially, who want to wire money overseas. But Thomas didn't use a word as genteel as "partner." Western Union pays him a "kickback," Thomas said, every time a customer made a wire transfer, just as he earned a "kickback" each time he sold one of the prepaid debit cards he peddles for a subsidiary of American Express.

"If I sell a card for $10.95, I get $5," he said. "Every time they swipe a card to make a purchase, something like a nickel or a dime or maybe a quarter kicks back to me"—depending on how much one of his customers spends on a transaction.

Cash advances represent another healthy source of Thomas's revenues. In most other states where payday loans are offered, customers can't take out back-to-back loans indefinitely but in Kansas they can. That cuts both ways, Thomas said. It's great for the bottom line if a customer simply pays another 15 percent commission every other week for months at a time before paying back a loan. The flip side is that there's nothing in the law to stop that customer from taking out a second or a third loan. Thomas imagines the customer who borrows $500, the maximum allowed under Kansas law. "That loan is costing him $75 every two weeks," Thomas said. That might not sound like much, he said, but $150 a month can swamp, say, the home health-care worker earning $8 an hour and taking home $1,000 per month.

"If one month he has trouble keeping up with his payments, he'll take out a second payday loan and then a third," he said. "After a while that's self-defeating. They're looming on bankruptcy and they just don't know it. And I'm not getting paid." Defaults eat up roughly one-fifth of his payday revenues—more or less the same number that the big chains report.

In the payday business, September and December are typically the best months of the year because of back-to-school and the holidays. But Thomas is also in the tax preparation business; that means January and February are the most lucrative for Daddy's Money.

Almost every enterprise that's part of the fringe economy takes a stab at the tax return business. That's something that Fesum Ogbazion griped about when we spoke in Dayton: all those pawnshops and check casher operations and even used car lots encroaching on his turf. Tim Thomas's experience at Daddy's Money shows why so many take the plunge. Thomas charges $65 for every return he fills out—good compensation, he said, for a job that typically takes him less than an hour. And while that's the end of the work he must do, that's just the start of the ways in which he is remunerated for his efforts.

The pages of *Cheklist*, the monthly magazine of the check-cashing industry, are marbled with the ads of companies pitching their services as a no-fuss way of making money in the tax business. Refund Today ("NO Tax Knowledge Necessary"), for instance, offers a product it calls "EZ Refund": Pay nothing out of pocket, its ad reads, and we provide the software you'll need and also the back office support. That means they take care of everything from electronically filing the completed tax return with the IRS to arranging the loan terms for those seeking a rapid refund. Under Thomas's deal, he earns $6 for every client who opts for a refund anticipation loan (most do, he said) and then at the end of the season receives a bonus check based on the volume of his RAL business. In recent years, that's meant an extra $2,000 to $3,000 in revenues.

The refund anticipation loan pays off in two additional ways. There's the extra check-cashing fees he earns from those who invariably choose to cash a check on the spot and also the corresponding boost in pawn sales. Because of the earned income tax credit, the tax season is the one time each year that many of the working poor feel rich, and his pawnshop is a bargain hunter's dream, a veritable warehouse crammed with flat-screen TVs, jewelry, video cameras, video games, and power tools—"everything except firearms," Thomas said. Not surprisingly, he said, the first two months of the year are his best on the pawn side of the business, which accounts for around half his revenues.

In other environments, Thomas might seem covetous. But here in Las Vegas, surrounded by fresh-scrubbed junior executives in shirts stamped with the names of some of the country's largest Poverty, Inc. brands, he comes across as the last modest man. He knows he could make a lot more money if he opened a second or a third store but then that would mean spending his days bouncing between stores and constantly fretting over new hires. Besides, what would he do with that extra money? "I'm not a greedy individual," he said. "I'm fine with the one store."

Modest" is not a term anyone would use to describe the ambitions of a thirty-two-year-old junior mogul named Fraser MacKechnie. MacKechnie is the chief operating officer of Amscot Financial, a family-run, all-purpose Poverty, Inc. enterprise (check cashing, payday loans, tax prep, money orders, prepaid credit cards) with more than 170 stores and 2,300 employees stretched across thirteen counties in central Florida. A tall, thin man with a wedge of blond hair, MacKechnie was featured in a panel discussion ("Marketing Strategies That Improve Perception and Profit") I attended on the first morning of the check cashers' convention. He spent thirty minutes sharing the tricks and tips that he, his father, and his brother have learned in operating what is widely considered one of the better run and more successful regional powerhouses.

MacKechnie began by stressing the "all-important" issue of "curb appeal." Aim to look like a McDonald's, he counseled; look to chains such as Starbucks for ideas. "We make a concerted effort to blend in and look like any national retailer," he offered. He also took on what might be described as the third rail of check cashing in the late 2000s—what he dubbed the "highly controversial issue" of direct deposit (I would attend a later workshop titled "Direct Deposit: Friend or Foe"). Many in the industry might fight direct deposit because it means losing the check-cashing fee, MacKechnie said, but at Amscot they've taken the opposite tack and offer their customers a direct deposit option. It has meant a short-term drop in revenues, MacKechnie acknowledged, but they also feel they're holding on to some customers as they move up the economic ladder. Think of the loyalty that builds, he counseled the three dozen or so people sitting in the audience. Invariably some of those customers will slide back down that ladder— especially in the current economy—"and then you'll be there to cash their unemployment checks." Think as well of the PR benefits. "It lets us present ourselves as more of an integrated financial institution," he said. "It helps give us a story when we talk to reporters."

If MacKechnie had one message to impart above all others, it was that today's Poverty, Inc. entrepreneur needs to become indispensable. Sell monthly commuter passes, lottery tickets, and postage stamps. Let people pay their parking tickets at your offices. You won't make much, if any, money on any of these items but customers will have extra reasons to stop by your stores and, more important, you'll find yourself with a strong set of friends when the industry is under attack. "We figure if we work with and become an arm of government," MacKechnie said, "they'll hopefully be less likely to do away with us as it will directly affect them." Similarly Amscot has offered its stores to local gas and electric companies anxious to shed the costs of operating satellite offices. "They're not much of a moneymaker for us," he said of these deals, "but they make us truly part of the fabric of the community."

Meeting with elected officials should be another priority. "It's not just about giving contributions," MacKechnie said. Sell your story. Show them the quality of your stores. Let them see what you do. "And then make sure you issue a press release about the visit," he said. MacKechnie figures that he, his brother, and their father have met with more than two hundred elected officials.

Throughout the weekend, the check cashers, payday lenders, and others taking the stage in Las Vegas patted themselves on the back for all they were doing on the philanthropy front. But sitting in the audience I often had the opposite reaction: That's the extent of your giving? The first time I had that feeling was listening to MacKechnie. The numbers he was talking seemed paltry for a company with Amscot's size and reach—$500 here, $500 there—and mainly he stressed the public relations advantage of sharing bits of their largesse. "Let the broader community know you care," he advised. "Make sure you send out a press release whenever you make a contribution." Later I checked and learned the company issued eleven such press releases in 2008, each announcing a $500 donation, or a total of $5,500. That worked out to about $32 per store.

MacKechnie had one more idea to share before turning over the microphone: Amscot has banned the "at times controversial phrase 'payday loan.'" They stopped using the term in promotional materials, he said, and they no longer use it in press releases. Instead they now offer a "life-line product" called a "cash advance." "We figure that way we can avoid some criticism by not being lumped in any time there's something negative written about payday," he said.

Mike Hodges of Nashville had made the same decision. When he started in the business in 1996, at the age of twenty-four, Hodges did nothing but payday loans. But by the time of the check cashers' show near the end of 2008, he was operating twenty stores and building a twenty-first and each provided, among other fee-generating services, check cashing, auto title loans, money transfers, and prepaid Visa cards. But though he might have started off in the payday business, that's not a word you'll hear watching one of the commercials his company, Advance Financial, runs on local television stations, and it's not a word you'll hear spoken by his clerks, all of whom have been instructed to use the term "cash advance." "The term 'payday' has become the black skull and crossbones of our industry," Hodges complained.

Hodges and his wife, Tina, who helps him run Advance Financial, were my luncheon companions on my first day at the convention. Mainly that meant listening to Mike Hodges rail about the big chains that run the payday industry. Payday is not an easy sell given what he described as a cultural bias against "the waitress with three kids who is short $200 on her rent," but industry leaders haven't helped their cause much. "It's like our industry is just now figuring out that we're not selling bottled water," he said. For a long time the big chains have been so focused on opening new markets that they have failed to do the hard work of educating the wider public. "They've put much more effort into lobbying and not enough into public relations," Hodges said. As a result, "We've let ourselves become easy targets at the hands of consumer advocates."

Despite that, business remained good inside Advance Financial through hard economic times, so much so that Tina Hodges's main complaint was a worldwide credit freeze that put their expansion plans on a shelf. I expressed amazement over twenty-one stores in a single metro area and Tina Hodges shrugged. "We could have a lot more," she told me. But with credit tight, any money committed to opening more stores means less money out on the streets. "With twenty stores, they're not rich yet," Steven Schlein told me when I brought up the Hodgeses the next time we met. "But they're making a good living." He wasn't much interested in talking about Mike Hodges's criticism but he was eager to learn more about Advance Financial. He was more impressed when I told him its stores offered much more than cash advances, including check cashing, debit cards, and beyond. He let out a little whistle of air. "Twenty stores is a lot," Schlein said. "The number I hear is $100,000 as a ballpark for profits per store. That's $2 million a year."

There was a small convention floor upstairs from where the workshops and the speeches were held. There large and familiar companies such as Western Union and H&R Block shared exhibit space with the more modest-sized booths occupied by small companies like Citylight Bullet Proof ("for all your bulletproof needs"), *Cheklist* magazine (the publication representing the "neighborhood financial services provider"), and the Rolland Safe Company. A veritable ecosystem had formed around the poverty industry, and walking the convention floor meant hearing from multiple competitors in any number of subspecialties, from debt collectors who had shown up in Las Vegas to offer their services to software makers there to peddle specialty products. Several companies sold themselves as offering better "card-scanning solutions," and at the booth for Acton Marketing, Zach Gabelhouse, the residential numbers genius for this Lincoln, Nebraska–based direct mail company, told me why his company was superior to the four or five other direct mail companies vying for the attention of conference attendees. The practice of microtargeting has meant that "prospecting"—the art of getting people in the door—is routine nowadays. "The real challenge is retention," Gablehouse said. "You need to maximize the household value of that customer. Where we come in is we help you to maximize your share of wallet."

Over the years there have been plenty of companies to do just that, starting with Western Union decades ago. As if intent on strutting its central place in the check-cashing industry, Western Union occupied a stretch of real estate in the middle of the convention floor so large that it would have been impossible to miss, even if the company hadn't bothered to hire an Elvis impersonator. Squadrons of salespeople dressed in the company's familiar yellow and black didn't talk to visitors to the booth one-on-one so much as they swarmed them in threes or fours. Western Union may be synonymous with the telegram, one explained to me, but the company had exited that business altogether a couple of years ago. Nowadays, the company, a global powerhouse that booked $5.3 billion in revenues in 2008 and $1.2 billion in pretax profits, makes nearly all its money wiring money across borders, primarily through deals with third parties. "We'll cut franchise deals with anyone who'll have us," another of the buzz team told me. "We've got deals with the big discount drugstore chains, with grocery stores, with clothing stores." But Western Union's best partners have been the country's check cashers and other Poverty, Inc. businesses, all of which earn a small amount of the $50 or so Western Union charges for every $1,000 a customer wires overseas. And that's only the start of the benefits, according to a Western Union brochure I took with me. Supposedly, three in every four people walking into a store to wire money spend money on a second product at that store.

Diversification has been the watchword of the forward-looking fringe financier in recent years, and any number of companies were in Las Vegas to help conference goers enhance their bottom line by broadening their offering of products. There were about a half-dozen tax preparers on the exhibit floor pitching the instant tax refund as the perfect way to goose annual revenues ("CHARGE to prepare returns and CHARGE to cash their check"). There were companies pitching prepaid phone cards and also several pushing gold buying as the ideal side business ("add significant income to your financial service center's bottom line at virtually no cost") in hard economic times, when more people would be needing access to quick cash. The largest crowds, though, seemed to be drawn to the booths of those peddling the debit cards that help Wichita's Tim Thomas live the good life.

Debit or prepaid credit cards have become a sensation inside the industry in recent years. A price sheet I picked up when visiting the booth of a company called CashPass, which sells a prepaid MasterCard, spelled out why. Sell more than 500 CashPass debit cards in a month and the enterprising check casher earns a 25 percent cut of all the charges that card generates. That includes an $11.95 setup fee, a $6.95 monthly fee, and more fees when a customer puts more cash on the card. Sell more than 1,000 and your cut is 30 percent. A CashPass representative was happy to translate those numbers into dollar figures for me: 1,000 cards on average means an extra $10,700 per month added to an entrepreneur's bottom line. The advantage to the customer is that with what in effect serves as a portable bank account, he or she has taken a step forward into the mainstream, albeit a stunningly pricey one.

Listening to speeches that weekend in Las Vegas meant hearing about any number of bogeymen. In his welcoming speech, the group's chairman, Joseph Coleman, singled out the FDIC and its hand-wringing over those 17 million or so Americans without a bank account, the so-called "unbanked." From the FDIC's point of view, the people who could least afford it were paying a surcharge on their wages—the Brookings Institution found that a worker bringing home $22,000 who doesn't have a bank account spends an average of $800 to $900 a year on check-cashing fees, or more than $1,000 annually if factoring in fees on money orders and bill-paying services—and the agency in recent years had been using its bully pulpit to pressure the banks under its charge to do more to reach moderate-income customers. Coleman couldn't bring himself to even use the term "unbanked." Banks charge noxiously high bounced-check fees and they revealed themselves to be so greedy they practically took down the global economy. His preferred term, to the delight of the crowd, was "the bank free."

Several speakers spoke about competitive threats posed by Walmart, which was moving aggressively into both the check-cashing and debit card businesses with a pair of low-priced products. It cost $3 to cash a payroll or government check at a Walmart and the retail giant was offering better terms on Visa debit cards as well. Other giant retailers were also starting to nibble around the edges of the market, and for those in the cash advance business there were the online payday lenders that charged considerably more than their brick-and-mortar counterparts but had nonetheless been gaining in popularity, accounting for roughly $3 billion of the $44 billion in payday loans made in 2007.

Maybe the weekend's gloomiest speaker was Bill Sellery, the group's top lobbyist. The news out of Washington wasn't good, Sellery told the crowd. Dick Durbin, the assistant majority leader in the U.S. Senate and, not incidentally, the senior senator representing Barack Obama's home state, had introduced a bill capping the national interest rates on subprime loans at 36 percent. That would affect the payday lenders and also auto title lenders and those in the pawn business. Several congress-men were working on similar legislation in the House. The only good news was that there had been so much bad news in the previous year, Sellery said, and so Congress probably wouldn't have much time for worrying about a group of industries on the economic fringes.

The news from state capitals around the United States was no less ominous. There were small threats to the industry, such as the occa-sional community voting to impose a moratorium on new check-cashing stores, payday lenders, and pawnshops, and larger threats like those in Ohio. So great was the unease over Ohio that when Ted Saunders, the chief executive of CheckSmart, the Columbus-based chain that had recently been sold to a private equity firm, appeared on a panel about mergers and acquisitions, he spent as much time talking about the elec-tion in his home state as he did his assigned topic.

The polls offered mixed news, Saunders told the group. "People out there have a very negative impression of our industry," he said. "It's really scary. Our data shows that we rank just below prostitutes and politicians in terms of popularity." But the problem—that people don't understand the value proposition we offer customers—could also prove the industry's saving grace. Focus groups showed their side "slightly ahead among people who have seen our commercials and understand our message," Saunders said. The key was raising enough money to deluge Ohioans with television ads. He reminded people that on the convention's first night there had been an appeal for every operator to donate $1,000 per store to help in Ohio and also Arizona, where there was a second, less pressing referendum on the ballot. (On the con-vention's second day, a different speaker suggested that every chain donate $50 per store to a FiSCA Scholarship Fund.) They were plan-ning on spending "in the high $30 million range," Saunders said, over the last ninety days of the campaign in the hopes Ohio would serve as their Maginot Line. "If we can beat back this attack, we take away this notion it'd be easy to put us out of business," Saunders said. "This can be our line in the sand."

Fifteen

Payday, the Sequel

OHIO, FALL 2008

B ill Faith doesn't walk into an office so much as he bursts through the door. He is a gale-force wind blowing through the corridors. Sitting in the office of one of his staff members while waiting for him to arrive, I heard Faith before I saw him. "We're going to do it!" a gravelly voice boomed as if amplified by a megaphone. "This is David versus Goliath!" he bellowed, talking to no one in particular. With election day a few weeks away, political junkies across the country were weighing the relative strengths of the Obama versus McCain get-out-the-vote efforts but Faith was preoccupied by Issue 5, the Ohio state referendum sponsored by the payday lenders. Everybody in the office had stopped working, taking in the show. "David is going to beat Goliath," Faith roared happily. "We're taking these giants down."

It seemed an odd day for Faith to be feeling optimistic. That morning, the office of Ohio's secretary of state released the most recent campaign disclosure forms. In the previous few months, the payday lenders had spent $13.8 million, compared to the $260,000 spent by the "Yes on

Issue 5" side. (Confusingly, though Issue 5 was paid for by the payday lenders, a yes vote was a vote in favor of imposing a 28 percent rate cap on the industry.) Worse, Faith and his allies had only $4,000 left in the bank with election day a few weeks away. But to Faith this glaring imbalance represented an occasion to score points—to cast a stone when the media would be paying attention to their down-ballot fight. He repeated his David-versus-Goliath line, tinkering with the phrasing, listening to how it sounded. A few hours later, "Yes on Issue 5" put out a press release telling reporters and editors that they could attribute the following quote to Faith: "This is a David versus Goliath battle. Voters need to know that a 'yes' vote on 5 lowers outrageous interest rates. It's the stone that stops the giant industry."

Before Faith's happy entrance, I had been talking with Suzanne Gravette Acker, the communications director for COHHIO, Faith's advocacy group. Gravette Acker, in contrast to her boss, was feeling jumpy about the payday ballot initiative. "They've hired really good lawyers," she said. "They've got really good strategists." She worried over the wording of the referendum ("it's so vague and confusing you don't know if you're supposed to vote yes or no"), and she fretted over the latest series of pro-payday television ads, which mentioned jobs and raised privacy issues but never mentioned the 391 percent APR. "They've done a great job of muddying the water," Gravette Acker said—and meanwhile the Yes side had spent all of $200,000 on a limited cable TV buy.

But Faith was having none of it. "Suzanne just needs a day off," Faith said, and then jokingly ordered her home. What more did they need to do, he asked, aside from reminding voters that those who were least able to afford it were paying triple-digit interest rates? "These people, they're vultures picking on the bones of working people," Faith said of the payday lenders. "And I don't see voters saying, 'Yeah, that's right, let's let these vultures continue to prey on hardworking people and seniors living on Social Security. Let them charge them 391 percent.'" He gave his head a shake and grunted out a phlegmy laugh. "Ya know?"

The industry enjoyed the element of surprise, of course. Even before the final vote in the Ohio Senate, those on the payday side were quietly reaching out to the big signature-gathering firms and lawyers and a couple of the state's better-known political operatives. But payday's advocates only learned that much sooner how much of an uphill climb they faced.

The lenders' first task was to gather the 250,000 signatures needed to get their referendum on the ballot. Normally that's a matter of writing a few big checks, but these were hardly normal circumstances, said CheckSmart CEO Ted Saunders: "Basically we had just been kicked out of the state. The *Columbus Dispatch* and *Plain Dealer* for months were telling people we're loan sharks, we're scumbags, we're just these awful people." Was it any wonder, then, that at least some of the low-wage people who were hired to pass their petitions sometimes resorted to fibbing?

Sandy Theis thought she had died and gone to heaven that day when she was shopping with her teenage son in a mall near Columbus and happened upon a man trying to convince passersby to sign a petition that would put the payday referendum on the ballot. Faith had hired Theis to handle the press for the Yes on 5 campaign and also help run the day-to-day operations. After listening to the petition carrier's pitch, she rushed home to grab a tape recorder. She captured two petition circulators on tape that day, both of whom utilized the same ready-made argument: We're here to shut down the payday lenders. The petition passers were being paid by the payday lenders, but they were giving the anti-payday argument. "These guys are legal loan sharks and we want to regulate them," one told Theis.

"But I thought it's the payday lenders using the ballot so they can keep charging 391 percent."

"No, ma'am," the man answered politely.

Ours is now a world in which taping someone is as simple as hitting the record button on a cell phone. That's what Robert Hagan did when he encountered a pair of circulators in his hometown of Youngstown. They too were claiming that the proposed initiative, if placed on the ballot, would lower the rates the state's beleaguered working class would pay for a payday loan, not raise them. Hagan, the state rep who had co-sponsored the original payday bill with Bill Batchelder, certainly knew better. So did his son, a student at Oberlin College, who claimed he had come across a trio of circulators spinning the same fabrications. Others told a similar story, including a city councilman from Toledo and a Columbus-area man named Peder Johanson, who was so incensed at the deception that he launched an "I Want My Name Back" campaign on YouTube.

The payday lenders would turn in more than 400,000 signatures, and after the secretary of state rejected 56 percent of those signatures (including undoubtedly "I'mGoingToFuckYou," which is how former Check 'n Go manager Chris Browning signed a petition being passed near her home), they gathered 200,000 more. In its campaign disclosure forms, the payday lenders reported spending $3.4 million to qualify their referendum for the ballot. Presumably that included the costly television ads the industry felt compelled to run asking people to at least keep an open mind and allow the voters of Ohio to decide on the future of payday in the state.

"That's how out of hand this all got," the payday trade association's Steven Schlein said. "We're spending money on ads just to get people to sign a petition."

At first, Schlein had been feeling optimistic about payday's chances with the voters. He had lived in California, and time and again had watched better-funded referendum campaigns swamp the opposition no matter what the issue. If we have the money, Schlein asked at an early campaign strategy meeting, what was there to worry about? He didn't like the answer he heard. We can run television ads for months. We can do weekly mailings. We can set up phone banks and do robocalls. But if the other side has the endorsements of the leading politicians and its top newspapers, they can trump our efforts with one or two good television ads in the final week.

Wooing the state's political establishment was out. The payday lenders were in a bind because they had already failed so miserably on that front. The industry could only watch helplessly as the Yes on 5 campaign trotted out its big political endorsements, starting with the first press event of the campaign, when two of the state's top Republicans, Jon Husted, the Speaker of the House, and Bill Harris, the Senate president, joined Ted Strickland, the Democratic governor, to endorse a Yes vote on 5. Later in the campaign, Faith and his allies would again show off their bipartisan muscle by convincing the Democratic and Republican candidates for attorney general to call a temporary truce in their campaign and join former AGs who were gathering to condemn the payday lenders and their practices. The payday lenders would win an endorsement from the Congress of Racial Equality, but though they played that up in press releases and in campaign materials, there was some question about the relevance of this once venerable civil rights organization, whose director, Roy Innis, had joined the Libertarian party in 1998 and endorsed fringe candidate Alan Keyes for president in 2000.

The payday lenders tried looking for friends among the state's newspaper editorial boards, but without much luck. Allan Jones may "still have a lot of hillbilly in him," Jared Davis told me, but it was Jones whom they sent to the *Cleveland Plain Dealer* to represent the industry in a sit-down with that paper's editorial board. Perhaps no one had explained to Jones that by design an editorial endorsement meeting generally means facing a small squad of editors and writers peppering a visitor with pointed questions, because Jones, fed up with what he described as "the most hostile questions I've ever heard," exploded partway through the meeting. "Y'all are the most biased group I've ever seen," he yelled at them, and then added for good measure that he thought the whole lot of them were full of shit. "Those people would not listen to reason, that's how antibusiness they are," Jones told me when we met in Cleveland, Tennessee.

In Cincinnati, Jared Davis and Jeff Kursman, Check 'n Go's spokesman, were no less disappointed in their hometown newspaper. The

Cincinnati Enquirer may be the most conservative large daily in the state but the reception they received was hardly warm. "We've been a business leader in this city for nearly twenty years, a major employer," Kursman said.

"Three thousand employees," Jared Davis interrupted.

"Three thousand employees. And what does the editor of the editorial page tell Mr. Davis? 'Look, you can show me all the statistics you want, you can show me all the numbers in the world, but we've made up our minds.'" The two of them shook their heads ruefully. "The whole experience made me wonder about the future of American journalism," Davis said.

"Journalism doesn't exist in the state of Ohio," Kursman sighed. The one newspaper of any size to endorse the industry's referendum was in Lima, a town of forty thousand in the state's northwest corner. "If someone is willing to accept the terms of these loans," the *Lima News* wrote archly, "that person ought to be free of government interference to do so." So inside the No on 5 campaign, they crossed their fingers and hoped that the Yes campaign wouldn't have enough money in the final weeks to afford even a decent mailer, let alone television money to trumpet their endorsements.

Ted Saunders is no one's idea of a charismatic speaker. Saunders will tell you that much himself. "I'm a numbers guy," he said when we met in CheckSmart's offices. He's someone who feels more at home poring over a spreadsheet than sitting opposite a foe in a political debate. "I didn't even run for student council," he said. "I was a total neophyte."

But the question was, if not him, who?

The payday ranks were depleted, to say the least. Angry that they had been so soundly defeated in the state legislature, Schlein's organization fired its longtime lobbyist. The head of the Ohio Association of Financial Service Centers, whom Jared Davis claimed had done more to bring payday to Ohio than anyone else, also dropped out of sight, presumably another casualty of their loss. Jared Davis proved willing to do as many radio shows as they threw at him, but no TV. "I don't like to do TV because of my Tourette's," he confessed. "My wife says get over it, but I don't like the way it looks so I don't do it." And the rest? Like most other businesspeople in the second half of 2008, they were preoccupied navigating the worst economic crisis since the Great Depression. Ohio was important but it was only one of dozens of states where the big chains had a presence. CheckSmart, in contrast, had its headquarters just outside Columbus and half of its stores were in the state.

So it fell to this mild-mannered technocrat who had only recently taken over as chief executive to square off against Bill Faith and his minions.

"Maybe I'm just a glutton for punishment," Saunders offered with a rueful smile. "I was willing."

Saunders is a slim man with thinning brown hair and the drab look of an accountant who has already spent twenty years on the job. Surprisingly, he was only thirty-five years of age. He in fact had worked as an accountant before taking a job at Stephens, Inc., the investment bank in Little Rock that had carved out a specialty in subprime businesses. While at Stephens, Saunders started doing work for Diamond Castle, a New York–based private equity firm that had raised $1.9 billion and announced in 2004 its intention to pursue "companies which serve the very large 'unbanked' or 'underbanked' population of the United States, estimated at approximately 70 million people." After Diamond Castle paid $268 million for CheckSmart in 2006, Saunders jumped when the new management offered him the job of chief financial officer. "This was going to be our vehicle," Saunders told me. With the purchase of CheckSmart, Diamond Castle wasn't just buying 175 payday and check-cashing stores; it was securing a platform on which to build.

"Fundamentally you have an entire sector of the population, whether people like it or not, living outside the American banking system," Saunders said. "And so long as those people are not welcome in the conventional banking system, and they're not served by the conventional banking system, there's going to be alternatives. That's just what America is." Using CheckSmart, Diamond Castle would snap up smaller chains as fast as they could, wring out redundancies, and eventually grow into an efficiently run giant of the poverty business. That at least was the theory.

The first challenge Diamond Castle faced in its plan to dominate this corner of the financial universe was that people were generally reluctant to sell because they too saw that there was still big money in the poverty business. "If you went through all our files, you'd see we tried quite diligently to expand this business," Saunders said. "But it was like the Wild West out there among the payday lenders and check cashers and pawnbrokers. These are people who have no fear and never had any fear." Saunders and his cohorts tried explaining that the industry was approaching a saturation point and, as a consequence, the better-funded, better-managed companies would crush the smaller players. But pretty much everyone they spoke with saw themselves as playing the role of the alpha company in that scenario. "Getting any of them to the point where they thought it made good economic sense to sell the business was next to impossible," Saunders said. By the time the global credit crunch put a sudden stop to their expansion plans, CheckSmart had grown to only around 250 stores, and most of those additional seventy-five stores were built rather than bought.

"It would be a fair statement that in retrospect we didn't have the greatest timing in the world," he said.

Saunders barely paid any attention when the state legislature was holding hearings about payday lending. "We were heading into this terrible economy, which meant more people were going to need this service, not less," he said. "I was thinking [the legislature] couldn't be so clueless as to cut people off just when the need was greatest." His promotion to CEO came at around the time the governor was signing the payday rate cap into law. So Saunders would need to navigate his company through the choppy waters of both a recession and a new regulatory environment at the same time he would take time to tape a segment for Fox News or argue for the industry's survival at small forums around the state.

"The combination of good employees who want to deliver a valued service and a customer who appreciates that service ought to be enough to create a business in America," he said. "But I don't know what's happened to our country." He brought up the new rule that dictated that no Ohioan could take out more than four payday loans in a year. "What if government in their infinite wisdom said you couldn't swipe your Visa card more than four or six times in a year? Well, that's what the legislature did to these other people over here," he said.

Saunders felt he owed it to his investors, his employees, and his customers to take to the stump. "If someone marched in tomorrow and took the company away, I could go do something else," he said. "I can't say that about everybody who works for me. I can't say what would happen to a lot of our customers." Like Billy Webster, Saunders had spent time working behind the counter before deciding to get into the business. "You spend three or four hours, without any cameras around, really talking to the people, and you become one hundred percent convinced that those people wanted the service and needed the service," he said. "But when people hear the word 'payday,' they immediately shut down. They become instantly closed-minded. They think, 'That's toxic, that's bad, that's awful.'

"If you've never had to use the product, it's easy to turn your nose up to it. People think, 'Only a fool. Only an uneducated person.'" And of course the media reinforced those negatives, he said, as did those "supposedly independent consumer organizations."

Saunders asked me if I knew the name Martin Eakes. I told him I did. "Then you understand what's really going on here," he said. I told him I wasn't sure I did. "You've got this group, CRL, which is supposed to be for what it sounds. Consumer protection. But it's funded by this credit union started by Martin Eakes, who just happens to be the head of the CRL. And it's this very same credit union that chased payday out of North Carolina in order to increase their fee revenues."

Saunders was hardly alone in making this argument. I was no more than two minutes into my first conversation with Kim Norris, the woman the payday lenders hired to run the No on 5 campaign, when she brought up the Center for Responsible Lending. "This is an attack on a very young industry that doesn't have the sophistication against this well-organized lobbying effort promoted by the credit unions and their front organization, the Center for Responsible Lending, which will say anything to get their way," Norris said. At the Ohioans for Financial Freedom website, sponsored by the No on 5 campaign, there was an entire section dedicated to "credit unions lies," which concluded: "It's pretty simple: credit unions see payday lenders as competition, and they have been spending millions on lobbyists to get their way."

And Bill Faith? To Norris he was "CRL's proxy in Ohio," a tool of the "credit unions who are trying to put their competitors out of business." To Saunders he was a hypocrite who had no right to call himself an advocate for the homeless. "This is a man who spent more money"— $200,000—"on one TV campaign about his pet issue than he's spent helping the homeless over the last two years," Saunders said. (According to Faith, COHHIO actually spent a combined $2.7 million in 2007 and 2008 on projects aimed at helping the homeless.) Later in our talk Saunders described Faith as "nothing more than a lobbyist who is very good at his job."

Payday lending operators might have seen their industry as young and overmatched, but they were certainly not without resources. The No on 5 campaign paid Strategic Public Partners Group, a Columbus-based political consultancy firm, nearly $1 million for its services and it spent tens of thousands more on State Street Consultants, which the *Columbus Dispatch* would describe as a "high-powered Columbus lobbying firm that . . . ruled Capitol Square." They would also pay Fleishman-Hillard, the giant communications consultancy, another $35,000 a month for Kim Norris's services. Through the end of September, they had already spent $1.6 million on mailings and purchased some $7 million in television ads.

Faith, in contrast, paid Sandy Theis, a former *Cleveland Plain Dealer* reporter, a flat fee of $7,500 for the campaign, and relied on the pro bono services of his longtime friend and media consultant, Greg Haas.

He had the part-time services of the COHHIO staff, just as the payday
lenders had their teams, but where the payday lenders spent hundreds
of thousands of dollars on polling, Haas had to beg to convince Faith to
spend a bit of their limited cash on a focus group.

That single focus group meeting held during the summer would
prove critical. For starters they learned that Ohioans had paid extraordinarily close attention to the legislative debate over payday. "We were
all basically stunned by how much people knew," Haas said. But most
important, it drove home the polarizing power of the triple-digit APR.
Any number of the participants hated this idea that limiting the number
of payday loans a person could take out in a year meant maintaining a
database that tracked loans by name. "The 'nanny government' stuff
really bothered people—until you mentioned the 391 percent," Haas
said. "People were suddenly, 'That's theft!'" It was after the focus group
meeting, Haas said, that the Yes on 5 campaign changed its name to
the "Is 391 Percent Too High? Vote YES on 5 Committee" so that the
391 percent would automatically be stamped on anything the campaign
produced.

"Bill decided we just have to keep pounding and pounding on that
391 percent," Haas said.

The payday lenders took more of a scatter shot approach. Sandy
Theis saw that as a sign of weakness. "They're changing topics every
few days," Theis told me a few weeks before election day, "which tells
me they're still searching for a message that has traction." Alternatively,
it also could have indicated that their polling revealed any number of
weaknesses in the anti-payday argument. As Greg Haas could have
predicted, the payday lenders hammered away at the database issue.
As written, the referendum wouldn't do anything to change what Ted
Saunders called the "Big Brother aspect" of the bill: The state would
still keep track of the number of loans people took out in a given year
even if the "no" side won. But it was also a potent issue, and so the lenders incessantly ran a television commercial reminding viewers of a few
of the state's more infamous data breaches. The industry also played
to antigovernment sentiments by slyly making fun of this idea that the

law required them to express the terms of a two-week loan as an APR. Imagine, the ad asked, if the authorities required rental car companies to advertise their rates as an annual rate: $10,585 a year for a compact rather than $29 a day. "Maybe they just think we're all stupid," the ad's tag line sneered.

But mainly the payday lenders played to people's fears. "Our polling shows that seventy percent of people are afraid of losing jobs," Ted Saunders had told his fellow payday lenders in Las Vegas. "So we're running a whole lot of ads about jobs." Set to ominous music, one showed a set of grainy black-and-white photos of what at quick glance looked like a kind of postapocalyptic Ohio. Ohio had lost hundreds of thousands of jobs in recent years, a narrator intones. "Is this the time to shut down an Ohio industry and eliminate another 6,000 jobs?" For a time, the No campaign took to calling Issue 5 the "job killing initiative."

That 6,000 number was a fabrication. Ohio had roughly 1,500 stores in the fall of 2008. Some had one employee; most of the rest employed two. Even accounting for an extra 150 roving district and regional managers, it didn't add up to anywhere near 6,000 Ohio jobs. And a restrictive rate cap wouldn't necessarily mean that every payday employee lost his or her job. By August, the state's consumer finance department had received nearly 1,100 license applications from existing payday stores looking to offer alternative loan products should Yes on Issue 5 prevail. People would lose jobs, no doubt, but nowhere near 6,000.

Yet that number grew even more elastic as the campaign wore on. "We're fighting to keep 10,000 good-paying jobs in the state," Kim Norris told an Associated Press reporter in the final weeks of the campaign. And from that point on, 10,000 became the new 6,000.

It was eleven days before the election, and Bill Faith was sick—he always catches a cold during these big campaigns, people around him told me—and he slurped and sneezed through this first interview. He fiddled with a pen on his desk and also paper clips and random papers. He rocked back and forth in his chair and then bent forward to peek at his BlackBerry. Sometimes he leaned in, it seemed, just to twirl it around. I wanted to hear about the campaign but he was curious to hear from me what it's like to chat with Allan Jones.

"They're evil," he said of the payday lenders. "They're Orwellian evil people. They are people without principles. They deserve to be beaten and jailed. They're thieves." Later he described them as the "new Mafia." They might not break kneecaps, he said, but they charge a higher vig.

Faith didn't have much of a rationale for how the executive director of a group called the Coalition on Homelessness and Housing in Ohio came to devote so much of his time—and his organization's time—to fighting the short-term cash advance business. "People were telling us some seniors were having a hard time paying their rent because they're taking out payday loans to help their kids make ends meet," he said. "People were at risk of losing their housing because of these things." But then he doesn't need to explain to anyone but his board of directors. COHHIO, a nonprofit, receives state and federal monies to help the homeless but those funds are earmarked for specific programs. It's the discretionary money he raises from foundations and wealthy individuals that he uses to pay for COHHIO's crusades, whether it's the fight against predatory mortgage lending or a two-year battle to cap the rates that a payday lender can charge. Over the years everyone from the IRS and HUD to various state agencies have audited him but he's never worried about what they may find. "I have an accounting guy to make sure we carefully segregate all our funds," he said.

In the end, there was no money for a last-minute advertising blitz. The opposition had spent a lot of time talking about Martin Eakes but the Center for Responsible Lending's presence in the campaign boiled down to the part-time help of a sole Durham-based CRL staffer. He proved an invaluable source for data and intelligence on the various payday companies but he hardly served as the campaign's mastermind. "None of the credit unions gave us a nickel," Faith said. "Zero." In the final days of the campaign, the Yes on 5 campaign had only enough money for a single statewide mailing.

But none of that mattered. NEARLY 2 MILLION OHIOANS STAND UP FOR

PAYDAY, read the headline over an Advance America press release posted the day after the election. Unfortunately for the payday lenders, Faith's side collected more than 3 million votes for a landslide 64 percent.

The Friday after the election the *Dayton Daily News* ran a recap story quoting a seventy-year-old Social Security recipient named Evelyn Reese who was disheartened to hear that Issue 5 had lost. "This is a terrible mess for people who live from week to week," Reese said.

Down in Cincinnati, Jared Davis and Jeff Kursman shook their heads over the *News* article. "The media finally quotes one of our customers talking about the value of our product," Kursman said.

"Once it's too late," Davis interjected.

"We never stood a chance," Kursman said.

Sixteen

Dayton after Dark

DAYTON, OHIO, 2008–2009

On a sunny and crisp autumn day, Jim McCarthy and I were on a driving tour of Dayton. Weeks earlier I had phoned McCarthy to talk about the impact of the poverty industry in one typical midwestern city, and McCarthy, an upbeat forty-three-year-old with bright blue eyes and a raucous Nathan Lane laugh, graciously offered to show me around. At that point I was new to Dayton, so he veered a few blocks out of his way to show me the preserved, pristine bicycle shop where the Wright Brothers built the first airplane to successfully take flight. He made sure I saw the broad lawns and handsome red brick buildings of the University of Dayton and, for a food break, he chose a revitalized neighborhood that would have felt familiar to anyone living in a regentrified section of Brooklyn, Chicago, or Oakland. McCarthy, who was born and raised in nearby Cincinnati, does his best to present his adopted hometown in the most favorable light, but block after block of boarded-up homes and a seemingly endless chain of strip malls dominated by the companies I had been writing about left my head whirling.

I had been forewarned. That morning I had pored over local maps with a woman in McCarthy's office named Anita Schmaltz, plotting possible routes. This was in October 2008 and Ohioans had yet to vote on Issue 5, by which the future of payday lending would be decided. I had told Schmaltz I was looking for neighborhoods thick with payday lenders, check cashers, instant tax companies, and consumer finance shops. She shrugged. If that were my criteria, she said, I might as well spin a dial because it made no difference in what direction we headed.

Schmaltz's finger traced the snakelike path of the Miami River, which bisects Dayton. Heading west meant passing through the city's black neighborhoods and, just over the city line, entering Trotwood, whose population in recent years had shifted from nearly all white to majority black. The poverty industry, she said, was particularly well represented in this suburb named, appropriately enough, after a character from a Dickens novel. A single street in Trotwood was home to no less than six payday shops, along with a Rent-A-Center and a Jackson Hewitt. The prospect of including Trotwood on our tour caused Schmaltz to sigh. That's where she and her husband owned a home.

Heading south would bring us to a set of first-ring suburbs that had fallen on hard times, starting with Kettering. Not long ago, Kettering was a nice middle-class community that many within Dayton aspired to. But that was before the metropolitan area experienced seven straight years of job losses, starting in 2001 and culminating with the June 2008 decision by General Motors to shut down the giant truck plant it operated in Moraine, directly to Kettering's west. "There's lots of payday in Kettering," Schmaltz said—and also in Moraine and West Carrollton and several more first-ring suburbs she named. But it doesn't stop there even as one proceeds farther south and begins the climb out of the Miami Valley. Allan Jones may have been the first payday lender to open a store in a newer, more prosperous-looking suburb called Miamisburg but he had hardly been the last. Eight competitors opened outlets in Miamisburg, along with Rent-A-Center and Aaron's. Jackson Hewitt and Liberty Tax each had two stores in town.

We ended up sticking mainly to the eastern half of the city and a sampling of predominantly white suburban towns. In recent years, the

Center for Responsible Lending has released a pair of studies claiming that there is a racial bias to the placement of payday stores. These reports enraged the likes of Billy Webster and Allan Jones and I can't say I blame them. They are hardly the most progressive group you'll ever meet. After the end of a long day with Allan Jones, I commented that Cleveland seemed a very white town. "That's why I can leave my keys in the car with the door unlocked," he answered. I started to muster a response but he interrupted me. "I'm just telling you the way it is," he said. "We have just enough so that our football and basketball teams are good." But the payday industry as a whole seems no more racist in its approach to business than a great white shark deciding between different shades of fish. A few years back, Policy Matters Ohio studied the geography of payday lending in Ohio. They thought they were going to show that lenders target black communities, but in fact the group found almost no correlation between race and store placement, researcher David Rothstein said. "The big surprise was in how payday had really taken off out in the suburbs and rural areas," he said.

After conferring with Schmaltz, McCarthy plotted out a route and pointed his 2002 gray Ford Focus east. We visited a few of east Dayton's more battered neighborhoods and then headed south to begin a loop around some of the city's first-ring suburbs. When I noticed three or four boarded-up homes on a block in the first neighborhood we visited, McCarthy waved off my whistle. "This is nothing," he warned. At the end of the 1990s, people in Dayton had been alarmed that the courts were seeing more than two thousand foreclosures a year in Montgomery County, which encompasses Dayton and some of the first-ring suburbs. But that number crossed four thousand in 2003 and then again in 2005. The city would be hit by another 5,200 foreclosures in 2008 and there were forecasts of five thousand more in 2009.

The various neighborhoods swim together. There's not really a name to that first neighborhood—the East Third Street community is the best McCarthy can manage—but in a way it made no difference. Each white working-class neighborhood was more or less a carbon copy of the other, a passing montage of modest-sized homes broken up by corners crowded with representatives of the poverty industry. Census data showed that the people who lived in the second neighborhood we visited, Linden Heights, were generally better educated than people living in the first, but the real difference, at the street level at least, seemed to be the proportion of homes for sale and the particular names of the stores that had taken root there. Both had a Jackson Hewitt and a Cashland payday store but whereas the first neighborhood had two check-cashing outlets and a Rent-A-Center, Linden Avenue, the main drag through Linden Heights, was home to a Check 'n Go, a CheckSmart, as well as an Aaron's and at least two instant tax shops.

Kettering was a lot like its city cousins except that the drive to or from a furniture rental store was a little leafier and more pleasant. Toby McKenzie opened the first payday store there in early 1997; Advance America and an outfit called Check Exchange opened stores the following year. Another four payday operators established a presence between 2003 and 2006, and Cash America, the pawn giant, opened a store in a Kettering strip mall. By the end of 2007, Ohio would rank first in the United States in foreclosure inventory and in Ohio (in short order, the state would be surpassed by Nevada, Arizona, and Florida) only Cuyahoga County (Cleveland) had a bigger foreclosure problem than Montgomery County (Dayton). Statistics like those helped to explain a fall in the average sales price of a home in Kettering from a peak of $160,000 to $100,000 in the first quarter of 2009. Not surprisingly, Kettering and Moraine and West Carrollton offered endless more views of neighborhoods studded with plywood and for-sale signs.

McCarthy took the scenic route along the river to head back north, but even a dramatic change in background offered only a partial respite from the gloom of our tour. He pointed to the vast empty space where for decades National Cash Register had operated a series of factory buildings. At that point, NCR, which did a robust $5.3 billion in business in 2008, still had its headquarters in Dayton but years ago it moved most of its manufacturing overseas—and then, in June 2009, the company abruptly announced it was moving its central offices to the Atlanta area. Other ghosts hover along the river, including a long list of tool-and-die makers that shut down years ago and a vast, six-story redbrick building now literally filled with junk, like loose mannequin arms and radio vacuum tubes collected by a company called Mendelson Liquidators. Farther north was an old GM radiator plant torn down to make room for something the city is optimistically calling "Tech Town." At the end of 2008, though, it seemed little more than thirty empty acres of good intentions.

Back in the city, more familiar Poverty, Inc. names occupy strip malls and storefronts and even an abandoned Pizza Hut now serves as a Cashland payday outlet. Yet perhaps the most startling sight on this portion of the tour are the bloated carcasses left behind by big-box stores that have abandoned Dayton in recent years, including a Builders Square, a Sun Appliance, and a Walmart. The mammoth shell that Walmart left behind, surrounded by an ocean of asphalt, must have been particularly galling. Dayton city officials had put together an attractive package of tax breaks to draw Walmart to this corner of the city, McCarthy told me, but as soon as the deal's term expired, the retail giant moved several miles north "in pursuit of another set of benefits from a different jurisdiction."

We entered Santa Clara, a white neighborhood that the *Dayton Daily News* had recently featured in a series that took a closer look at the destructiveness of the subprime mortgage meltdown. Here Ken McCall, a reporter with the *News*, discovered a four-block stretch he dubbed the "ground zero" of the area's foreclosure crisis. It's here in Santa Clara where I learned why McCarthy had previously shrugged at the sight of a few boarded-up houses. On a single block in Santa Clara, fifteen of twenty-eight properties had been sold at auction in the previous thirty-nine months, and an average of ten families lost homes during that period on the other three blocks the *News* featured. This was once a solidly middle-class neighborhood seemingly built on bedrock. Now anyone can buy a 1,500-square-foot house there for $30,000—if they don't mind the drug dealers who now brazenly sell their wares on a street corner.

McCarthy headed toward Wright-Patterson Air Force Base, a sprawling facility that employs some twenty-two thousand people, most of them young and modestly paid, many of them non-military. He wanted to make sure I saw Huber Heights, and not because this once model suburb built in the 1950s heralds itself as "America's largest community of brick homes." The concentration of name-brand Poverty, Inc. outposts in this one town, which McCarthy dubs Dayton's only truly integrated neighborhood, is at once astonishing and overwhelming. A partial list includes Rent-A-Center, Jackson Hewitt, H&R Block, ACE Cash Express, Advance America, Check 'n Go, Check Into Cash, CheckSmart, QC Holdings, and Cashland. In all, the state has issued fourteen licenses to payday operators in Huber Heights. CitiFinancial has its offices a few blocks from the town border and it was at a Household Finance in Huber Heights where Tommy Myers said he got "took for a screwin'."

McCarthy lives not far from here and can remember Huber Heights as a thriving community. But the nearby giant Delco factory shuttered its doors in 2007 and all those people he described as earning $75,000 or $80,000 with overtime could no longer make the payment on their $600-a-month gas guzzlers or the adjustable rate mortgages they could barely afford in flush times. "I hate to say it because it's cliché, but it really *was* the perfect storm," McCarthy said. "You had all this predatory lending going on at the same time all these people were living beyond their means and overconsuming." When the job losses hit, he said, it all turned very ugly very quickly.

One perspective on how the poverty business has grown so vast in so short a period of time holds that corporate America has so thoroughly chewed up the nation's once-solid middle class that the country's poor and working poor were pretty much the last consumer segment left to exploit. Witness the credit card industry: The charge card is barely fifty years old but whereas the country was a collective $20 billion in debt to credit card companies in the mid-1970s, that figure would exceed $600 billion by the end of the 1990s. Looking for fresh fields to harvest and inspired by the profits posted by the pioneers of the sub-prime charge card, the big banks began peddling credit to those on the economy's fringes.

Elizabeth Warren, a Harvard Law School professor who has written extensively about consumer debt, would learn firsthand about the financial value of the customer who is barely making ends meet. When she was talking with a group of senior executives from Citigroup about how the bank where they worked might lower its default rate by more accurately determining which customers could least afford to carry credit card debt, a man at the back of the room interrupted her. Cutting off our most marginal customers, he told her, is out of the question because it would mean giving up a large portion of the bank's profits. Warren quotes a MasterCard executive who described for her the perfect credit card customer. It's someone who has recently emerged from bankruptcy protection because it will be years before they are permitted under the law to file for bankruptcy again yet they also have what he described as a "taste for credit." (At the end of 2008, Warren would be named chairwoman of the five-person oversight committee Congress created to oversee spending of the $700 billion TARP bailout money.)

The tax preparation business has followed a similar arc. For years those running H&R Block, which was founded in 1955 and went public in 1962, were happy to stick to the core business of preparing tax returns for the middle class. As long as there was still a long list of cities and towns to conquer, they could simply open more storefronts each year to reliably post the double-digit growth revenues that Wall Street expected. But by 1978, confronting a map of the country that was more or less filled in, Block tried moving into the temp agency business (their logic being that a corporation that earned virtually all of its revenues during a four-month period was already in the temporary employee business) and then in 1980 purchased CompuServe, at the time a computer time-share company. Block even tried getting into the legal services business in a short-lived partnership with Joel Hyatt. But it wasn't until the second half of the 1980s that the company wowed Wall Street with the refund anticipation loan. Block's long-stagnant stock price soared by 118 percent over the next four tax seasons.

The subprime mortgage market, however, followed the opposite trajectory. It proved so successful among the working poor that it was reinvented and repurposed for middle-class borrowers. These borrowers, because they had deep scars in their credit records, or because they were self-employed and could not produce the W-2s needed to verify their income, or simply because they wanted more house than their income could justify, were offered mortgages on less favorable terms than conventional borrowers. A problem once isolated on Dayton's black west side spread to the white east side and first-ring suburbs and quickly climbed up the hills in search of people living in higher tax brackets. By 2007, every county in the Miami Valley experienced a triple-digit increase in foreclosure filings since 1995—except Warren County, an exurb to the south that saw a four-digit increase of more than 1,000 percent in foreclosure filings.

The cast of companies making these loans changed as well. Subprime pioneers like Household Finance didn't drop out of the game but they weren't the same powerhouses that reigned during the 1990s. Most of the big consumer finance companies, for instance, no longer sold credit insurance, and if they did, they no longer folded it into the principal of a loan and financed it at shocking rates. And while the middle class might be perfectly happy to use a subprime product to buy the house they coveted, they certainly weren't visiting some make-believe banker in a box in a strip mall as Tommy Myers had done. The era that Kathleen Keest would call the "third wave " of subprime finance was dawning, and the early years of the new century would see the mortgage broker emerge as a central player in the home loan business, selling to a new crop of companies.

Any list of the most successful third-wave companies would have to include Ameriquest Mortgage, the lender that so aggressively fought Vincent Fort and Roy Barnes in Georgia and the outfit that the *Wall Street Journal* would single out when looking at the role lobbying money played in the subprime meltdown. Ameriquest's founder was Roland Arnall, an Eastern European Jew born in 1939 to a family that survived the war by pretending to be Roman Catholic. In Los Angeles after the war, a young Arnall got his start in business selling flowers on the street and eventually had enough money to start buying real estate. He pounced when Congress eased the restrictions on savings and loans in the early 1980s and then jumped on the mortgage lending boom in the mid-1990s. In 1996, Arnall paid a $4 million fine to the U.S. Justice Department to settle a lawsuit accusing his company of exploiting minority borrowers and the elderly. He declared that he was a changed man and promised that Ameriquest would serve as a model for the industry. In 2006, after raising $12 million on behalf of George Bush and other Republican causes, the president named Arnall the American ambassador to the Netherlands. By that point he had a net worth of $3 billion. He owned a $30 million estate in Los Angeles and a $46 million ranch in Aspen but also proved a generous philanthropist, making large donations to local animal shelters and hospitals and serving as co-founder of the Simon Wiesenthal Center in Los Angeles.

Like Household and the other consumer finance companies that preceded them into the subprime field, Ameriquest and rivals like New Century, Option One, and Countrywide Financial did not have depositors like a traditional bank would. Instead these operations arranged what in the trade are called "warehouse lines"—outsized lines of credit for businesses needing access to tens of millions of dollars in ready cash that Ameriquest used to make home loans to individual borrowers. But unlike the consumer finance shops, Ameriquest and its ilk did not hold these loans but immediately sold them at a quick profit to big investment banks like Bear Stearns, Lehman Brothers, or Merrill Lynch. (Sometimes they sold them to middlemen who put together big pools of these loans on behalf of its Wall Street brethren.) Bear, Lehman, Merrill, or other big investment houses on Wall Street would in turn sell pieces of these repackaged mortgages to pension funds, state and municipal entities, and other clients who thought they were buying something safe and reliable, as the A ratings bestowed on them by the big rating agencies implied. No subprime mortgage lender proved more proficient at this game than Arnall. In 2004, Ameriquest made $55 billion in subprime loans, topping the league tables published by *Inside B&C Lending*. The company would again rank first in 2005 with $54 billion in subprime loans, $15 billion better than Countrywide Financial, its closest competitor, and two or three times the loan volume of Household or CitiFinancial.

"Associates, Household, CitiFinancial, and the Money Store proved to be very good at subprime lending," Jim McCarthy said. "But Ameriquest became the experts at it." Where the old-line companies focused primarily on refinancings and home equity lines of credit, Ameriquest included new financings in its offering.

The three hundred retail offices that Ameriquest maintained in thirty-eight states might have been better appointed than those of Household or CitiFinancial, but Ameriquest at its core seemed familiar to McCarthy and his fellow housing advocates. Early in 2005, three years before personalities on the cable news networks started talking about mortgage-backed securities and credit default swaps, the *Los Angeles Times* ran a story by E. Scott Reckard and Mike Hudson revealing the darker side of this huge lender in its backyard. Ameriquest, the paper reported, seemed little more than a collection of "boiler rooms" scattered across the country, each stuffed with loan agents cold calling borrowers and then burdening them with higher rates than promised and fees they never bothered to disclose in loan agreements. In a suburban Minneapolis office, an agent named Mark Bomchill told of colleagues so eager to cross into six-figure salary territory that they forged documents. They were spurred along, Bomchill said, by a "little Hitler" of a manager who hounded them to sell more loans—in between reminders of how easily they could be replaced. Other former salespeople told much the same story. It didn't matter to Ameriquest's bottom line whether customers could afford the high-cost loans they were being sold, because they would be off the books long before a borrower defaulted. "Proud sponsor of the American dream" was the Ameriquest motto but Ameriquest paid $325 million in 2005 to settle actions against it taken by forty-nine states and the District of Columbia, suggesting that for many its financings proved to be nightmarish.

Ameriquest, of course, was hardly alone in its relentless, reckless pursuit of borrowers and profits. Massachusetts Attorney General Martha Coakley singled out Option One Mortgage in 2008 when she sued that company, alleging that it engaged in "unfair and deceptive conduct on a broad scale by selling extremely risky loan products that the companies knew or should have known were destined to fail to Massachusetts consumers." The complaint also charged that Option One specifically targeted black and Latino borrowers in its marketing push and routinely charged them with higher points and fees than similarly situated whites. Agents for Option One, it seemed, were particularly fond of "no doc" (no documentation) and "low doc" loans and also so-called "2/28" adjustable rate mortgages, sometimes called "explodable ARMs." Often borrowers could afford the monthly payments during the first two years because a teaser rate remained in effect but not once the interest reset at a higher rate. "Brokers and agents for Option One often promised borrowers they could simply refinance before the ARM adjustment," the Massachusetts complaint read, "without disclosing that such refinancing was entirely dependent on continued home price appreciation and other factors." Yet Option One did not even make the top three in customer complaints with the Federal Trade Commission. Ameriquest was the clear leader, with Full Spectrum Lending (Countrywide's subprime subsidiary) in second and New Century in third place.

Which subprime lender ranked as the worst? I asked that question of a wide range of people, from the banking analysts I met at an FDIC event in Washington, D.C., to the wide array of consumer activists I encountered across the country. Ameriquest was the clear winner in my unscientific straw poll but Countrywide, a latecomer to the subprime sweepstakes, received more than a few votes, and many chose CitiFinancial (Jim McCarthy's pick), New Century, and Option One. The CRL's Mike Calhoun named Countrywide ("you wouldn't believe some of the stuff they were pushing out the door," he said). Kevin Byers, a CPA and financial consultant whom Kathleen Keest had commended to me as her "favorite forensic accountant" ("he's the only person I know who reads SEC filings for fun," Keest said), cast Countrywide as the "most aggressive" of all the aggressive lenders attacking the subprime market in the 2000s.

Countrywide CEO Angelo Mozilo, as tawny as a movie star, the George Hamilton of subprime mortgage lending, had initially resisted the temptations of the subprime market. But the profits were too alluring and once the company made the jump, Mozilo seemed determined to make his company number one. "Countrywide wanted to lead the market and so they adopted whatever product innovation was out there," said Byers, who runs a consulting firm in Atlanta called Parkside Associates. They were happy to put people in a high-priced product nicknamed the NINJA loan (No Income, No Job, No Assets, also called a "liar's loan" because it essentially invited a borrower to obtain a loan with virtually no documentation) and they paid what they needed to pay to convince brokers to steer borrowers to a higher-cost loan from Countrywide. In 2009, the Securities and Exchange Commission charged Mozilo with stock fraud, citing email messages in which Mozilo himself referred to some of his products as "toxic" and "poison." Mozilo, who had received as much as $33 million in annual compensation and cashed in hundreds of millions in options, was also charged with insider trading.

There were other culprits, of course, starting with all those mortgage brokers willing to accept fees for steering clients into the 2/28 teaser loans they couldn't possibly afford in year three. "The brokers were the drivers, as far as I'm concerned," said Chuck Roedersheimer, a bankruptcy attorney I met in Dayton who specializes in cases involving home foreclosure. They worked on commissions, Roedersheimer said, that could reach 3 or 4 percent of the loan's value if it included a generous yield spread premium—the bonuses a lender gave brokers who steered borrowers into higher priced, more profitable loans. Early on, Option One was among those lenders refusing to pay a yield spread premium, essentially a bribe for putting people into higher-priced loans. "But then brokers stopped sending them business," the Center for Responsible Lending's Mike Calhoun said. "So they turned around and endorsed yield spread premiums because that's what they needed to do to compete." (A study commissioned by the *Wall Street Journal* found that more than half of the borrowers taking out a subprime loan between 2000 and 2006 had a credit score high enough to qualify them for a conventional rate loan.) Mortgage broker might once have been considered an honorable profession, but by the start of the 2000s it seemed nothing more than a quick way to become rich. "Literally you saw people going from used car dealer to mortgage broker," Jim McCarthy said.

Yet the system worked after a fashion—as long as home prices continued to rise at a brisk rate. The broker was happy to put a homeowner holding an adjustable rate mortgage about to reset into a new mortgage if a $300,000 house was now worth $350,000, as was the lender. Everyone earned another fee, and the ultimate stakeholders would even hold collateral that was appreciating in value. There would only be a problem if home prices fell. Without the ability to refinance, people would be trapped in adjustable rate mortgages they couldn't really afford and as more families were forced into foreclosure, prices would fall further, widening the gap between the amount owed on a property and the price it would fetch at a sheriff's sale. Only then would it seem as if everyone had been living in a perversely rosy world.

"Losses were remarkably low given the crazy lending they were doing," Mike Calhoun said, "but that was because they were doing even crazier stuff, putting off foreclosures by refinancing people into even less sustainable loans." The most maddening part, Calhoun said, was that the more lenders loosened their terms, the more it reinforced a perception that there was nothing wrong. Home ownership was on the rise, the stock market was soaring, and politicians on both sides of the aisle were happily accepting campaign contributions from these rich new benefactors. "It was a hard time to say this giant storm is building but it's beyond the horizon," Calhoun said.

In places like Ohio that weren't experiencing the same boom in home prices as other parts of the country, consumer advocates started talking about another problem: appraisal inflation. For Beth Deutscher, an early member of the Predatory Lending Solutions Project that Jim McCarthy helped put together, the case that alerted her to the problem involved two sisters in their sixties, both legally blind and living on a fixed income. The sisters were in a house in such poor shape that the dining room sloped downhill, Deutscher said, and cracks were visible in the foundation. Yet somehow they owed a lender $100,000 after a broker sweet-talked them into signing papers they couldn't read for a loan they couldn't afford. Initially Deutscher, who by this time was running an organization she helped found called the Home Ownership Center of Greater Dayton, read the appraiser's report and wondered if the crazy real estate inflation taking place in other locales had hit Dayton. The house to her seemed worth less than half that $100,000. But the case of the sisters taught her that as bad as waves one and two of the subprime mortgage fiasco had been, there were still new shocks to be had in wave three. Select appraisers, it seemed, were happy to enrich themselves by fabricating a report when a lender needed the justification for an outsized loan.

"With that case it started to become clear that lenders are not afraid to loan more than a house was worth," Deutscher said. "It became all about maximizing the up-front profit and then moving on to the next loan, with no conscience about how that was going to play out."

The big rating agencies would play similarly destructive roles as well—and not out of ignorance, Kevin Byers told me when I visited him in Atlanta. To make his point he grabbed a stack of reports he keeps handy in a desk drawer. One is from Moody's and is dated May 2005. It explores what its analysts called the "payment shock risk" associated with the 2/28s as lenders continued to lower the teaser rates to make loans seem more affordable. "The resulting differences in potential payment increase," the analysts note, will have a "meaningful" impact on the financial soundness of these loans. Another, written by two Standard & Poor's analysts in April 2005, explores what the pair describe as the "continuing quest to help keep the loan origination flowing." Lenders are resorting to any number of new products to keep loan volume up, they wrote, including mortgages that mean people will own less of their home over time rather than more and the repurposing of interest-only loans for the subprime market, a product that really only made sense for a rich client who can afford the balloon payment on the other end. "There is growing concern around the increased usage of these mortgages," they wrote.

"It's not like they didn't know that all this was going on," Byers said. "They just didn't want to do anything about it because they had a vested interest." The institutions putting together these packages loaded with toxic loans were the very ones paying the credit agencies to evaluate the creditworthiness of the loans, and so the agencies would liberally hand out top ratings while relegating their concerns to the occasional research report. "I think they saw their role as ending once they put the investor community on notice that there are structural issues that they need to watch out for," Byers said. The attorney general of Ohio was among those suing the major credit rating agencies, claiming their stamping of a triple-A rating on high-risk and wobbly securities cost state retirement and pension funds more than $450 million in losses.

Alan Greenspan shares some of the blame—a lot of the blame, according to some. Congress had deputized the Federal Reserve to enforce a sense of fair play inside the subprime market but the Fed chair steadfastly maintained a hands-off approach even as subprime grew from 5 percent of the mortgage market in 2001 to a 29 percent share by 2006. Worse, Greenspan kept interest rates historically low through the first half of the decade—at 1 percent in 2003, the lowest rate in half a century. "I'm sitting there watching Greenspan continuing to lower interest rates," Kathleen Keest said, "and I'm going, 'I thought your job was to take the punch bowl away and you're pouring more rum into it.'" Federal Reserve Governor Edward Gramlich would rebuke Greenspan for showing no interest in investigating the predatory behavior of the subprime lenders.

There were those who said Wall Street was primarily responsible. Their insatiable appetite for these loans—the *New Yorker*'s Connie Bruck called it Wall Street's "addiction"—kept everyone motivated. But then one can also fault those wanting to buy small tranches of a mortgage-backed bond for keeping demand high. And to say "Wall Street" is to miss out on a broader range of culprits. In the mid-2000s, it seemed every major financial institution in the world had a hand in this dirty business. By 2006, Wells Fargo, through its Wells Fargo Home Mortgage unit, ranked as a top-ten subprime lender, as did Citigroup, which ranked fourth. Washington Mutual placed eleventh on that same list and Chase Home Financial, a division of JPMorgan Chase, seventeenth. HSBC, the London-based financial giant that had purchased Household Finance, was number one on the list in 2006 after its subsidiary, Household Finance, regained the top spot with $53 billion in subprime loans. A chastened Ameriquest, which paid a $325 million settlement earlier that year, fell to seventh.

And the big financial conglomerates were hardly the only major corporations to aggressively jump into the subprime mortgage business. The money H&R Block made offering refund anticipation loans had apparently given the tax preparation giant a taste for subprime profits because in 1997 it paid $190 million for Option One and in short order transformed it into a top-tier subprime lender. General Motors aggressively entered the subprime market through its GMAC unit, which bundled together nearly $26 billion in mortgage-backed securities in 2006, and General Electric owned WMC, a subprime lender that made $33 billion in mortgage loans in 2006, ranking it fifth on the *Inside B&C Lending* list.

Glen Pizzolorusso, a WMC sales manager, gave a sense of what life was like in the middle of the credit cyclone when he agreed to an interview in 2008 with the radio show *This American Life*. Pizzolorusso, in his mid-twenties, seemed to be living the life of a mini-celebrity. He bought $1,000 bottles of Cristal champagne at bottle clubs in Manhattan and rubbed shoulders with the likes of Christina Aguilera and Cuba Gooding, Jr. He bought a penthouse on Manhattan's Upper East Side and a $1.5 million house in Connecticut and owned a Porsche and two Mercedes to get him back and forth. He was making between $75,000 and $100,000 per month and suspected something might be seriously wrong in his life when one month he was paid $25,000 and that wasn't enough to cover his expenses. "I did what YOU do every day, try to be the best at my job," he wrote on a blog he created to defend himself after his story appeared on the radio. He didn't create the rules, he said, and the corporation he worked for had stayed within the law. His sole regret, he wrote, was that he had spent his money so foolishly.

The first overt sign of trouble came in February 2007, when HSBC announced that it was writing down its subprime mortgage holdings by more than $10 billion. The housing market had peaked in 2006 and began its inexorable decline, and in short order HSBC would not be the only large institution to announce a loss in the double-digit billions. By the time the banks were lining up for TARP handouts from the federal government in the fall of 2008, the U.S. stock markets had lost more than $8 trillion in value. Finally, the country woke up to the problem that Bill Brennan, Martin Eakes, Jim McCarthy, and others had been warning about for years.

In Dayton, it fell to people like McCarthy and Beth Deutscher and Deutscher's old employer, Consumer Credit Counseling Services, to handle the fallout. The civil courts also absorbed much of the burden; by 2006, foreclosures represented 49 percent of the civil caseload in Montgomery County. Bankruptcy attorneys like Chuck Roedersheimer worked to sort out the mess.

Roedersheimer worked at Thompson & DeVeny, located a few miles from downtown on a street crowded with insurance agents, medical professionals, and fast-food purveyors. There a basic bankruptcy could be had for a couple of thousand dollars. Business in recent months had been very good at Thompson & DeVeny, Thompson told me prior to my arrival in December 2008, but that turned out to be a major understatement. I entered the waiting area in a low-slung bunkerlike building and found no seats. A loud-voiced receptionist called out people's names as if we were all crowded in a bus terminal. The firm has three lawyers, Roedersheimer told me, and they were seeing as many as two hundred new people a month and taking on forty to fifty as clients. He figured he saw two or three clients a day but the other two lawyers (the firm has since added two young associates), well versed in the intricacies of bankruptcy law and unburdened by the complexities of the subprime loans that were his specialty, were seeing ten a day.

The phone rang constantly during the hour I spent with Roedersheimer. He took several calls, from a judge and from opposing counsel, but that only gave me more time to behold the veritable skyline of paper that dominated his office. Stacks of folders were piled high on his desk and there were more sitting on a credenza behind him. One reached so high I feared Roedersheimer would be lost in an avalanche if it fell. There were files stacked on the floor next to him and more piled behind me and on every chair in the room except his and mine. There were more mentions of Ameriquest in those stacks than any other lenders, Roedersheimer said, but Option One and CitiFinancial were also well represented. He seemed to hold American General Finance, AIG's subprime mortgage division, with a special contempt but that might be because AIG played so hideous a role in the subprime mess through its sale of a subprime insurance product (the so-called "credit default swaps") that didn't come close to covering the losses when disaster hit.

Roedersheimer is a slight man with short gray hair and pouchy Fred Basset eyes. He walks with a slight slouch as if carrying his client's collective burdens on his back. For twenty-six years he oversaw procurement contracts for the U.S. Defense Department, and though he had risen to assistant regional counsel, he left because he couldn't take the commute anymore, 170 miles roundtrip to Columbus five days a week. In 2001 he took a job with the local legal aid office in

Dayton, hoping to carve out a specialty in subprime mortgage loans, but the funding for that project lasted only a few years. Among those clients he took with him when he left legal aid was an elderly couple from Kettering (he had worked as a bricklayer; she had retired from the phone company) who had been talked into so many refinancings that they owed $126,000 on a house that was worth maybe $80,000. "One of the things you look for when you deal with predatory lending is can the person afford the loan when all is said and done," Roedersheimer said. Because this couple couldn't, he was able to get the woman (her husband had since passed away) some money from their mortgage broker and also another $5,000 from an appraiser who had worked on her mortgage application.

But such outcomes are depressingly rare, Roedersheimer said. "Unless there's out-and-out fraud, if people signed the papers, there's not much I can do for them," he said. He gets people the bankruptcy that brought the client to the office and that's about it. Sometimes, he said, he can't believe the shamelessness of lenders, but often he can't fathom how little people understand basic finances, his more middle-class clientele included. Clients took out home equity loans not appreciating that they were risking their home on their ability to pay. He shook his head over all those who used payday loans to try to forestall the inevitable, not recognizing that they were only digging a deeper hole for themselves. But if he's learned anything in his five-plus years handling bankruptcies, it's that people will use whatever they have at their disposal—a rich brother, a credit card, the corner pawnbroker—if it means holding on for one more month.

Before someone can complete bankruptcy proceedings, he or she must first attend a short financial education course taught by people like Ken Binzer, a retired military educator working for Dayton's Consumer Credit Counseling Services. To Binzer, the requirement that people endure at least two hours of class time so they can better handle their finances is about the only good thing to come out of the otherwise pro-lender Bankruptcy Abuse Prevention and Consumer Protection Act that George W. Bush signed into law early in his second term. Even people who theoretically have nothing are vulnerable, he said, because of those who might be the ultimate financial vultures of the poverty business: those who view a declaration of personal bankruptcy as a profit opportunity. The worst, Binzer said, are the car dealerships that comb the legal records for the names of those who have recently filed.

Binzer asked his class how many had received an offer from an auto dealer since initiating bankruptcy proceedings. "Almost always one hundred percent of the hands go up," he said. Often people emerge from a bankruptcy without a vehicle but a ready market of prospective customers needing transportation is only one reason the dealers are so eager for their business. There are solicitations from new car companies and solicitations from those selling used cars but invariably the come-ons are all the same. "They'll offer them a loan at eighteen to twenty-two to twenty-five percent but make it sound affordable by giving a person eight years to pay back the loan," he said. Interestingly, Binzer said, eight years is precisely the amount of time a person must wait before filing for another Chapter 7.

L ate in the afternoon of my Dayton drive-along with Jim McCarthy, he asked if I would "indulge him" and visit a neighborhood not on our tour. I had asked him to show me the city's white working-class neighborhood but he wanted me to see at least a small patch of the predominantly African-American west side. Later, Fesum Ogbazion, the CEO of Dayton's Instant Tax Service, would tell me that if it weren't for the instant-tax mills and the payday lenders, the check cashers, and the occasional pawnbroker, there would be no businesses operating in poor minority communities other than a few convenience stores and the ubiquitous hair and nail shops. His claim was an exaggeration but only a slight one. It was on the black side of town where all these low-rent credit shops had first taken root and it seemed every major payday chain had at least one outlet on the west side of the river, and most seemed to have two. Cashland operated no less than five payday stores in west Dayton. Even the Sunoco station we passed shortly after crossing the river sported a sign advertising its check-cashing services, allowing the proprietor to charge up to 3 percent of the face value of a check.

McCarthy drove slowly through a west side neighborhood called University Row (the streets have names like Harvard and Amherst). Many of the homes are magnificent, or at least they were not that long ago: wooden beauties with leaded glass and architectural touches like turrets and gables and wraparound porches. I had gasped earlier in the day when I saw three or four boarded-up houses clumped near one another and there were those few blocks in a row in Santa Clara where nearly half the homes had been foreclosed. Here, however, it seemed that half the homes on *every* block had been abandoned. Paint was peeling, exteriors were crumbling, multiple windows were broken, lawns were overgrown, and the occasional roof had buckled in. This is a place, McCarthy said, that not so long ago he would have described as a stable, solidly working-class community. No longer. "We're seeing the sex trade here," McCarthy said as he drove. "There's drug stuff going on inside a lot of these boarded-up properties."

And there are similar communities elsewhere in the country. One, South Ozone Park, a predominantly black neighborhood near New York's Kennedy Airport, is populated by postal workers, bus drivers, teachers, and clerks. These people were solidly middle class and yet it was South Ozone Park and several other black enclaves in the southeast corner of Queens that the *New York Daily News* declared the "ground zero of New York's subprime mess." For decades the story of neighborhoods like these was their stability; houses weren't sold so much as passed down from generation to generation. But that was before the mortgage brokers set up shop in the early 2000s. In South Ozone Park, the Neighborhood Housing Services of New York City, an organization that offers financial education and affordable lending products, started to see changes in South Ozone Park and several of the neighborhoods around it. Soon, Sarah Gerecke, the group's CEO, told me, where less than 5 percent of the homes in South Ozone Park would change hands in a given year, that number rose to 20 percent. By 2008, she said, the turnover rate on some blocks was approaching 50 percent.

"When you look at communities like South Ozone Park," Gerecke said, "you can't help but think that abusive lending was often more racial than economic." Gerecke's claim has been substantiated by any number of studies, including a May 2006 report by the Center for Responsible Lending that demonstrated a significant racial bias in subprime mortgage lending even taking into account income and credit score.

In the car with McCarthy, looking at all those once-beautiful homes now serving as nothing more than well-dressed drug houses, I couldn't help speculating about whether I was seeing a vision of the future. It was here, in communities like Dayton's west side, where the subprime mortgage disaster that would engulf the country first reared itself. It's here where the disaster has had the longest to play itself out—and it was clear as we wound up our tour that it's far from over.

Borrowed Time

NEW YORK, FALL 2009

Allan Jones had opened 1,300 payday stores yet through much of our two days together in Cleveland he bellyached how it could have been more. Several times he brought up Europe. Advance America operated stores in the United Kingdom; Check 'n Go bought a small chain in Scotland. The payday loan was becoming so popular in the UK that Kevin Brennan, its consumer minister, told the BBC he was "concerned that so many people are relying on these forms of high-cost lending." But Jones had never been to Europe, so in the summer of 2007 he and his family spent several weeks hopscotching their way across the continent, never staying in one place for more than two days. "I was trying to learn culture," he said. "Trying to get myself up to speed. So basically it was up and out with the tour guide at nine each morning and go through five." By the time the trip was over, everyone was happy to be home and Jones expressed no desire to ever return.

"I was all set to take the plunge but I was afraid of Europe," he said. Instead he opened some stores in Texas, a state he had always avoided because the rules required a payday lender to partner with a local bank. "I was ignorant of Europe," Jones said. "But Texas I understand, I told myself. Why go to Europe if you haven't been to Texas yet?" He found a partner bank and together they opened sixty stores.

"I can't tell you how many times I kicked myself for that decision," Jones said with a deep sigh. Texas has been a consistent money loser and Europe makes him nostalgic for the United States in the mid-1990s, when most of the country was still virgin territory. "I could really use that money," he said of the cash he's not collecting because of his failure to open any stores overseas. His money is so tied up in planes and yachts and real estate and cars and horses, he moaned at one point, that there were still projects around his property he wanted to take care of, starting with the paving of the roadway leading up to his house, but he didn't want to dip into his savings to do so.

"There's this big misconception out there that payday is more lucrative than it is in reality," he said. "People have this idea that I must be richer than I am."

To make his point, Jones pulled out the small calculator he carries in a pocket. We were near the end of lunch on our first day together and he pushed aside the plate of food and started to punch in numbers. The average Check Into Cash store, he said, makes roughly $1,500 a month in profits. There are four and one-third weeks in the typical month, so he divided $1,500 by 4.3. He then divided that number by the 44 hours in a week that his stores are typically open. That worked out to $7.93 an hour.

"Does that sound excessive to you?" he asked, fixing me with a level gaze. "That's practically minimum-wage rates."

Rather than answer, I asked to borrow his calculator. He slid it across the table and I plugged in the $1,500 in profits he had just told me a store makes in a month. I multiplied that by 12 months. His average store generated $18,000 a year—after paying salaries and factoring in bad loans and even incidentals like his payments to Jones Airways for the use of his own jets. I multiplied that $18,000 times his 1,300 stores and held up the number for Jones to see: $23.4 million. He had given away a 2.5 percent ownership stake so I subtracted that amount. That left him with $22.8 million in after-tax profits.

I tried to engage Jones in a discussion of how much might be enough. Jones responded that he had the opposite worry: His empire was shrinking. The Ohio vote had taken place three months earlier but he was still angry about it as if it had taken place the day before. By that time he had already shut down forty of his ninety-four stores there—using his numbers, that represented roughly $720,000 in lost profits. And then there were the stores he had recently closed in Oregon and New Hampshire. When I mentioned that hard economic times would drive up demand at those stores that were still open, he frowned: A recession would probably mean a spike in defaults, he said sourly. He mentioned the millions he had spent buying a dude ranch in Jackson Hole he now wishes he hadn't. I kept fiddling with his calculator to figure out his earnings if he punched the clock like so many of his customers do. Based on a 44-hour week, he made just a shade under $10,000 an hour in 2008. Around the country, headlines blared the news of rising unemployment rates and every day the papers were bringing more news of people losing homes through foreclosures. He had just had a strong January, Jones acknowledged, but even if things slowed down considerably over the rest of 2009, he seemed to be at least one American who could be able to survive a pay cut.

There was a time I was unsure what to think of the payday loan. Not everyone can tap a rich friend or family member for a few hundred dollars to hold them over until payday, and of course credit cards are their own quicksand. The interest rates on a payday loan were horrifically high but they seemed largely irrelevant on loans that lasted two weeks. Besides, what's a single mom making $22,000 a year supposed to do when her car breaks down and she has no cash left in her bank account?

I can remember the exact moment when my view started to harden in opposition to the payday loan. I was on an airplane streaking west toward Dayton when I came across a report by the former Ohio attorney general (he would resign in May 2008 over a sex scandal) that included the testimonies of former payday employees like Chris Browning. As they told it, the payday loan wasn't an every-once-in-a-while product that customers reserved for emergencies, as their bosses would have people believe, but rather a monthly reality for well over half their customers. In that scenario, an annual percentage rate of 391 percent wasn't some theoretical number but a good gauge of the price too many people were paying for credit.

"I left the industry when I saw that the rollovers were as high as they were." That's what Jerry Robinson told me when I visited with him in Atlanta. Robinson had helped Toby McKenzie decide to get into the payday business, and as a banker for Stephens, Inc., he had been one of the industry's early cheerleaders. But the industry had become a victim of its own success. "There's just too many stores. That's the bottom line," Robinson said. "Customers have two loans, then three loans, then five."

Billy Webster tended to agree: Too many entrepreneurs had gotten into the business and, as a result, it was too easy for borrowers to end up owing money to several stores at once. The shame of it, Webster said, was that the industry might have avoided some of these problems if it had been more open to reforms like the one he helped to negotiate in Florida. The state government there maintains a database to ensure that no borrower has more than one payday loan out at a time (and caps rates at $10 per $100) and yet entrepreneurs like the MacKechnies of Amscot Financial, with all its stores in central Florida, are thriving. But people inside the industry such as Allan Jones (and also Jerry Robinson) slammed Webster for caving in to payday's critics. "The industry's worst instinct has been to confuse reform with prohibition," Webster said. By the middle of 2009, Advance America had counted fifteen pending bills in Congress and another 173 around the country that would have an impact on its business—and the man now sitting in the Oval Office had, as a candidate for president, promised to "empower more Americans in the fight against predatory lending" by capping "outlandish interest rates." Advance America had earned $30 million in profits in the second half of 2008, and then booked another $26 million in profits in the first quarter of 2009, yet its stock was down by more than 75 percent from its high because of uncertainty about the payday loan.

"It's hard to invest in the future earnings of a company if you don't know if it's going to have a future," Webster said. To guard against further erosion of its market, the payday lenders collectively have forty company-paid lobbyists on staff and contract with another seventy-five lobbyists working in thirty-four states, the head of its trade organization told *Cheklist* magazine.

Inside the payday industry, they see a business less profitable than it had once been and conclude they can't be ripping people off. With more competition and a lowering of the rates so that $15 per $100 is pretty much the standard in most states (exceptions include Montana, where lenders tend to charge $20 for every $100 borrowed, and Missouri, where they tend to charge $25 per $100), the days of 20 percent or more profit margins are over. Yet payday is still plenty profitable. Advance America, for instance, reported a profit margin of 8 percent in 2008. That meant the company had a higher profit margin than Hewlett-Packard, Target, Office Depot, or even Morgan Stanley. In fact, despite the increased competition and greater regulatory prescriptions, Advance America's profit margin would place it ahead of more than 60 percent of the companies in the Fortune 500.

Still, the lenders are right when they argue that the economics of the stand-alone payday shop don't work with a 36 percent rate cap. That works out to a fee of $1.12 per $100 borrowed rather than $15, which wouldn't even begin to cover fixed costs such as salaries and store leases. But then why is there something sacrosanct about the free-standing payday store? McDonald's would no doubt be a money loser if its franchises carried nothing except hamburgers, but they also sell fries and shakes and desserts and other concoctions to help pay for the cost of the restaurant and the salaries of the people who work there. The State Employees' Credit Union of North Carolina, one of the country's largest (the state's teachers are eligible), has been making payday loans since 2001. They charge a fee that works out to an annual percentage rate of 12 percent and yet the credit union's CEO, Jim Blaine, describes the product as "the single most profitable loan we make." But of course their tellers do more than just write payday loans, and their branches are supported by revenues from a wide range of services, from car and home loans to more routine banking functions.

The payday lenders would diversify their offerings—eventually. In April 2008, Allan Jones first started experimenting with check cashing at select stores, and by the time I visited him in February 2009, check cashing was available at around half his stores, along with wire transfers through Western Union. Advance America announced in 2008 that it had cut a similar deal with MoneyGram; at the same time, the company began selling prepaid debit cards and Visa gift cards at all of its stores. Check 'n Go had experimented with the tax refund anticipation loan at its stores years earlier then dropped the practice. But it too began offering check-cashing and wire transfer services at select stores and announced in 2009 that it would offer car title loans in states where they were permitted to do so by law. "Before we were just focused on taking care of our customer," Allan Jones said. "Now we're trying to survive."

Or trying to thwart the will of the people. Despite the express wishes of the Ohio state legislature and more than 60 percent of the electorate, all the big payday lenders were still making short-term cash loans in Ohio. Incredibly, some were charging rates that worked out to more than 391 percent annually. "Like mosquitoes adapting to a new bug spray," wrote Thomas Suddes, a columnist for the *Cleveland Plain Dealer*.

The lenders had found any number of clever ways to do so. Most had applied for licenses either under the state's Small Loan Act or the Mortgage Loan Act. A business couldn't charge more than 28 percent interest under either of these acts but there was no preventing a lender from charging a loan origination fee or making a borrower pay a fee for a credit check. The more aggressive companies went one step further, issuing the advances in the form of a check and then charging a steep fee to cash it. Under this new system, the APR depended on the amount of the loan and the audacity of the lender but one local business figured out that it could charge as much as 423 percent under the Small Loan Act on a $100 loan and 680 percent under the mortgage loan law. Bill Batchelder and others were working on legislation that would eliminate what Bill Faith and others dubbed "loopholes" in the law but they could be certain that the payday lenders would not be leaving Ohio anytime soon. It had taken North Carolina five years to finally drive them out of the state.

If it was in an airplane somewhere over Pennsylvania where I started thinking differently about the payday loan, then it was in a meeting room in the bowels of the Mandalay Bay resort during the annual meeting of the check cashers in 2008 that I began to liken the entire Poverty, Inc. industry to those energy companies whose strip-mining destroyed vast tracts of wilderness areas until the practice was made illegal in the 1980s. There, Jim Higgins, the Vincent Gardenia look-alike, was teaching the smaller operators the tricks of the trade, from raffled-off iPods to the payment of kickbacks to local businesspeople who send them business.

"A dentist sends you a reminder card." That's what Check 'n Go's Jeff Kursman said when we talked about his company's practice of phoning people who haven't been to one of their stores in the previous sixty days. "Some haircut places do it also." In Ohio, I would come across a company, Heartland Cash Advance, that has its managers start phoning customers who haven't been into the store for thirty days. And why not, asked Larry Hauser, the owner of Heartland. "I call my customers every week for the same reason a car-servicing company sends you a message when it's time to get your oil changed," he said.

I was reminded, and not for the first time, of an interview I had done a couple of years earlier with Gary Loveman, the CEO of Harrah's, when I was a staff reporter at the New York Times writing frequently about the gambling industry. Loveman, who has a Ph.D. from MIT and for years had taught at the Harvard Business School, had moved over to Harrah's in 1998 as kind of a real-life experiment: After years of studying how some of the country's more successful companies used marketing and new technologies to grow their businesses, could he apply that book knowledge to a once-profitable casino chain that had grown fat and moribund? Among the innovations Loveman introduced to the casino industry was the use of sophisticated data mining tools to better understand the gambling habits of individual customers and market to them accordingly, and the introduction of a rewards program so effective that in time every other big casino chain would appropriate the idea. When we spoke, Loveman seemed particularly impressed by the marketing genius of the credit card companies and he told me they frequently served as a model as he strove to turn the gambler who visited a Harrah's property three or five times a year into one who visited eight, ten, or twelve times the next year and gambled more with each successive stay. By the time we sat down over breakfast at one of his properties on the Las Vegas Strip, Loveman was widely hailed as the man who brought the casino into the twenty-first century. Yet as I listened to him, I grew horrified by the cold efficiency with which Harrah's systematically harvested ever more money from its most loyal customers.

I had a similar feeling sitting through Higgins's ninety-minute presentation on tips for turning the $1,000 customer into one who spends $3,000. We spoke after his talk and Higgins, like Loveman, was anything but defensive. These were legitimate businesses, he said, run by legitimate people, doing what any other business would do to increase its profits. Maybe. But his talk and others like it left me thinking that it wasn't a fair fight being waged on the rougher fringes of the financial universe. On one side, you had the policy wonks, consumer advocates, and the other well-intentioned reformers pushing their pilot programs for the unbanked and advocating for better financial literacy education. On the other side, there were the pseudo-bankers in their strip mall storefronts wielding a powerful arsenal of weapons they learned from the likes of Jim Higgins. Short of government intervention, the consumer advocacy side didn't stand a chance.

en Bernanke took over as chairman of the Federal Reserve in February 2006. A Republican who had served as chairman of President Bush's Council of Economic Advisers just prior to his promotion
to the top spot at the Fed, Bernanke was no one's idea of a consumer
champion. Yet he was a vast improvement over Alan Greenspan, at least
in the fight against predatory lending. His campaign against what he
ultimately called "unfair and deceptive" loans began with a series of
public hearings into mortgage lending the Fed held in the summer of
2006. At the end of 2007, the Fed issued a new set of rules governing
any mortgage carrying an interest rate just 1.5 percent higher than the
average rate paid by prime borrowers—its new definition of a "higher-
priced" loan. Under the new rules, lenders can no longer make a higher-
priced mortgage without regard for a borrower's ability to pay. The Fed
restricted the use of prepayment penalties in higher-priced mortgages
and banned the use of "stated income" loans—the so-called liar loans
that required no proof of income. The Fed also prohibited lenders and
mortgage brokers from advertising only the lower teaser rates on an adjustable rate mortgage.

The Center for Responsible Lending and other consumer groups
praised the Fed for what the CRL dubbed a return to "common-sense
business practices" in subprime lending—and then castigated the Fed
board of governors for not going far enough. Mike Calhoun, CRL's
president, criticized the Fed for failing to rein in option ARMs—the
very product that had made Herb and Marion Sandler billionaires—and
called on the Fed governors to do something about yield spread premiums. It was hard to justify these payments that were nothing but kickbacks lenders paid mortgage brokers to put borrowers in costlier loans.
North Carolina had banned yield spread premiums. It was time for the
Fed to do the same, Calhoun said.

In time, the Fed would propose such a ban (the comments period
ended on New Year's Eve 2009, clearing the way for action). Its governors would announce new rules for the overdraft fees banks charge (in

particular the overdraft protection plans in which banks automatically enroll people) and also the credit cards they issue. Again, the CRL would criticize the Fed for not going far enough on these last two issues. The failures of the Fed on credit card reform would be moot as Congress would take on the issue with passage of a credit cardholders' "bill of rights" in 2008. The new law, which went into effect in early 2010, protects cardholders from capricious interest rate increases and clamps down on the fees card issuers can charge. "The Fed's overdraft rules were a small step but at least a bank now has to ask if someone wants this expensive small-loan product," the CRL's Kathleen Day said.

Even Alan Greenspan would provide a bit of pleasure to people inside the CRL when he appeared before Congress to talk about the subprime meltdown. As far back as 2000, Greenspan showed he recognized that there was something amiss in the mortgage business. "Of concern," he said in a speech he gave in March of that year in front of the National Community Reinvestment Coalition, "are abusive lending practices that target specific neighborhoods or vulnerable segments of the population and can result in unaffordable payments, equity stripping, and foreclosures." Yet as a young man, Greenspan had sharpened his political philosophy in the living room of Ayn Rand, and he believed deeply in a hands-off approach to the market. "I have found a flaw" in my thinking, Greenspan confessed when appearing in front of the House Committee on Oversight and Government Reform. His free-market ideology, he acknowledged, ended up being the wrong one for the circumstances. The market didn't self-correct, as he had assumed it would, a humbled Greenspan said in his testimony. "I was shocked," he admitted. Kathleen Keest had been so ecstatic to see the former Fed chairman, once hailed as the world's greatest central banker, taken down a peg or two that she had taped to her office door news articles reporting on Greenspan's testimony.

The payday lenders, the check cashers, and others catering to those on the economic fringes had been worried that somehow a crackdown on subprime mortgage lenders could threaten the way they conduct business. They were right to worry. The centerpiece of the Obama

administration's financial reform package was an idea that Elizabeth
Warren of Harvard first proposed in mid-2007: a Consumer Financial
Protection Agency, or CFPA. The impetus behind this new regulatory
body may have been the need to rein in abusive mortgage practices and
complex products such as collateralized debt obligations that Warren
Buffett had dubbed "financial weapons of mass destruction." But this
proposed, new consumer protection agency for financial products would
also have jurisdiction over payday loans, the pawn business, subprime
credit card companies, and pretty much any Poverty, Inc. enterprise.
The CFPA consolidated enforcement into a single, stand-alone agency
that would have broad authority to investigate and react to abuses. The
agency would also promote better financial education. Predictably, virtually every business in this sector lined up against the Obama proposal. How could they not in the face of a new federal agency that
would suddenly be poking into their business? The CFPA was "redun-
dant," a "waste of money" (actually, under Obama's plan, the businesses
being regulated would be assessed a fee to pay for the agency), and an
"extra layer of bureaucracy." Lynn DeVault, the Allan Jones lieutenant
heading up the payday lender trade organization, told *Cheklist* that her
group had quadrupled its federal lobbying budget.

The scope of this proposed new regulatory body was made plain
by the breadth of interests aligned against it, a roster that included
banks and payday lenders, of course, but also pawnbrokers, car dealers, real estate developers, the U.S. Chamber of Commerce, and even
utility companies. By the time the debate over the agency began in mid-
October, the financial services industry had already spent more than
$220 million lobbying against Obama's proposed agency.

FEDERAL AGENCY A NEW THREAT—that was the headline in the fall
2009 issue of *Cheklist*. The author of the article checked in with the
check cashers, a pawn chain, and a payday proprietor. There may have
been a time when the poverty industry wasn't a single entity so much
as splintered, competing interests fighting over the same clusters of
customers. But the pawnbrokers became check cashers and the check
cashers ventured into payday, as did rent-to-own. And more recently

the payday lenders started getting into check cashing, money orders, refund anticipation tax loans, and any other business that might bring in additional revenues. They all learned the same tricks for maximizing revenues from the same sources, each category of business grew plump with profits due to the same set of broader economic factors: stagnating wages while home and health prices soared, the loss of good-paying manufacturing jobs, the widening gap between the wealthy and those on the bottom half of the wage pyramid that economists have been observing for thirty years. If nothing else, the fight against a new consumer agency underscored the unified nature of the country's Poverty, Inc. sector—and its clout. JPMorgan Chase underwrites the loans for a large share of the instant tax market, the country's biggest banks funded the growth of the payday industry, and pretty much every large investment bank has had its hand in one of these businesses or another. And what are overdraft fees, which generated $24 billion for the banks in 2008 according to the CRL, but another way a business is feasting off those living on the financial margins?

"If it was just us, we'd get killed here," payday spokesman Steven Schlein said of Obama's proposal for a consumer agency. But the interests of his clients and the country's largest financial institutions are aligned. "Our hope is that the banks will beat this bill back," Schlein said. As written, the Consumer Financial Protection Agency Act of 2009 didn't give this new agency the power to cap interest rates. But it was Schlein's great worry, and the worry of many within the Poverty, Inc. field, that an interest rate cap will be slipped in at the last minute or tacked on to a completely unrelated piece of legislation.

Obama said he wanted a financial reform package signed by the end of 2009 but that deadline came and went—and with it the Democrats' filibuster-proof majority in the Senate. The House had done its part, authorizing the CFPA in legislation it dubbed the Wall Street Reform and Consumer Protection Act. Barney Frank, the liberal congressman from Massachusetts and chair of the House Financial Services Committee, had angered consumer activists by granting the federal government the power to preempt the states from regulating the national banks in some circumstances, but President Obama, anxious to see legislation pass by year's end, immediately issued a press statement lauding the committee for its swift action.

The House bill passed without a single Republican vote. A rival proposal passed out of the Senate Banking Committee, chaired by Connecticut's Christopher Dodd, but with health-care reform taking center stage and other issues crowding out the agenda, the full Senate failed to vote on the measure by year's end. Then, shortly into 2010, Dodd announced he would not be running for reelection, introducing another X factor into the debate. Early in 2009, the *Los Angeles Times* had reported that Dodd had raised more than $44,000 in campaign funds from high-interest lenders like payday and pawn, and later that spring there were news accounts of the senator eating dinner with members of the industry group representing the online payday lenders. Despite a reputation for being too cozy with the banks and other financial institutions under his committee's jurisdiction, or perhaps because of it, Dodd announced his support for a consumer regulatory agency shortly thereafter. What the lame-duck senator might do now that he wasn't worried about raising more money or winning votes—and whether Obama's proposed new agency could survive a filibuster threat—was anyone's guess.

Ameriquest would be the first big subprime lender to flop. Its ignoble end in mid-2007 came when the company posted a curt message on its website informing people it would be taking no new applications for loans. Its assets would be sold, fittingly, to Citigroup. JPMorgan sold off much of its subprime mortgage holdings at the start of 2007 and, not long afterward, H&R Block and General Electric put its subprime mortgage units up for sale. But, finding no buyers, the two companies shut them down and absorbed the losses. Wells Fargo made a similar announcement, and New Century, which made $37 billion in loans in 2006, declared bankruptcy the next year. In 2008, Bank of America purchased Countrywide and JPMorgan Chase bought Washington Mutual. What was left of the subprime lenders boiled down to billions of dollars in debts and a raft of legal cases, including the lawsuit the city of Baltimore filed against Wells Fargo accusing the bank of steering black customers into subprime loans even when they qualified for lower-rate mortgages and home equity lines of credit. (A federal judge dismissed the charges against Wells at the start of 2010.) Perhaps the most shocking news of all came when HSBC announced, in March 2009, that it was shutting down Household Finance, despite the $14 billion it had paid for the company just a half-dozen years earlier.

Yet no bank seemed to take it on the chin as hard as Citigroup. Citi would remain on government life support longer than most of its competitors, and the stock price of this once-mighty global institution that as recently as May 2007 traded for more than $50 a share dropped to $1.02 a share—a 98 percent plunge. Citigroup's primary problem was that it had full exposure on both sides of the subprime debacle: Through CitiFinancial, it was one of the country's leading subprime mortgage originators and on the investment banking side its people had aggressively pursued a derivative product called a collateralized debt obligation that was based on underlying portfolios of mortgages. Citigroup wrote off tens of billions of dollars in bad mortgages and a new CEO split the company in two: those units they would keep and those they would sell once there was money back in the system. This second category included any number of divisions (insurance, the brokerage business) that Sandy Weill had brought to Citigroup. Citi would cut 110,000 jobs (around one-third of its workforce) and sell off $350 billion in assets by the start of 2010.

Yet there was little joy inside the Center for Responsible Lending over the demise of the predatory subprime lender. The value of real estate in the United States had shrunk by $1 trillion in a matter of months, and there was more bad news coming as the rates would reset on all those explodable ARMs written in 2006 and early 2007. There was another new foreclosure every thirteen seconds through the early months of 2009, the Mortgage Bankers Association reported, and while the Obama administration promised help, it was slow in coming. Under its $75 billion Home Affordable Modification Program, created in

March 2009, the government announced that it would pay mortgage companies $1,000 for each loan they modified and then another $1,000 a year for up to three years. But as 2009 was coming to a close, the institutions controlling these loans had renegotiated the home loans for only a tiny fraction of the 4 million eligible homeowners—66,000 in ten months. The CRL estimated that homeowners in neighborhoods with a high ratio of subprime loans saw the collective worth of their homes drop $500 billion in value because of nearby foreclosures.

"In the last twenty-five years, the United States made tremendous progress integrating poor families into the middle class, largely through home ownership," Martin Eakes told me. "But now we'll lose about half of that progress because of subprime abuses that were permitted to continue despite the best efforts of a lot of people. The subprime lenders have basically destroyed the communities that we were targeting. It's a tragedy." Compounding that tragedy, Eakes said, were the likes of Rush Limbaugh, Dick Cheney, and editorial writers for the *Wall Street Journal* repeatedly blaming the Community Reinvestment Act, or CRA, which required banks to make loans in any neighborhood where they had branches, as the cause of the crisis. It was absurd to blame a law that was written more than thirty years ago and didn't apply to many of the biggest subprime lenders, including Ameriquest, Countrywide, and Household Finance. Yet Neil Cavuto declared on the Fox Business Network in the middle of the subprime meltdown in the second half of 2008, "Loaning to minorities and risky folks is a disaster."

"If the extremists succeed in putting forward this view, then we'll lose all hope for the next generation," Eakes said. Equally disconcerting were those blaming the poor for the financial woes facing both Fannie Mae and Freddie Mac. Fannie and Freddie both played a big role in helping to cause the Great Recession of 2008. In September of that year, the federal government felt obliged to announce a $200 billion rescue of the two government-sponsored mortgage finance companies. But its true motivation for buying up all those home mortgages and either holding them in a portfolio or reselling them to Wall Street investors seemed less about helping those of modest means purchase a home—a large portion of those subprime loans, after all, involved middle-class and upper-middle-class borrowers—and more about profits and remaining relevant. Both Fannie and Freddie had gone public in 1989 and the seemingly unquenchable appetite for subprime loans in the 2000s seemed primarily about justifying the hefty salaries and even bigger bonuses the executives paid themselves.

There was at least one subprime lender still in business: Self-Help. Its own loan portfolio was performing blessedly well despite the global financial meltdown. By September 2009, roughly 4 percent of the country's prime borrowers were delinquent on their mortgage payments compared to 20 percent of subprime borrowers. At Self-Help, that figure was 8 percent. The mortgages Self-Help bought on the secondary market it created in the mid-1990s were also faring much better than the typical subprime loan, in no small part because of the standards the organization used when evaluating a portfolio. Self-Help, Eakes said, would only buy portfolios where the points and fees were in line with conventional loans and would avoid writing mortgages that included onerous terms, such as a prepayment penalty. "We've always been about creating sustainable loans," Eakes said.

There are still people, and not just Allan Jones, who blame Eakes and Self-Help at least in part for the subprime meltdown. Self-Help, after all, created the first subprime market and it was Self-Help who pushed Wachovia so hard to enter subprime lending (the bank ultimately hit bottom because of subprime). One problem with that argument is that Self-Help ended up being dwarfed by the larger subprime market. Over fifteen years, Self-Help bought $6 billion worth of subprime loans on the open market—or what Ameriquest, Countrywide, or Household Finance wrote individually in two months in 2005. "We were just a flea on this giant elephant," Eakes said. Self-Help's David Beck also disputed the notion that Self-Help's secondary market served as a kind of gateway drug, giving established banks a taste for subprime. "The dirty little secret about subprime was already out there," Beck said. "We didn't have to give banks any idea of the obscene profits they could be making because they already knew."

Despite its successes, Self-Help's allies weren't universal in their praise of the group. "They told me when we were fighting to save the Georgia Fair Lending Act, 'We'll negotiate to one iota of something just to be able to say we have a victory,'" Bill Brennan said of the role the CRL played in Georgia after the defeat of Roy Barnes. "We ended up dropping out of negotiations way before them. To be honest about it, we were appalled they were continuing to negotiate long after the bill had been gutted beyond recognition."

Vincent Fort was even harsher in his assessment of CRL. "I'm down here dealing with people every day talking about foreclosures and predatory lending," Fort said, "but here this group flies in here, they've received tens of millions of dollars from some predatory lenders, and they're working on a bill with Republicans that's a total piece of shit because they want to go back and say 'We've accomplished this.' I wasn't very happy with the CRL."

Then there's the perspective of those who are part of a group that *Newsweek* dubbed the "ethical subprime lenders": community development financial institutions and other nonprofits mainly. These lenders expose as overly simplistic the claim that the CRA was to blame for the global financial meltdown of 2008 or Neil Cavuto's line that lending to minorities or those with blemished credit is a "disaster." "Even amid the worst housing crisis since the 1930s," *Newsweek*'s Daniel Gross wrote near the end of 2008, "many of these institutions sport healthy payback rates. They haven't bankrupted their customers or their shareholders. Nor have they rushed to Washington begging for bailouts." One person quoted in the article, Cliff Rosenthal, the head of an organization representing more than two hundred credit unions that lend primarily in low-income communities, said that delinquent loans were about 3.1 percent of assets in the middle of 2008 compared to a national delinquency rate at the time of 18.7 percent among subprime loans. The article also quoted Mike Loftin, the head of Homewise, a Santa Fe, New Mexico–based nonprofit that lends exclusively to first-time, working-class homebuyers. Of the five hundred loans on Homewise's books in the fall of 2008, only 0.6 percent were ninety days late, Loftin said, compared with 2.4 percent of all prime mortgages nationwide.

Loftin is a good friend and I've been hearing about his group since the early 1990s, when he took over as its executive director. Technically, Homewise is not a subprime lender. His group focuses on potential homeowners with blemished credit scores but rather than put them in loans with a higher interest rate, Homewise provides prospective home-buyers financial counseling and also helps them get into the habit of setting aside some savings each month. (The Home Ownership Center of Greater Dayton, Beth Deutscher's group, has the same approach as Homewise.) Typically it takes six months to a year for the serious home-buyer to boost his or her credit score and also scrape together the 2 percent down payment his organization wants to see before making a loan. "If customers build a savings habit to save that money on a modest income," Loftin told *Newsweek*, "it says a lot about them and their fi-nancial discipline."

Loftin thinks the world of Martin Eakes. I've heard him describe Eakes as having a rare moral clarity in a jaded world and he expresses great admiration for Eakes's effectiveness, his creativity, and his integ-rity. He'll hear Eakes speak and he'll feel invigorated. "He has this abil-ity to remind us why we do what we do," he said. The two have often been featured speakers at the same conferences and usually find them-selves on the same side of an issue. The exception is the use of sub-prime loans. Through the subprime boom, Loftin watched as more than a few nonprofits embraced such loans. Colleagues confessed to him that they were moving into subprime because that's where the action was and boasted about the fees they were earning writing those loans. He saw groups he had respected profoundly lose their way as they accepted money from Ameriquest, Citigroup, and other large lenders. Eakes never did so but it was Eakes who had been an inspiration for many and Eakes who served as the pied piper for responsible subprime lending. "Martin has to take some of the blame for giving credence to this notion that the best or only way to serve lower-income households is to charge them more," Loftin said. From his perspective, the real shame of it was that all the energies of a group as talented and creative as Self-Help went into the development and growth of the subprime home loan.

Loftin trained as community organizer, and seems to have a preternatural ability to pose the kind of fundamental questions that get you thinking differently about an issue that had been settled in your mind. "Risk-based pricing" is supposed to be one of the great innovations in finance. Where in the old days, only those with good credit could secure a loan, risk-based pricing meant the extension of credit to everyone—so long as you're willing to pay more to cover the greater risk in lending money to you. "The underlying logic of subprime mortgages and payday loans is the same: that the only way to expand credit to minorities and lower-income people is to dumb-down credit standards and charge them more for the added risk," Loftin said. "But there are other tools in the box"—including financial literacy. "No one is born with poor credit," he continued, "and teaching people how to manage their finances is a tool that has proven itself to work and to work over the long haul." But it's easier and quicker to charge people more than to go through the hard work of teaching people good habits.

"To the extent that 'responsible subprime lenders,' including Martin, gave credence to the notion that the best or only way to serve lower-income households is to charge them more, they have to take some of the blame for what happened," Loftin said.

Mortgage brokers need to make a living. All those former subprime salesmen need to put food on the table—and who better to help a distressed borrower negotiate a loan modification than those who proved so adept at negotiating the tricky shoals of this world in the first place? The *New York Times*'s Peter Goodman even found a group of mortgage brokers and lenders working in the very same offices on Wilshire Boulevard in Los Angeles where they made their fortunes during the boom. Now they were the Federal Loan Modification Law Center (FedMod for short) and selling their services to those who found themselves in arrears on subprime loans. "We just changed the script and changed the product we were selling," one of the brokers told Goodman. They certainly had a compelling selling point. "We're able to help you out because we understand your lender," this broker told prospective clients.

But whether those borrowers are any better off after paying a fee of up to $3,500 for help is another question. By mid-2009, the Better Business Bureau was receiving hundreds of complaints about FedMod and similar companies. FedMod's managing partner confessed to Goodman that the business had largely been a bust as far as rescuing people but, he claimed, it wasn't for a lack of trying. But there were reasons to doubt his sincerity, starting with the former FedMod salesman who told Goodman he wanted to talk with him because he felt so bad about the small part he had played in a business he considered unethical: "Our job was to get the money in and then we're done. But I never saw one client come out of it with a successful loan modification." In April 2009, the FTC sued FedMod, charging that they often did little or nothing to help their customers. The FTC sent warning letters to another seventy-one similar companies and ended up filing charges against at least seven of them.

The problem with reporting on the poverty business is that it's so broad and multifaceted. There are newfangled businesses like FedMod and old standbys experiencing a resurgence in hard economic times: debt collectors and those in the debt consolidation business ("Bill collectors got you down? Find yourself in debt? We can help.") and their close cousins, companies promising people a higher FICO score—for a fee, of course. Boosting a credit score is not hard to do, at least temporarily. You challenge every ding on a person's credit report; some are suspended while the dispute is investigated, and meanwhile a person's credit score goes up. The problem is that it plummets back down a couple of months later when all the black marks are returned to a person's credit record—but now they're worse off because they just wasted $500 on a bit of financial cosmetic surgery.

There are any number of strange but seemingly lucrative splinters that are part of the poverty industry. There are those in the business of buying large legal settlements from those who otherwise would be paid in monthly or annual payments (one, Peachtree Financial, tells potential customers that it "helps people who are holding structured settlements or annuity products enjoy the benefits of receiving their money faster") and also the lucrative world of subprime student loans. As recently as ten years ago, most college kids received low-cost, federally guaranteed student loans with interest rates in the 6–8 percent range. But the private lenders moved in with products that included 10 percent origination fees and interest rates as high as 15 or 18 percent. A report put together by investigators for the Congressional Committee on Education and by Andrew Cuomo, New York's attorney general, found "troubling, deceptive, and often illegal practices" among these lenders.

The auto title loan is confined mainly to the South and is tiny compared to the payday sector. But it's still a half-a-billion-dollar-a-year business and so controversial that even Allan Jones and Billy Webster question the morality of this product that lets people risk their car when they feel trapped and in desperate need of a short-term loan. Similarly, rent-to-own. "It's an awful business," Clay Taber, an Aaron's franchisee from 2003 to 2008, told me. Taber, unlike most other entrepreneurs I would speak with, doesn't pretend there was anything noble about this idea of renting people their televisions and dining room sets by the month. "I was looking at this as an annuitized income," he confessed—a reliable source of easy money for him and a group of investors he had put together. But he ended up the slumlord who thought life would be as easy as cashing checks once a month—except he forgot to factor in that it might bother him seeing the way people lived.

"You go hang flyers at public housing projects but these people have never been trained to pay bills," Taber said. "You tell them, 'You give me $100 and that TV will be in your house later today.' That's your hook." But that $100 was still a big hurdle for some so he and his people did as the corporate office suggested, Taber said, and ran "99 cents" sales. "The basic idea is for only a dollar, you get the item in their house, and then you'd just hammer them with payments for twenty-four months," he said. He would occasionally call the home office for advice. "Basically their attitude was 'You do whatever you have to do to get your money.'" Taber described himself as so disgusted by his experience running three stores in Canada that he has sued the company. Maybe most frightening is that by all accounts, the rent-to-own business had already cleaned itself up by the time Taber became a franchisee.

At around the same time the payday lenders hired Steven Schlein and his firm to try to dress up the image of the industry, Allan Jones decided it was time to hedge his bets. He knew nothing about selling cars but he certainly knew the poverty industry, and so in 2005 he took the plunge into the used car business by opening several lots in and around Cleveland. A year or so later, he opened the first of two pawnshops.

Jones told me he hated the used car business. He did it in part to help the man who had married his daughter and it only brought headaches from day one. "It's really the collections business," Jones said. "A lot of these people have weekly payments so you need to be on them after every paycheck." It's even more labor intensive than payday, he said. "These people, they don't send in their checks, they stop by the lot on their way someplace," Jones said. "So you have to stop whatever you're doing, call up the file, and mark their payments." Under Tennessee law, he can charge an interest rate of 21 percent, but that's too low, he complained, given the customers he deals with. He estimated that one in four loans were past due, and invariably a portion of those were going to be written off as losses.

"I might give 'em to you for free if you'll take 'em off my hands," he told me in a woe-is-me voice that had become familiar. "They ain't worth nothing." Earlier in his career, Jerry Robinson had run Just Right Auto Sales, a ten-lot used auto business. Everyone needs a car, Robinson said when I visited him in Atlanta, and in hard economic times "this will be a fabulous business for the next five years." When I mentioned this to Jones, he responded by calling Robinson "an idiot."

Pawnshops, though, had been a different story entirely. He had always looked at pawn, he said, as a "lower-class business," but then

Cash America, the pawn giant, made an offer for Check Into Cash and he opened his eyes. He ended up saying no to them but the experience taught him that he was missing a big opportunity to make a lot of money.

"The rule of thumb with pawn is you pledge three times collateral," he said. So if one of his clerks thinks they can sell a flat-screen TV for $300, they will loan that person $100. That borrower pays a little more than $20 a month in interest on that $100 (Tennessee allows pawnshops to charge a 256 percent APR); meanwhile, the pawned item remains in the shop's back room as long as that customer keeps current with his or her loan. If that customer can't repay the loan or decides not to, the shop puts the item up for sale. "I make money if they can pay off the loan," Jones said. "I make money if they can't pay off the loan." At the start of 2009, he was operating two U.S. Pawn shops and was looking to open more. He only wished that it hadn't taken him so long to recognize the potential of pawn. "If I have one regret, it was that I didn't get into pawn earlier," he said. Payday might be under siege but with more people out of work and in need of quick cash, the pawn business is booming.

"I didn't know I was in a fight for my life when I got in 'em," he said of his two pawnshops, "but since I am, I'm glad I got 'em." Check Into Cash started with one store and fifteen years later he was up to 1,300. Who's to say he can't do it again?

Notes on Sources

This book is based primarily on interviews—with the people I write about as well as with their confederates and their critics. But as the text melds journalism with history, I also build on the work of others who began investigating the subjects before I did. I mention some fellow writers and publications in the body of this work but largely I waited until this section of the book to make reference to my aids. I did this to help the flow of the narrative, just as I often wove statistics into the body of the book without full sourcing for the sake of readability. I offer credit and citations below.

Prologue

Caseload statistics for the Dayton area's Predatory Lending Solutions Project were culled from the annual reports the Miami Valley Fair Housing Center assembled for county officials. For the cases that helped to spur Christine Gregoire, then Washington state's attorney general, to action I relied on an article in the *Seattle Times* written by Peter Lewis. Data on Household Finance—its revenues, profits, and the number of people included in its $484 million settlement—were obtained from public filings and also news stories about the company.

One

My sketch of Jack Daugherty, the pawn pioneer, relied largely on a terrific profile of him written by Bill Minutaglio and published first in the *Dallas Morning News* and then, in 1996, in Mike Hudson's anthology, *Merchants of Misery*. The National Pawnbrokers Association estimated that the average size of a pawn loan in 2009 was $90 and also helped me to estimate the size of the pawn industry; the early history of rent-to-own was courtesy of its trade association, the Association of Progressive Rental Organizations, which also placed the size of the rent-to-own industry at $7 billion. Every year the investment bank Stephens, Inc. publishes an annual report about the payday industry. That report and Stephens analyst David Burtzlaff served as my primary sources for data about the size of the U.S. payday market. FiSCA, the trade association for the country's check cashers, provided data on its industry. To help me estimate the size of the various Poverty, Inc. industries, I spoke with several financial analysts who monitor what they tend to call the specialty finance sector, including Burtzlaff, Richard Shane of Jefferies & Co., and John Stilmar of SunTrust Robinson Humphrey.

Edmund Andrews's book is called *Busted: Life Inside the Great Mortgage Meltdown*.

Two

A quartet of reporters did stellar work investigating Fleet Finance: Mitchell Zuckoff and Peter S. Canellos at the *Boston Globe,* Jill Vejnoska at the *Atlanta Journal-Constitution*, and Mike Hudson, then a research fellow for the Alicia Patterson Foundation. The work of all four helped to inform my reporting on Fleet. Profiles of Bruce Marks that appeared in *BusinessWeek* (by Geoffrey Smith) and the *Wall Street Journal* (by Suzanne Alexander Ryan and John R. Wilke) shortly after the Fleet fight helped in my characterization of his role in that battle. An article by James Greiff in the *Charlotte Observer* at the start of 1993 provided me with a snapshot of Chrysler First at the time of the NationsBank purchase and alerted me to the two-hundred-plus lawsuits this sub-prime lender faced at the time.

Three

Allan Jones was my primary source for information about the early days of Check Into Cash but the "red herring"—the S-1 every company must file with the Securities and Exchange Commission when announc-ing its intentions of going public—it filed at the end of the 1990s also proved a rich source of information. It was while reading the company's S-1 that I discovered that Jones paid himself $360,000 a month for use of his own jets (plus extra for flying time), for instance, and also found many details, financial and otherwise, of Check Into Cash through the 1990s. At Check 'n Go, Jared Davis would give me as much time as I wanted but David Davis, his brother, would not so much as say hello to me even when he walked into the room to ask Jared a question. Daniel Brook wrote a lively account of James Eaton and the earliest days of payday in *Harper's* in an article titled "Usury County: Welcome to the Birthplace of Payday Lending." Rodney Ho authored the early profile of the payday lending industry that appeared in the *Wall Street Journal*.

Four

The Marshall Eakes quote about his brother's refusal to give up ap-pears in a terrific profile of Eakes by Jim Nesbitt of the *Raleigh News & Observer,* published when the paper named him its 2005 "Tar Heel of the Year." Eakes's "we beg for it" quote appeared in the *Durham Herald-Sun.* Any number of publications, including the *News & Observer,* the *Winston-Salem Journal,* the *Triad Business Weekly,* and *Southern Ex-posure*, which all published early profiles of Self-Help that also proved helpful. Also notable was the column that Tony Snow wrote about his old friend in *USA Today* in 1996.

Five

Freddie Rogers's case was featured in articles appearing in both the

Durham Herald-Sun and the *Raleigh News & Observer*, written respectively by Christopher Kirkpatrick and Carol Frey. Jeff Bailey wrote the 1997 *Wall Street Journal* article about Bennie Roberts, the retired quarry worker who ended up owing $45,000 on a $1,250 loan. An in-depth account of the fight Peter Skillern and his allies waged against NationsBank appeared in 1998 in the *Independent Weekly*, based in Durham. That piece was written by Barry Yeoman and proved helpful in my depiction of Skillern, as did a profile of him written by Frank Norton that appeared in the *News & Observer* in 2006. The tidbit about Eakes handing out seven thousand copies of Associates videotape appeared in an entertaining and informative profile of Eakes written by Chris Serres for the *News & Observer* in 2000.

Six

As was the case with Allan Jones's Check Into Cash, Advance America's S-1 offered up a trove of information about the company's early growth and its financials. Also helpful were Susan Orr's lengthy profile of Billy Webster that appeared in the *Spartanburg Herald-Journal* in 2005, and C. Grant Jackson's profile of George Johnson in the *State*, Columbia's primary daily newspaper. "Strife inside the family": Eventually the tensions between the Davis brothers and their father prompted Allen Davis, in February 2005, to sue his sons for control of the company. "Passed the 10,000-store mark by 2001"—that is according to a study of the payday industry conducted by the Federal Reserve Bank of Philadelphia. Mark Anderson was the *Sacramento Business Journal* reporter who noticed all these cash advance stores in his midst in 1998.

Seven

The *Dayton Daily News* proved an excellent resource in the re-creation of the fight over subprime lending in its city. At the end of the 1990s, reporter Marcus Franklin wrote an excellent piece on the impact of the payday loan business on Dayton. Franklin also reported on the hearing where Pam Shackelford and Suriffa Rice both spoke. Jim Bebbington's in-depth profile of Dean Lovelace in the *Daily News* helped me round out my profile of Lovelace, and Bebbington, among others at the *Daily News*, did a commendable job covering the debate over Lovelace's proposal to curb high-cost home loans inside the city limits. That list also includes Eddie Roth, who, in the late 1990s and early 2000s, wrote a series of editorials for the *Daily News* decrying subprime abuses and calling on elected officials at all levels of government to do something about this festering problem, and Ken McCall, who wrote about the Gloria Thorpe case.

The University of Dayton's Center for Business and Economic Research conducted the study that found that at least 30 percent (and as many as 40 percent) of all refinancings had been initiated by the lender and also provided the data showing that subprime home equity loans had quadrupled in the Dayton area between 1997 and 1999. Lee Schear declined several requests for an interview, though in 2002 he sat down with Caleb Stephens of the *Dayton Business Journal* for a profile under the headline "Classic Entrepreneur."

The best account I found of Senator Grassley's hearing into predatory lending was written by the *New York Times*'s Richard W. Stevenson, which is where I first learned about Ormond and Rosie Jackson of Brooklyn and Helen Ferguson of Washington, D.C. Critical to my portrait of Phil Gramm was the terrific piece Eric Lipton and Stephen Labaton wrote for the *Times* in 2008 as part of "The Reckoning" series the paper ran that year. The *Times* article was my source for the revelation that the country's banks gave Gramm more in campaign contributions than any other senator and it was through this impressive in-depth piece that I first learned about Florence Gramm.

Eight

Richard A. Oppel, Jr., wrote that great piece investigating Associates for the *Dallas Morning News*—and then, after moving to the *New York Times*, he did an admirable job (along with fellow reporter Patrick McGeehan) covering the ongoing battle over Citigroup's decision to purchase this controversial subprime lender. Julie Flaherty was the reporter who interviewed Eakes for the *Times*'s Sunday business section and

Robert Julavits was the author of the *American Banker* article that accurately predicted that Citigroup was going to have an enormous fight on its hands with its proposed purchase. Also useful were reports by Kathleen Day in the *Washington Post* and Paul Beckett in the *Wall Street Journal*. At the website of the Inner City Press, run by activist-lawyer Matthew Lee, I first learned about a pair of former CitiFinancial employees named Michele Handzel and Gail Kubiniec and also about Kelly Raleigh, who went to work for Commercial Credit in 1990.

There are any number of good sources on Sandy Weill, including a terrific and memorable profile written by Roger Lowenstein that appeared in the *Times*'s Sunday magazine in August 2000—just weeks before the Associates purchase. Monica Langley, the author of *Tearing Down the Walls*, a lively and informative account of Weill's rise to the top, was the source for two anecdotes in this chapter: the displeasure expressed by Weill's personal assistant, Alison Falls, when she learned her boss, post–American Express, was thinking of getting into the consumer finance business, and the reaction of James Calvano, the former president of Avis, who also expressed his incredulity. Weill, it turns out, was one of the few subprime lenders who declined to speak with me. Also of note: Mike Hudson's piece appearing in *Southern Poverty*, in the summer of 2003, "Banking on Misery: Citigroup, Wall Street, and the Fleecing of the South," winner of the prestigious Polk Award. And Lawrence Richter Quinn's 1998 article for *Mortgage Banking* documenting the purchase of subprime lenders by brand-name banks.

Nine

In a 2007 interview with Jonathan D. Epstein of the *Buffalo News*, John Hewitt spoke at length about getting into the refund anticipation loan business. He described the working poor as "low hanging fruit," and described himself as a mathematician so good "I was the best I ever met." The homegrown *Virginian-Pilot* did a diligent job covering Jackson Hewitt and served as the source for Keith Alessi's quote about needing to "find ways of attacking entire metropolitan areas." Details about Jackson Hewitt's tax loan business—the costs associated with a RAL and its revenue figures in 1997—were culled from a well-done feature by Jerry Knight at the *Washington Post*. Also helpful was a Jackson Hewitt feature written by Len Strazewski for *Franchise Times*.

The *Dayton Daily News* profile of Fesum Ogbazion and his company, Instant Tax Service, was written by Jim Bohman. Geert DeLombaerde profiled Ogbazion in 2001 in the *Business Courier of Cincinnati* shorly after he sold his first business. And for the brief section about Andrew Kahr and the birth of the subprime credit card, I'm indebted to my former colleague Joe Nocera for his wonderful book, *A Piece of the Action: How the Middle Class Joined the Money Class*.

Ten

The Ohio Department of Commerce generously provided me with a town-by-town, store-by-store listing of every payday enterprise in the state that included the date each was granted a license and each one's location.

Eleven

Again, the *Atlanta Journal-Constitution* proved an invaluable resource. Especially impressive was the work of Maureen Downey, a columnist and editorial writer who for my money deserves a retroactive Pulitzer for her outrage over subprime mortgage lending in the early 2000s and the lengths the lenders went to foil the state's attempts to check their mortgage business. The *Journal-Constitution* was my source for historical foreclosure data in Atlanta. Glenn R. Simpson, one of the *Wall Street Journal*'s star investigative reporters wrote about Ameriquest and Wright Andrews at the end of 2007, and Clark Howard was the consumer reporter who declared Atlanta under siege by predatory lenders. *Newsweek*'s Michael Hirsh wrote a nice coda about the Georgia bill that almost was, and *BusinessWeek* took John D. Hawke, Jr., to task in a memorable piece written by Robert Berner and Brian Grow, published in October 2008.

Dennis Hevesi of the *New York Times* wrote a revealing and in-depth 2002 feature looking at predatory lending in New York City. That piece included data from the Federal Reserve showing a sevenfold jump in subprime mortgages between 1993 and 2000 and the 68 percent spike in foreclosures. John Sugg was the author of the *Creative Loafing* article, also appearing in 2002, that featured the Iveys of Atlanta and quoted Fort.

Twelve

The annual reports on the payday industry produced each year by Stephens, Inc. were my source for the growth of the payday lending industry through the decade. The 2005 "like bears on a trout stream" study was conducted by Steven Graves, an assistant professor of geography at California State University–Northridge, and Christopher Peterson, an assistant professor at the Levin College of Law at the University of Florida. There were several good sources on subprime credit cards, including a study by Chi Chi Wu and Rick Jurgens at the National Consumer Law Center titled "Fee-Harvesters: Low-Credit, High-Cost Cards Bleed Consumers."

The *BusinessWeek* article about what the magazine dubbed the "medical debt revolution" ran on its cover in November 2007 and was written by Brian Grow and Robert Berner. At the *American Banker*, Jeff Horwitz's research into World Savings, the Sandlers, and option ARMs proved invaluable. Victoria McGrane wrote the *Politico* profile of the Center for Responsible Lending that declared the organization the main intellectual engine driving the Democratic response to the housing crisis, and a *BusinessWeek* writer named Eamon Javers wrote both the "pit bull of public relations" profile of Eric Dezenhall and the piece examining the stealth sponsorship of commentators such as Tom Lehman of Indiana Wesleyan University. An article by Jenny Anderson at the *Times* as well as *Alpha* magazine—and of course Gregory Zuckerman's writings about John Paulson in the *Wall Street Journal* and his book, *The Greatest Trade Ever*—were the sources for John Paulson's extraordinary success.

Thirteen

Dayna Baird, the chief lobbyist for large lenders like Household and CitiFinancial, was quoted as praising the Ohio legislature's 2002 bill in a *Dayton Daily News* article written by Laura A. Bischoff. The article covering the Predatory Lending Study Committee's visit to Dayton was written by the *Daily News*'s Ken McCall. The lengthy profile of Faith that the *Cleveland Plain Dealer* ran when naming him its 2003 "Ohioan of the Year" was written by Bill Sloat. In that piece I found the quote from Barb Poppe, Faith's wife, about her husband's intensity and ability to get into "the zone." I found the Joy Padgett quote in the August 2007 volume of *Stateline Midwest*, a newsletter published by the Council of State Governments.

I spoke with Martha Clay and Rachel Robinson, the attorney who rescued the Clays before they lost their home to foreclosure. The *Columbus Dispatch*'s Geoff Dutton and Doug Haddix also wrote a terrific profile of the Clays while the state legislature was debating a hard-hitting predatory lending bill. Reporter Bobby Warren told Peggy Daugherty's story in the *Wooster Daily-Record*, and a report written by the attorney general's office, along with interviews with attendees, served as the foundation for my write-up of the hearings into payday lending sponsored by the attorney general around the state. Aaron Marshall is the *Cleveland Plain Dealer* reporter who broke the story about Otto Beatty, the husband of Joyce Beatty, the House minority leader, and his ties to a payday lender. Data on registered lobbyists and their affiliations are listed at the website maintained by the Joint Legislative Ethics Committee and the Office of the Legislative Inspector General. Particularly useful in my depiction of the legislative fight over payday was Jim Siegel's coverage of the wrangling, which appeared in the *Columbus Dispatch* and the political blog he maintains, and Laura A. Bischoff's coverage of state politics in the *Dayton Daily News*.

Fourteen

Matt Fellowes, founder and CEO of a new company called Hello Wallet, is a former scholar at the Brookings Institution who studied the high cost of being poor; it was Fellowes who calculated how much the typical cash checking customer pays in fees over a year. The estimated size of the unbanked in the United States comes from the FDIC, via Fellowes.

Sixteen

The country was collectively $19.5 billion in credit card debt in 1975 compared to $587 billion in 1998, according to the Federal Reserve. Elizabeth Warren told the story of her meeting with bank executives in the 2006 documentary *Maxed Out*, James Scurlock's entertaining investigation of debt in America.

At the *Dayton Daily News*, Lynn Hulsey and Ken McCall wrote a fine series of articles about the area's foreclosure problem. An article by the *Los Angeles Times*'s E. Scott Reckard was the source of the revelation that Roland Arnall and his wife gave $12 million to Republicans between 2004 and March 2008, and it was Reckard and Mike Hudson, in the terrific piece they wrote exposing Ameriquest's business practices, who checked on the volume of customer complaints to the Federal Trade Commission between 2000 and 2004—and discovered that Option One didn't even make the top three.

Connie Bruck wrote a great piece, published in 2009, about Angelo Mozilo and Countrywide for the *New Yorker*. That built on a series of prize-worthy articles about Countrywide written the previous year by my former colleague Gretchen Morgenson at the *Times*. For rankings of the top subprime lenders, I relied on data provided by *Inside B&C Lending*. Glen Pizzolorusso was featured in an award-winning radio broadcast called "The Giant Pool of Money" by Alex Blumberg and Adam Davidson, broadcast on *This American Life*. (A longer version of the interview appeared in *GQ*.)

Epilogue

Sheryl Harris, a columnist for the *Cleveland Plain Dealer*, wrote at length about the ways payday lenders tried to repackage the payday loan so it remains legal under Ohio law, despite a legislative fight and a ballot initiative, as did Bob Driehaus in the *New York Times*. Larry Hauser, the payday entrepreneur who has his employees call customers every thirty days, explained his policy in an interview with the *Wall Street Journal*'s Easha Anand, and I found Alan Greenspan's 2000 statement to the National Community Reinvestment Coalition in *Shortchanged*, a book published in 2005 and written by Howard Karger, a social policy professor at the University of Houston. An article by the *Times*'s Stephen Labaton in mid-October 2009 was the source for the claim that the financial services industry had spent $220 million lobbying against Obama's proposed financial oversight board. Also at the *Times*, Peter Goodman and Sewell Chan kept close tabs on the federal government's efforts to help homeowners facing foreclosures and Eric Dash kept tally of Citigroup's post-crash job losses and selloffs. The data about the lucrative world of student loans was gleaned from a terrific article by Kathy Kristof appearing in *Forbes* in 2009 and called "The Great College Hoax."

Acknowledgments

This project began with a conversation about the pioneers of sub-prime: What are the various ways they have devised to make money off those of modest means? So first and foremost I want to thank Hollis Heimbouch for broaching the topic, planting a seed, and then standing back as I ventured to make the idea my own.

I was fortunate to have worked on this book with two talented and committed editors, Hollis and Bill Strachan. This is my third book with Bill, and he more than earned his keep on this go-round. He read a thicker version of this work and then patiently helped me forge through what belongs inside these covers and what was better lost to the recycling bin. Once that was settled, he gave the slimmed-down manuscript I handed in a good buffing. I couldn't imagine doing a book without Elizabeth Kaplan, my longtime agent and friend. She's a source of support and good counsel and, not incidentally, keeps me in business. Tom Pitoniak belongs to that unsung breed known as the copy editor, who double-checks and fixes while adding that final coat of polish, and thanks again to my mother, Naomi Rivlin, proofreader extraordinaire. I also want to thank Cristina Maldonado and Stephanie Atlan, who both provided research help.

My friend and editor, John Raeside, read early chapters and late ones; his ideas and suggestions can be found throughout these pages. I married into a theater family and finally found the term for the role he plays in my writing life: John is my *dramaturge*.

Others read this book in various forms and I owe them my deep gratitude: Randy Stross, Peter Goodman, Mike Buchman, Alissa Quart, Sue Matteucci, Mike Loftin, and Mike Kelly.

This book might have been born during an expensive breakfast in midtown Manhattan but it was shaped in Wellfleet, Cape Cod, and then birthed there during an intense final five weeks. So thank you Aylette Jenness, for your hospitality on the front end of this project, and Dina Harris, my mother-in-law, on the back end. I also want to thank Kevin Morison, Ellen Leander, and Carl for their hospitality during my trips to Washington, D.C., and Sonia Resika for a special assist.

I'm indebted to the scores of people I spent time with in this investigation into the poverty industry. Many people were generous with their time and their knowledge yet their names don't appear within the covers of this book. Others gave me hours of their time—and then end up with only a quote or two. That's not to say the time I spent was any less important as it proved invaluable to my immersion in this world.

Which brings me last, but hardly least, to Daisy and Oliver. I was a new husband at the start of this project and then, ten months later (TMI?), a new father. There's nothing like a newborn to keep a person focused and disciplined, at least when he's not feeling cross-eyed from a lack of sleep. So often did Oliver Daniel see his father sitting in front of a computer that in one picture he seems to be posing his hands, as if at work at a keyboard. And, finally, Daisy Walker, my wife and companion, she of the big heart and kind soul and the sweet smile who never grew weary from this book even long after I had. She was a great sounding board when I received conflicting advice and a patient listener when I needed propping up. I'll never be able to thank her enough, though I look forward to trying.

Index